Flavia Brizio-Skov is Professor of Italian at the University of Tennessee where she teaches modern literature and cinema. She received her PhD in Comparative Literature from the University of Washington, Seattle, and has published numerous articles in Italian, American, French, Spanish and Portuguese journals. She is also the author of a study of Lalla Romano (*La scrittura e la memoria: Lalla Romano*, 1993), a critical monograph on Antonio Tabucchi (*Antonio Tabucchi: navigazioni in un universo narrativo*, 2002), and editor of *Reconstructing Societies in the Aftermath of War: Memory, Identity, and Reconcilliation* (2004).

POPULAR ITALIAN CINEMA

Culture and Politics in a Postwar Society

Edited by
Flavia Brizio-Skov

I.B. TAURIS

LONDON · NEW YORK

Published in 2011 by I.B.Tauris & Co Ltd
6 Salem Road, London W2 4BU
175 Fifth Avenue, New York NY 10010
www.ibtauris.com

Distributed in the United States and Canada Exclusively by Palgrave Macmillan
175 Fifth Avenue, New York NY 10010

International Library of Visual Clulture, Vol. 5
ISBN 978 1 84515 572 4

A full CIP record for this book is available from the British Library
A full CIP record for this book is available from the Library of Congress

Library of Congress Catalog Card Number: available

Printed and bound in Great Britain by CPI Antony Rowe, Chippenham from camera-ready
copy edited and supplied by the author

MIX
Paper from
responsible sources
FSC® C013604

To David and Esmerald who made it all ... possible

Brucio nel tempo

CONTENTS

LIST OF PHOTOGRAPHS

NOTES ON CONTRIBUTORS

ANDREA BINI received his degree in Philosophy in 2003 from the Sapienza University of Rome. In 2006 he received his Master's in Film and Media Studies from the University of Texas at Austin. In 2006, he published his Italian thesis with the title *Kant & Carabellese* (Luiss University Press). He is currently working on a PhD on Italian cinema at the University of California, Los Angeles.

FRANK BURKE is a Professor in the Department of Film and Media, Queen's University (Canada). His work embraces Italian, American, and Italian-American cinema. He has published three books on Fellini's films in English and has contributed to two Italian volumes on the director. He has authored or edited approximately 60 other publications related to his three areas of interest and has been contracted by the Edinburgh University Press to produce a study on Italian cinema.

FLAVIA LAVIOSA is Senior Lecturer in the Department of Italian Studies at Wellesley College in Massachusetts. Her research interests are in women's studies, Italian cinema, and southern Italy. Her articles have appeared in several publications and she has also contributed essays and chapters on Italian directors and representations of the South to various anthologies.

ACKNOWLEDGMENTS

My teaching and my research gave rise to *Popular Italian Cinema,* and I wish to thank those near and far who assisted in its production including many of my students whose interest and insight gave me the idea for this book.

First I must acknowledge the fine work and the patience of the contributors, colleagues and friends whose essays appear in this volume. They spent time and energy in corresponding with me during a span of five years, and they never complained. Secondly, I want to thank the internal and external readers whose thorough reports stand as proof to the intensive work that members of our profession perform anonymously and all too often without the proper recognition and remuneration. I am especially indebted to Dr. Millicent Marcus and to Dr. Mark Pietralunga for taking the time to write nice reviews of the present work.

A special thanks goes to Dr. Erec Koch, Chair of the Department of Modern Foreign Languages and Literatures, who has always been very supportive and encouraging of my endeavors and to the University of Tennessee for granting a sabbatical leave that allowed me to finish this project in a timely manner and for helping in the copy editing of the manuscript.

I also am indebted to the many colleagues (Dr. Sal DiMaria, Dr. David Fairservice, Dr. Susanna Delfino etc.) who read the chapters during various phases of the writing process and whose comments I treasured. My special gratitude also goes to Edgar Miller, my copy editor, whose long experience in the field of editing made the navigation through the maze of publishing regulations a more pleasant sailing.

Finally, I would like to thank Dr. Paolo Ciarlo of the *Letimbro Computers*, because without his technological support and expertise, during my staying in Italy, the completion of this project would have been very difficult if not impossible.

INTRODUCTION

Flavia Brizio-Skov

The idea of this volume stems from the desire of four scholars to collaborate on their similar research interests. We felt the need to read and interpret Italian popular culture and cinema against the grain, and the urge to dispel the lingering misconception that has considered any form of popular culture as edible entertainment for the masses.

We believe that culture is the expression of a particular way of life, and the cultural analysis of the *texts* produced at the time is a way to reconstitute, reconstruct and recapture that particular way of life.[1] Popular *texts* such as songs, films, rituals succeed only when they meet the emotional requirements of the popular audience. Obviously the lived culture of a particular time and place is accessible only to those living in that time and place, but the recorded culture, from art to everyday facts, is the culture of a period. There is only one factor connecting lived culture and period culture, the culture of the selective tradition: the forming of the canon. However, a great deal is lost between the lived culture and its reconstitution via cultural analysis because the selection is based on contemporary interests, and therefore the relevance of past works is always, to a certain extent, unforeseeable. The canon often excludes large portions of the *texts*. Sometimes, they get included much later. But even when that happens, the damage is often difficult to repair, not because of the everlasting effect of the disparaging opinions of the critics, but because, as has happened with the Italian genre cinema, the critics for years forgot these products, they glossed over them, they ignored them, they lumped them together into the infamous category of popular entertainment, and the stigma seems to be permanent. Serious studies of the western Italian style, for example, did not appear till the mid 1980s, almost two decades after these films ceased to be produced, and for that reason, even to this day, such texts have not yet been granted a complete rehabilitation.

The present work, therefore, wants to re-evaluate the past, showing how popular cinema was not one of evasion and of escapism, but, rather, a cinema in tune with the political and social changes that occurred in Italy at the time: a cinema that kept alive and thriving the old, conservative values of the prewar monarchic-fascist *Italietta*, and also a cinema that registered ahead of time the turmoil and the rebellion that was going to afflict Italy in the 1960s and 1970s. The chapters of this volume underscore the discrepancy between the popular genre cinema that met the emotional requirement of the audience and was greatly appreciated by the public, and the critics who misjudged it for ideological and political reasons. Most of these studies not only deal with the subject matter in depth, but also span across a vast cultural horizon so that they can really be considered exhaustive on the subject in question.

We are confident that this volume will contribute greatly to the field of both Italian cultural studies and cinema studies for the novelty of the critical approaches and the variety of the subjects. The groundbreaking nature of this work is testified by its ability to show how important the study of genres is for Italian cinema, how essential it is to show that, on the one hand, the *texts* in question attempt to win the *reader* to a particular world view and, on the other, how the same texts, rituals and customs, bind together the social order, in a sort of Althusserian way, offering pleasure and relief from its demands. We also point out how many of these texts and rituals manage to somehow achieve a plurality of messages that range from the more conservative and pro-establishment to the more rebellious and pro-revolutionary, therefore constituting a family of *hybrid texts*.

Starting from these premises, John Storey claims that all texts are ultimately political, because they offer competing ideological significations of the way the world is.[2] Every text, therefore attempts to entice the reader to see the world in a particular way; it tries to push the reader/spectator in a particular direction. Basically all texts are ideological or, put another way, culture and ideology often cover the same ground. Therefore, this study of popular culture and cinema aims at reconstructing all the inescapable relations of power and politics that mark the culture/ideology of a specific time, both nationally and internationally. The so-called "formula cinema," or genre cinema, is used as a tool to penetrate successfully into a large portion of our culture. According to Gramsci's hegemony theory, popular culture is the site of the struggle between the forces of resistance of subordinate groups and the forces of incorporation associated with dominant groups in society.[3] Texts and practices of popular culture as a result move between two poles, resistance and incorporation, and also between the discourse of the text and the discourse of the reader, who brings his own cultural formation and his historical moment to the reading. This is because, as Benjamin suggests, the meaning of a cultural text is produced at consumption not at production. Of course, there is always a discrepancy between the use of a text or practice by the public and the use intended by the producers. Cinema is a highly profitable commercial enterprise, and as a consequence we need to keep in mind that a filmic text tends to mirror attitudes and sentiments that are already there consciously and/or unconsciously, but, on the other hand, we cannot forget that it also tends to create new areas in which these attitudes can be projected. The popular filmic texts analyzed in this volume tell us not so much, for example, about ancient mythology (peplum films) or the Far West (spaghetti western): They tell us about the people who created them and the society that enjoyed them.

Moreover, the present book fits into a smaller and less populated area of cultural studies that comprises those works that study Italian culture, but are written in English. The number of publications in the English-speaking world on cultural studies is enormous, especially because cultural studies was born in Birmingham, England, and then migrated successfully throughout the Anglo-Saxon world and to the United States and Australia. However, cultural studies did not spread with the same speed to the rest of Europe. In Italy, the persistent Crocean heritage of the division between "low" and "high" culture delayed the development of this kind of work. Nowadays, nevertheless, cultural studies thrive in Italy. Besides the pioneering work by Umberto Eco (*Apocalittici e integrati*, 1964) and now Dal Lago's body of work (*Descrizione di una battaglia. Rituali del calcio*, 1990), to cite the most well-known examples, there are many contributions to this field (in Italian usually occurring under the umbrella of *Scienze della Comunicazione*).[4] However, because the production of Italian cultural studies written in English is not a vast one, we would like to map it, following chronologically the appearance of the most significant books from 1990 on, hoping to create a niche that would make manifest the contribution of the present study to the field.

In 1990 Baranski and Lumley edited a volume entitled *Culture and Conflict in Postwar Italy* that is a touchstone for Italian cultural studies written in English.[5] The book analyzes the cultural transformations that happened in Italy starting from the Second World War, concentrating on key words such as "mass," "popular" and "culture." "Culture" is interpreted in an anthropological sense as a "way of life" and not as a separate sphere of human activity. The book is divided into five parts that deal respectively with history (history, culture, language), catholic and communist subcultures (religion, politics, social movements), role of the intellectuals (mass culture and intellectuals), commercial cinema (cinema and design in postwar Italy) and television. The two editors make an interesting distinction between "mass culture" and "popular culture," comparing the English definitions with the Italian ones: *cultura di massa* and *cultura popolare*. Usually *cultura di massa* means everything that is produced in society for hegemonic goals in a Marxist sense, or, better, everything that is "fed to the masses," while *cultura popolare* has a positive Gramscian connotation and should be read as "culture of the people, born from the people for the people." Therefore, *cultura popolare* would be the culture that opposes the elitist culture of the dominant classes, and, at least in the first decade of the postwar period the leftist intellectuals tried to promote a culture that could prevent the effects of homogenization caused by the mass culture imported from the United States. Lumley and Baranski, on the other hand, also affirm that Italian culture becomes "mass culture" in the years that follow the economic boom of 1958–63. We could not agree more with this statement. In this study, in fact, we have based our analysis of the filmic texts keeping in mind Spinazzola's distinction between *cinema popolare* and *cinema di massa*. Spinazzola says that "the works targeting the consumption of the lower classes belong to popular cinema; mass cinema instead is aimed at the unification of the audience, both upper and lower classes, and it is in a certain way classless."[6] We can for that reason conclude that after the economic boom (1958–63) the distinction between popular and mass culture is no longer possible in Italy. See, for example, the pepla films of the 1950s that still fall into Spinazzola's category of *cultura popolare* (i.e. films fed to the lower classes) while the spaghetti western of the 1960s are already "mass culture," a product appealing to men and women of any class, bourgeoisie and proletariat.

Before entering more deeply into the mapping of this cultural field, we need to make a brief diversion and talk about the pioneering works of Umberto Eco. It is impossible to talk about Italian cultural studies without coming to terms with Umberto Eco's legacy. *Apocalittici e integrati* published in 1964 is an international point of reference in the study of mass culture. Eco's book was a revolutionary text. It managed to defeat the widespread hostility on the part of Italian intellectuals (from left and as well as right) toward the so-called homogenization of the American-led invasion of mass culture, or against the invasion of low culture at the expense of real culture, where *real* should be read as *high* culture, i.e., the expression of the highest form of the human spirit as in the works of the great masters (the "canon"). Eco tried to look anthropologically at cultural production. Shultz's cartoons, the comic strip of Superman, television programs etc., are seen as products of a certain culture that can reveal a lot about itself. Eco also never forgets that behind production there is also distribution and consumption.

From the 1960s on, Eco extensively dealt with "mass culture" from a theoretical point of view, studying those texts which portray the Manichean opposition between Good and Evil; concentrating his attention on comic or filmic characters that, being divided into neat, simple and opposed categories, give life to a cultural production that, according to the critic, negates the complexity of reality. See the happy ending of many filmic texts which convey a falsely ordered view of the world, negating its complexity, as well as the continuous becoming of history. Eco deconstructs the "signs" to reveal the ideological effects of mass communication, in opposition to which there are the "open works," i.e., those texts that break the norm and open themselves to multiple interpretations and, in so doing, question the real, uncovering its hidden meanings.[7]

In 1994, David Forgacs published *Italian Culture in the Industrial Era*.[8] In this important work, the author examined the long-term development of the culture industries, and their relations with the state. His study is a brief but interesting history of the cultural modernization of Italy in the century after 1880. Forgacs focuses mostly on the development of the industries engaged in the production and distribution of cultural products, such as books, newspapers, magazines, films, radio and television. He contends that, even if it is common belief that mass culture arrived in Italy with the economic boom of the late 1950s and early 1960s, there are scholars who believe that the phenomenon started in 1880 with the first wave of industrialization and that another followed in the 1930s with the advent of radio. Forgacs reinserts the study of products and producers within the circuit production-distribution-consumption, with an emphasis on the linkages between cultural industries and political power from the turn of the nineteenth century to the 1970s. He bases his study on three notions: that social consent is actively organized by cultural means in civil society and not just by legitimation by the state (political society); that social cohesion works through a cementing together of blocks or alliances of different social groups rather than being the work of a single dominant class; and that these blocks need to be actively constructed. Because they are impermanent, they can be destabilized and re-stabilized by changing the relations of force within and outside society. According to Forgacs, the study of culture has been heavily conditioned by politics in Italy because from the very beginning the dominant parties managed to control public broadcasting, making it evident that the ones who own and control the cultural industries remain in power. This, as a consequence, has also impeded the development of a cultural studies approach.

Italian Cultural Studies—An Introduction (1996), edited by Forgacs and Lumley, opened up the field of cultural research, giving the scholar of cultural studies a wider horizon.[9] The book is divided in parts that cover subjects as seemingly diverse as anthropological fieldworks (geographies, political identities, gender relations), media (press, cinema, television), fashion and music (culture and society). The contributors carefully avoided any rankings between high and low culture, and looked at a variety of cultural materials, always keeping in mind that culture is a set of signifying practices and symbolic social forms, looking at it from the standpoint of the dominated classes and not from the side of the dominant classes.

Between 1996 and today many collaborative studies on Italian cultural have been published. I will mention only some of these works, not because the remaining ones are not interesting—quite the contrary—but because these collections often cover the same topics, from cinema to fashion, from problems of national identities to cuisine, from literature to religion, from language to sport. Therefore, for obvious reasons, it would be impossible to analyze in detail this varied production. From all these volumes I want to single out *The Cambridge Companion to Modern Italian Culture* (2001), edited by Baranski and West, which offers a good perspective on the multifaceted complexity of modern Italian culture.[10] If, on one hand, its thematic richness can run the risk of fragmenting the general discourse, on the other hand, this richness prevents the compartmentalization of the topics. As Baranski and West say in the Introduction: "In a book which attempts to provide an introduction to 'modern Italian culture,' both Rossellini the film maker and Berlusconi the media entrepreneur have to be found a niche."[11] That is to say that the selection tries to keep a balanced mixture of high and low culture. The same would be true for *Italian Cultural Studies* (2001), another collaborative book edited by Parati and Lawton. Here the material is divided into two sections, a more theoretical one and more practical one; the key word of the volume is "interdisciplinary" in order to, as the editors point out, "explore new methodologies in defining a culture as a set of intertwining strategies and of inter-relations."[12]

There is a group of volumes dealing with Italian cultural studies that offer collections of essays written both in Italian and in English. In 1998 *Annali d'Italianistica* dedicated its entire Volume 16 to Italian cultural studies. Quoting Lawrence Grossberg et al. in his thoughtful Forward, Dombroski states that the main problem affecting the area of cultural studies has been the lack of a discourse that shares "a commitment to examining cultural practices from the point of view of their intricacies with, and, within relations of power,"[13] including the relations of power that the critic himself has within those relations. He points out the necessity of establishing some markers to a field that runs the risk of becoming "anything anyone wants."[14] We could not agree more with Dombroski's warning. In writing the present essays, in fact, we have kept in mind that culture and ideology coincide.

In 2003 Antonio Vitti and Roberta Morosini edited *In Search of Italia — Saggi sulla cultura dell'Italia contemporanea.*[15] Three out of the 12 essays are in English, the rest are in Italian. These studies are written by scholars who, facing the many ideological and political changes that have occurred in Italy since the advent of the Second Republic (1992), try to understand a nation that, for some of them who emigrated abroad, remains a puzzle. The authors are, therefore, motivated by scholarly interests and by a desire to make sense of the intense cultural, political, and social modifications that Italy has been undergoing in the recent past. The topics are varied and concentrate on contemporary culture: from Francesco Guccini's novels to the national Bicycle Tour (Giro d'Italia), from contemporary cinema to the status of the spoken language of today etc. In the same year, Vitti also edited another volume, *Incontri con il cinema italiano.* In the Preface, Vitti indicates that he wants to re-direct the attention of the reader away from the traditional cinematic canon, i.e., away from the production of the great masters such as Antonioni, Visconti, De Sica, Fellini, Pasolini, Bertolucci, toward a blending of cinema and cultural studies, in order to examine the "historical landscape" of Italy through the lens of cinema from its origins to the present. Many of the essays (both in English and in Italian) deal with films of contemporary directors who focus on immigration and political corruption, as well as the many economic problems from which the national cinematic industry suffers today.

In 2005, Anthony Tamburri edited *Italian Cultural Studies 2002.*[16] Tamburri, quoting Stuart Hall in his introduction, makes clear that cultural studies is a mode of analysis which takes at its focal point "the changing way of life of societies and groups and the networks of meanings that individuals and groups use to make sense of and to communicate with each other."[17] He stresses the intertwining and inter-relations of everything that pertains to culture, specifying that cultural studies is not a "mere description of the cultural emergent that aim to give voice to the 'experience' of those who have been denied a space to talk,"[18] but an explanation that will foster change in the conditions that have blocked those voices from talking. The political stance of cultural studies could not be stated more clearly, together with the premise that cultural studies breaks the traditional boundaries among the disciplines, because it is interdisciplinary in nature, and as a consequence it presupposes a study of a broad context or of the "cultural cluster" into which the particular text is studied. According to Tamburri, globalization, multiculturalism, interdisciplinarity are the key terms of cultural studies, now that all the planet's societies are linked in a world system and enmeshed in a global movement of difference and power.

In 2006 Norma Bouchard edited *Negotiating Italian Identities* as a special issue of the journal *Annali d'Italianistica* entirely devoted to exploring the dynamics of Italian identities from the postwar period to the present.[19] The volume is a selection of articles written in English and in Italian. As the title suggests, and as Bouchard states in her opening essay, "Negotiating Italian Identities," cultural studies has "placed the issue of identity at the core of its enquiry, conceptualizing it as a continuous set of ever-evolving subject positions negotiated and articulated within the wider contexts and sites of acculturation that are available to us at any given stage of our personal and public histories."[20] The dramatic economic, social and political transformations that have affected Italy since its formation in 1860 and up to the Second Republic (1992) presented a panorama in which particularistic identity formations appeared, last but not least the new subnational identities such as the emergence of the *Lega Nord* and *Lega Lombarda*. Local, national and supranational identities are explored in relation to high- and low-print culture, media culture, patterns of consumption of everyday life, ritualized forms of behavior and lifestyles, sites of memory and forgetfulness. Some of these studies investigate processes of identities in relation to large socio-political developments, others in relation to diasporic, regional, gendered, class and generational changes using diverse methodologies. If some of the scholars address issues connected with formalizations of identities propelled by modern industrialization, the cultural revolution of 1968, the rise of the *Leghe* and of supra-national communities, and the immigration to Italy from abroad, others discuss symbolic practices from fashion to popular music, from documentaries to journalism.

We hope that the overview of the above volumes will help the reader to situate the present study within the field of Italian cultural studies and, at the same time, we trust that this overview will make evident the many points of contact and of departure from the above mentioned works and will highlight our contribution to the field, having covered some new ground. In writing the essays we tried to appeal to a wide audience, ranging from students to specialists of Italian cultural studies. The reader will notice that in our essays we are more interested in the *reception* rather than in the *production* of mass popular culture; therefore, we concentrated on the reception of popular genre cinema and on specific cultural phenomena following a chronological approach. For this reason we started in the 1950s with the sword-and-sandal epics, and we progressed from there, tracing the development of popular genre cinema through the decades: the horror, the spaghetti western and the birth of the comedy Italian style. We also felt the need to study a popular ritual, *tarantismo*, from its origins to the present, as an example, in a Gramscian sense, of *cultura popolare nata dal popolo per il popolo* (popular culture born from the people for the people). The last section deals with violence and comprises two types of violence: violence in the western genre and violence against women. We felt the urge to deal with violence because on the one hand it is the intrinsic and inescapable fiber that holds together the history of the western genre, and because on the other, in spite of the sexual revolution, the onset of feminism, and the advent of the so-called "emancipation of women," the problem persists in Italian society. We decided to look at what kind of "image of woman" these films created at the symbolic level.

Popular Genre Cinema

In "The Italian Sword-and-Sandal Cinema from *Fabiola* (1949) to

Hercules and the Captive Women (1961): Texts and Contexts," Frank Burke addresses a genre (the sword-and-sandal film) and a *filone* (strand) or sub-genre (the pseudo-mythical Italian peplum of the late 1950s and early 1960s) in such a way as to reveal how the issues and meanings generated within a seemingly repeatable formula change according to the historical and cultural moments in which examples of that formula arise. He discusses how, for instance, a 1949 film, *Fabiola,* differs markedly in tone, characterization, and subject matter from two 1962 pepla, *The Colossus of Rhodes* and *Hercules and the Captive Women,* because of the historical and cultural landscape from which they emerge. In so doing, he links what seems to be a relatively insignificant popular culture phenomenon to major shifts in Italy and in the confluence of Italian and American cultural politics following the Second World War. His approach is interdisciplinary, embodying issues of history, culture, politics, ideology, gender, genre, sexual orientation, production, and reception, in the context of film textual analysis. The essay insists that meaning arises only within a cultural field, and focuses on the relationship of cultural production to power (the politics of the sword-and-sandal film, as it were). Finally, the essay as a whole strongly focuses on popular culture and, in particular, on a cluster of films (the pepla) that undermine the classics by treating Greek mythology and history with the utmost irreverence, thus unsettling the boundaries between high and low culture.

In "Horror Cinema: the Emancipation of Women and Urban Anxiety," Andrea Bini analyzes the birth, evolution, and decline of the horror genre in Italian cinema in the postwar years and the way in which this cinema incorporated the changes of Italian society. The first decade (1956–66) is characterized by Gothic films, in which, instead of traditional male monsters and villains, sexually active women (vampire-witches) become the forces menacing the patriarchal system. The female monster is the outcome of a crisis experienced by a rural society uprooted by the economic boom and the frantic modernization of the 1950s and the early 1960s. The Italian horror film undergoes a rebirth in the 1970s with the Italian *giallo,* and its contemporary settings and explicit gore (1969–77). Bini shows how this unexpected commercial achievement cannot be explained by looking only at male anxiety due to the spreading of sexual liberation and feminist movements; instead, it should be examined with an eye on the growing urban anxiety caused by the transformation of the Italian cities into anonymous megalopolis between 1969 and 1979.

Flavia Brizio-Skov, in "Dollars, Bullets, and Success: The Spaghetti Western Phenomenon," puts in motion a rehabilitation of the western Italian style, trying to find the reasons behind the enormous success of the spaghetti western, a phenomenon that clearly goes beyond the narrow label of edible mass consumption product. There are many studies on the spaghetti westerns, first of all the seminal volume written by Sir Christopher Frayling titled *Spaghetti Westerns*.[21] However, an in-depth analysis of the phenomenal success of this genre has not yet appeared. What is required is a close look at the socio-political fiber of Italy as well as making hypotheses on the ideological tendencies of the audience of the time. The goal of this chapter is to provide convincing explanations of how these films satisfied the sense of rebellion and the rite of passage from nineteenth century conservative-monarchic-fascist values to the modern capitalistic values created by the sudden industrialization of the country in the 1960s, and how these apparently contradictory elements met the expectations of a large spectrum of spectators.

In "The Birth of the Comedy Italian Style," Andrea Bini focuses, in the context of postwar Italian cinema, on the beginning of the most successful Italian genre (or sub-genre) of the 1960s: the *commedia all'italiana* (comedy Italian style). Going against mainstream critical opinion that situates this cinematic production in the wake of *Neorealismo Rosa* (Rosy Neorealism), a series of light, happy-ending comedies of the 1950s commonly considered its direct forerunners, Bini demonstrates how this critical view does not account for the biting satire of the *commedia all'italiana*. The predecessors of this genre must be found in other, much bleaker comedies of the 1940s and early 1950s directed by Roberto Rossellini, Federico Fellini and Mario Monicelli. This cinematic production—as well as other films starring the young actor Alberto Sordi—created on screen the image of a country whose social bonds had collapsed after the war, a country in which the intense process of industrialization and urbanization due to the "economic miracle" had created high levels of social distress, favoring the formation of a new breed of self-indulgent and opportunistic Italian males. Unsurprisingly, the first comedies Italian style became box-office successes and established themselves as a special genre only in the 1960s. In these years, in fact, they found a large audience in the new urban middle-class that was willing to laugh at itself insofar as it saw itself as the leading protagonist of the new prosperity.

Ritual and Cinema

Flavia Laviosa, in "Tarantula Myths and Music: Popular Culture and Ancient Rituals in Italian Cinema," examines Southern Italian tarantism, a fascinating ritual with mythical-symbolic and magic-religious aspects that has generated interest for centuries. The historical, anthropological and ethno-musicological overview of the present-day rituals connected with this ancient phenomenon illustrates the topic from a composite cultural studies perspective. This chapter offers an in-depth analysis of the stylistic and thematic choices of feature and documentary films portraying tarantism. More specifically, the author examines the films *Flavia, the Heretic* (*Flavia, la monaca musulmana,* 1974) by Gianfranco Mingozzi; *La sposa di San Paolo* (1990; no English title available) by Gabriella Rosaleva; *Pizzicata* (1996) and *Life Blood* (*Sangue vivo,* 2000) by Edoardo Winspeare. Although tarantism is extinct today, the myth of the spider is re-interpreted through music festivals and theater performances in the Salento region. Laviosa explores how and why the music and dance *pizzica* have exploded in the past 20 years, thus generating the artistic expressions of *new*-tarantism. Finally, the author focuses on whether this current popularity of tarantism is only the result of commercial exploitation, or if it is the product of the reappropriation of Southern Italian popular culture by the people.

Violence and Cinema

Brizio-Skov continues her analysis of the spaghetti western in "Popular Cinema and Violence: The Western Genre." Starting from the point of view that a complete rehabilitation of the spaghetti western is not possible without its insertion into the genesis of the western genre, the author demonstrates that the western Italian style is not really a sub-genre, but an indispensable moment in the development of the whole genre. With its innovations the spaghetti western changes the classic western formula, allowing the birth of the post-western. The subversive qualities of the spaghetti western, with its altering of the classic western justification of violence, has not been studied sufficiently. This essay seeks to help fill that void by demonstrating how the American post-westerns of today would not exist without Sergio Leone's films and the films of his best followers. The spaghetti western's transformation of the concept of violence, a fundamental ingredient of any western film, has facilitated the genre re-reading of the history of America. This transformation has opened profound gaps in the monolithic faith of the American concept of justice, triggering a shift in ideological perspective that is evident in the post-westerns, a shift that begins with Sam Peckinpah's seminal film, *The Wild Bunch* (1969), and continues to the present.

In "Women's Drama, Men's Business: Sexual Violence Against Women in Italian Cinema and Media," Flavia Laviosa brings together several aspects—legal, political, cultural, sociological and psychological—of sexual violence against women in Italy, thus examining the phenomenon across disciplines and through a cultural studies approach that aims at re-creating the psychology of the victims of sexual violence within the framework of trauma theory. The novelty of this chapter consists in addressing this aberrant behavior from multiple perspectives and manifestations. First, the author gives a historical overview of the international and Italian feminist debate on the definitions and forms of sexual violence; second, she analyzes how gang-rape has been represented in Italian cinema, performed in theater, and covered by the media; and third, she discusses how Italian institutions, the legal system, and women's organizations have dealt with such behavior, while exposing the widespread cultural acceptance and the legal tolerance towards this crime. The texts examined are four feature films: two versions of *Two Women* (*La ciociara*, Vittorio De Sica, 1960 and Dino Risi, 1989), *The Most Beautiful Wife* (*La sposa più bella* Damiano Damiani, 1970), *The Pack* (*Il Branco*, Marco Risi, 1994) and *The Wedding Dress* (*Il vestito da sposa*, Fiorella Infascelli, 2003); a theater play *The Rape* (*Lo stupro*, Franca Rame, 1975); media coverage of *The Circeo Massacre* (1975) and a documentary of an actual rape trial, *Trial for Rape* (*Processo per stupro*, Loredana Dordi, 1979).

NOTES

1   On cultural studies theory for Gramsci Culture see *Ideology and Social Process*, Tony Bennett, Colin Mercer and Janet Woolacott, eds. (London, Batsford, 1981); on cultural studies theory see John Fiske *Reading the Popular* (London, Unwin Hyman, 1989); *An Introduction Guide to Cultural Theory and Popular Culture*, John Storey, ed. (Athens, University of Georgia Press, 1993); *Resistance through Rituals*, Stuart Hall and Tony Jefferson, eds. (London, Hutchinson, 1976); and *Cultural Studies*, Lawrence Grossberg et all, eds. (London, Routledge, 1992).

2   John Storey, ed., *An Introduction Guide to Cultural Theory and Popular Culture* (Athens, University of Georgia Press, 1993).

3   Antonio Gramsci, *Antonio Gramsci: Prison Notebooks* (New York, Columbia UP, 1996); *Quaderni del Carcere* (Torino, Einaudi Editore, 1975); Antonio Santucci ed., *Le opere. Antologia di tutti gli scritti* (Roma, Editori Riuniti, 1997).

4   Umberto Eco, *Opera aperta* (Milano, Bompiani. 1962); *Apocalittici e integrati*, (Milano, Bompiani 1964); *Il superuomo di massa* (Milano, Bompiani, 1978). *Si veda anche* De Martino, Passerini, Portelli.

5   Zygmunt G. Baranski and Robert Lumley, eds. *Culture and Conflict in Postwar Italy—Essays on Mass and Popular Culture* (London, Macmillan Press, 1990).

6   "*Al cinema popolare appartengono le opere destinate al consumo esclusivo delle classi subalterne; il cinema di massa è invece programmato in vista di una unificazione del pubblico, borghese e proletario, e appare perciò dotato di valenza interclassista.*" The translation is mine. Vittorio Spinazzola, *Cinema e pubblico-Lo spettacolo filmico in Italia* 1945–65 (Milano, Bompiani, 1974): 348.

7   Umberto Eco, *Apocalypse Postponed*, Robert Lumley ed. (London, BFI Publishing, 1994).

8   David Forgacs, *Italian Culture in the Industrial Era 1880–1980—Cultural Industries, Politics and the Public* (Manchester, Manchester UP, 1990).

9   David Forgacs and Robert Lumley, eds. *Italian Cultural Studies-An Introduction* (Oxford, Oxford UP, 1996).

10 Zygmunt G. Baranski and Rebecca West eds., *The Cambridge Companion to Modern Italian Culture* (Cambridge, Cambridge UP, 2001).

11 Ibidem: 3.
12 Graziella Parati and Ben Lawton eds. *Italian Cultural Studies* (Boca Raton, Bordighera Press, 2001): ix.
13 Robert S. Dombroski and Dino S. Cervigni eds., *Italian Cultural Studies, Annali d'Italianistica*, vol. 16 (1998), Chapel Hill, North Carolina: 13.
14 Dombroski: 13. See also Lawrence Grossberg, Cary Nelson and Paula Treichler, eds. *Cultural Studies* (New York, Routledge, 1992).
15 Antonio Vitti and Roberta Morosini, eds. *In Search of Italia—Saggi sulla cultura dell'Italia contemporanea* (Pesaro. Metauro Edizioni, 2003).
16 This volume, *Italian Cultural Studies 2002* (Boca Raton, Florida, Bordighera Press, 2005) as *Italian Cultural Studies 2001*, edited by Graziella Parati and Ben Lawton (Lafayette, Indiana, Bordighera Press, 2001), stem from papers delivered at the annual conference of the Italian Cultural Studies Association (ICSA). The association has held a number of conferences through the years, at Dartmouth College, Purdue University, Boca Raton.
17 Anthony Tamburri, ed., *Italian Cutlural Studies 2002* (Boca Raton, Bordighera Press, 2005): iii.
18 Tamburri: iii.
19 Norma Bouchard, ed. *Negotiating Italian Identities, Annali d'Italianistica*, vol. 24 (2006), Chapel Hill, North Carolina.
20 Bouchad: 11.
20 Christopher Frayling, *Spaghetti Westerns* (London, I.B.Tauris, 1998).

1

THE ITALIAN SWORD-AND-SANDAL FILM FROM *FABIOLA* TO *HERCULES AND THE CAPTIVE WOMEN*

Texts and Contexts

Frank Burke

The Italian peplum (sword and sandal) was an extraordinary mini genre or *filone* of the late 1950s and early 1960s. It was ushered in by *Hercules* (*Le fatiche di Ercole*, Pietro Francisci, 1957) and consisted largely of tales based loosely on Greco-Roman mythology with heroes played by body-builders (usually American) such as Steve Reeves. The subgenre also encompasses films that were loosely based on history, e.g., *The Giant of Marathon* (*La battaglia di Maratona,* Jacques Tourneur and Mario Bava, 1959), and on biblical subjects, e.g., *Samson* (*Sansone,* Gianfranco Parolini, 1962). The peplum spawned at least 200 movies over a seven-year period and derived its name from French critics, in reference to the type of tunic often worn by its characters, at least in the pseudo-mythological and pseudo-historical films. The *filone* has not attracted much critical attention. This is largely because of its absurdity (or what I would rather term "absurdism"). Featuring cartoon-like characters and situations in live-action cinema, ridiculous monsters and sci-fi effects, and musclemen wielding boulders of *papier mâché*, the peplum appears at first glance to be nothing more than a box-office ploy in spectacular bad taste. Moreover, it seems a sadly escapist moment in Italian film, particularly after the renowned seriousness of neorealism and when compared with the Italian "art" cinema of Fellini, Antonioni, Visconti, and others. However, as with even the most frivolously intentioned of popular culture phenomena, the peplum does meaningful cultural work, reflecting and embodying significant economic, social, and ideological realities as an integral part of precisely that which it seems to be fleeing. I would like here to address that work. In particular, by expanding my chronological parameters to include three pre-pepla sword-and-sandal films—*Fabiola* (*Fabiola*, Alessandro Blasetti, 1949), *Sins of Rome* (*Spartaco*, Riccardo Freda, 1952), and *Ulysses* (*Ulysses*, Mario Camerini, 1954)—as well addressing three bona fide pepla—*Hercules, The Colossus of Rhodes* (*Il Colosso di Rodi*, Sergio Leone, 1961), and *Hercules and the Captive Women* (*Ercole alla conquista d'Atlantide*, Vittorio Cottafavi, 1961)—I would like to chart a trajectory of significant changes within the Italian situation, reading the films in relation to history and vice versa. As the films move from stories of compromised or failed revolution (*Fabiola, Sins of Rome*) to tales of (monarchical) restoration (*Ulysses, Hercules*), they reflect the increasing conservatism of the postwar period: the disappearance of Resistance aspirations and values and the onset of 1950s conformism. The common people, central to *Fabiola* and *Sins of Rome*, disappear as the succeeding two films escape into a classical world that, particularly in the case of the peplum, seems far distant not only from the realist settings of neorealism but also from the fictionalized-history-with-contemporary-relevance that characterizes the first two. On the other hand, and consistent with the normal evolution of genres, the peplum acquires a certain degree of self-reflexivity, becoming in certain instances strikingly anti-reactionary. *The Colossus of Rhodes* and *Hercules and the Captive Women* are not just silly, they are seriously silly, parodying their own escapism and allowing for compelling critiques of the extreme limitations posed by the Americanization of politics at the end of and following the Second World War. In so doing, they point to the strong politicization of Italian film and society that characterizes the later 1960s. At the same time, the six films chart a movement beyond an isolated Italian context as Italian cinema increasingly negotiates American cultural influence and a host of American-driven values associated with late capitalism, consumerism, and nascent postmodernity. By *Ulysses*, the effects of Americanization materialize; by *The Colossus of Rhodes* so does Italian resistance to those effects.

The film with the most overt links (albeit allegorical) to a social and political reality is Alessandro Blasetti's *Fabiola*. The biggest box office success in Italy following its release, *Fabiola* was very loosely based on a nineteenth-century novel, *Fabiola o La Chiesa delle catacombe* by English Cardinal Nicholas Wiseman, and details Christian revolution on historical, political, religious, and personal levels, all four of which dovetail by the film's end. The story situates itself historically at the moment when Constantine, experiencing a vision before his triumph over Massenzio at the Battle of Milvian Bridge, brings religious tolerance to Rome and the Roman Empire, marking in effect the legal and political legitimization of Christianity in Western society. The social backdrop of the film is a Christian "revolution," with converts multiplying daily and forever changing the fabric of the Roman Empire. The spiritual odyssey of the protagonists, Rhual and Fabiola, draws them ever closer to the revolution, as they evolve in selflessness and transcendent love to the point of their own conversion in the arena. Fabiola's conversion then has a culminative, centrifugal effect. The moment she closes her eyes and makes the sign of the cross, accepting Christianity, the social transformation

In *Fabiola* (1949), the title character (Michèle Morgan) closes her eyes and makes the sign of the cross at the moment of her conversion.

that has been occurring around her completes itself. First, gladiators who were about to kill Rhual throw down their swords. Then the throngs in the arena unite in clamorous confirmation of her (and their) newfound Christianity. Moreover, when Fabiola confirms her faith in a Christian hereafter by willing her own death (she tells a soldier under orders of the anti-Christian Roman prefect to kill her and Rhual), the legions of Constantine suddenly appear. Fabiola's death is averted, and the film concludes with the image of Constantine's insignia which recalls his vision and his motto *in hoc signo vinces* ("in this sign you will conquer"). The progression of events at the end lead to the implication that Constantine represents God's arrival on the scene or, more theologically, the fulfillment of His presence in the world, actuated by the virtuous actions of the film's hero and heroine and of their ever-growing ranks of Christian compatriots.

The film is clearly couched in Catholic terms and notions, consistent with the fact that it was produced by the Catholic production company Universalia with funding by the Vatican. However, its revolutionary thrust and representation of a mass social movement do not accord with any contemporary (1940s) religious movement, but with a significant discourse of revolution and radical change associated with communism and emerging out of the partisan movement. This discourse was particularly prominent in the ambit of Italian cinema and, in particular, in discussions around neorealism on the part of left-wing film critics. There was talk of a new society about to be born from the newly strengthened left as a result of its heroic role in the resistance, and the immediate postwar period was invoked as the "springtime" of a new Italy (Overbey, passim).

Consistent with this, and based in part on Blasetti's own comments about the film, both Gian Piero Brunetta and Maria Wyke see the film as an allegory less of Christian values than of communist sympathy. Brunetta states that "the ideological preoccupation" is to "make the situation of early Christians emotionally equatable to that of present-day communism" (454, trans. mine), and Wyke asserts that "through the narration of ancient religious persecution, (*Fabiola*) addresses not only the wartime violence inflicted on victims of and rebels against Nazism, but also the post-war intolerance exhibited toward Italian communism" (55). In fact, the scenes of Christian persecution trigger associations with Fascist *squadristi* attacks against Socialists and Nazi massacres of partisans (as well of course as Nazi persecution of the Jews) and, in this respect, are intended to be multiply evocative and applicable to a persecuted left as well as to fourth-century Christian martyrs. (The film's self-dedication—"to the wronged, the persecuted, and the victims of injustice"—conveys this sense of multiple applicability.) The scenes of secret meeting places and growing solidarity in the face of oppression also recall the clandestine evolution of the Resistance.

In this respect, the film represents a plea for tolerance in response to the powerful backlash experienced by the left after its initial moment of strength in the postwar. The backlash was fuelled in part by the conservative interests of the Italian employer classes, aided (paradoxically given the film's origins) by the Catholic Church, and supported by the political and economic interference of a hysterically anti-communist American government. It led to the expulsion of the left from the Italian government in 1947 and its disastrous defeat at the hands of the Vatican- and U.S.-supported Christian Democrats in the elections of 1948. The backlash reflected strong polarization which, along with massive social unrest, created, at the time of the making of *Fabiola*, one of the many moments in Italian history in which the country seemed headed toward civil war (Ginsborg: 110).

So in certain ways, *Fabiola* was intended as a progressive film, whose message seemed to be that there was nothing to fear in dramatic social change; that in fact communist and Christian social aims were largely equatable; and that acceptance, tolerance, and mutual cohabitation were infinitely preferable to hostility, disunity, and violence. This message reflected the moments of social unification (fleeting though they proved) that marked the Italian experience toward the end of the war, when the Resistance (largely through the Committees of National Liberation) brought together people from across the political spectrum to aid in the fight for freedom. It also reflected broad-spectrum participation in the politics of the immediate postwar, perhaps best reflected in the drafting and approval of Italy's constitution. The extent to which the film sought to resonate beyond a purely Christian or Catholic context was consistent with the fact that Universalia, while funded by the Vatican and largely viewed as a Catholic production company, was small "c" catholic in the films it produced and in its support for filmmakers of varying political affiliations—so much so that film and cultural studies scholar Enrica Capussotti actually describes Universalia as "tied to the left."[1] However, as my summary of the film's plot should have made clear, "revolution" or massive social change is ideologically managed in such a way as to ultimately deny communist-style revolution or even radical reform. Any change that occurs is top down. Not only is Constantine the *deus-ex-machina* who secures the "revolution" at the end (reconfirming monarchy despite the referendum of 1946 that had secured republicanism for Italy), but Fabiola herself is a noblewoman who is heavily dependent throughout the film on the memory and influence of her wealthy and influential father who was killed at the hands of conniving anti-Christian and anti-Constantine politicians. And of course, the ultimate top down change agent is God Himself, working through the divine providence that, by film's end, seems to have been behind every seemingly chance meeting and unrelated event that preceded and coalesced into such a glorious conclusion. This is confirmed by much of the iconography of the film, in particular the evocation of *in hoc signo vinces*, which ultimately effaces any contemporary communist-centered allegory in favor of a traditional Christian reading of pilgrims in progress and God's grace acting upon them.

Concomitantly, the social hierarchy remains largely as it was at the end. The ruling classes are still in charge. The under classes are no longer persecuted, and we are led to believe that slavery will end. However, there is no significant equalization or redistribution of wealth or power.

Given its equation of Christian and socialist/communist experience, we might conclude that, just as the film seeks to render social transformation unthreatening to conservative social forces, it seeks to make social continuity, and in particular stratification, unthreatening to the left. Monarchy can be revolutionary and the ruling classes can undergo a transformation of consciousness.

However, read in the light of subsequent history, the film fails in its attempts at depicting a version of the "umbrella" harmony to which the Resistance had briefly given rise. At worst, it seems, in retrospect, a celebration of Italian Christian Democrat values: the restoration of pre-war privilege dressed up as democratic freedom and as the never-to-be-fulfilled promise of social reform. Nonetheless *Fabiola* stands apart from all the other films I will be addressing in this essay in articulating, even in the most compromised of ways, the possibility of a mass social movement.

The second film under consideration is Riccardo Freda's *Sins of Rome*, released in 1952. Whereas *Fabiola* was born out of the experience of the Resistance and immediate postwar period, *Sins of Rome* emerges from a period in which the left has long been excluded from power and the Christian Democrats have begun to establish a hegemony that will last nearly 50 years. Neorealism has lost its impetus, partly through strategies of fiscal and ideological suppression on the part of the government. Italy has entered into a period of conformism so hauntingly portrayed in Frederico Fellini's *I Vitelloni* (1953) and is moving rapidly toward the Economic Miracle or "Boom" (1958–63) that will signify the triumph of American capitalism over anything even remotely radical, as the principal means of social integration. Despite this, the story of *Sins of Rome* is rooted in an actual revolutionary moment in Roman history (which serves as a source for American adaptations that culminate in Stanley Kubrick's *Spartacus*, 1960) and was significantly resurrected from an 1874 Italian novel by Raffaello Giovagnoli. Centering on a slave rebellion, it seemed to offer, at the outset of the 1950s, the possibility of envisioning a return to the heady notions of postwar social change. This seemed even more the case when the prison notebooks of the extraordinary Communist thinker Antonio Gramsci were published between 1948 and 1951 and took the novel as an example of the potential for a national popular literature. In fact, influenced by Gramsci's response to the novel, the Italian Communist Party magazine *Vie Nuove* serialized it during the first half of 1952. (See Wyke: 34 ff.)

At first glance, the film seems to support communist investment in the novel and its hero. Rome and the Romans are presented as Fascistic. The growing community of Spartaco's rebels, gathering in the countryside, clearly evoke the Italian resistance fighters who helped liberate Italy at the end of the Second World War. And Spartaco himself, as Wyke puts it, "is reconfigured ... in the mold of an

Italian partisan fighting in the resistance movement ..." (53). However, unlike the partisan movement, Spartaco's rebellion ends not only in failure but devastation. Moreover, the film dramatically de-heroizes the protagonist, focusing on his "temptations ... self-doubt, and ... failing" (Wyke: 55). In fact, Spartaco, having founded the revolutionary movement, ends up betraying it. He leaves his followers, and his love Amitys, to go on a reconnaissance mission that ends up with him in the arms of the noblewoman Sabina, daughter of his Roman enemy Crassus,[2] which allows Spartaco's subordinate Octavio to foment dissatisfaction among the slaves. Shortly after returning to the rebels, Spartaco is again lured to the world of Sabina and Crassus by the Sabina's claim that the Crassus wants to make a deal. While Spartaco wastes time haggling with Crassus (who makes clear that Sabina made up the deal-making ploy and that he himself is not really interested), Octavio and Amitys incite the slaves into a suicidal mission against the Romans, and by the time Spartaco makes ready to return, a massacre is in progress that decimates his troops and ends the rebellion. As he tells Amitys, who finds him dying on the field of battle: "It's too late. I betrayed you all ... I made promises I didn't keep. I led you to disaster not to victory. This is the end of our road. All is lost." There is more than a bit of irony in Spartaco's egoism: he did not lead his people to anything; he was just not around. The consequences of his actions are underscored in a long and haunting aerial shot and pan, including two dissolves to heighten the sense of time and space, as Amitys walks through a seemingly endless battlefield of dead bodies in search of Spartaco. Although there are obviously Roman dead as well, the overwhelming sensation is of the annihilation of the rebel movement.

Freda's representation of the revolutionaries is damning. Not only is their leader easily seduced by the pleasures associated with established power, but the leadership of the slaves is riven by conflict (Octavio vs. Spartaco) virtually the moment the rebellion is born.[3] The rest of the slaves are sheep, easily led in one or direction or another, depending on who dictates orders. Analogies with both Soviet and Italian communism are, of course, not difficult to find (For the latter, see Wyke: 56).

The film offers an ironically happy ending. Amitys claims: "Even if this battle is lost, the fight will go on until victory is ours. Be at peace, your example will be followed. The flame you've lit is still burning. It will burn until the world is free." However, it is obvious that Spartaco's example has been appalling and that there are no followers in sight to continue the fight. The concluding "optimism" seems to be Freda miming and in fact parodying the end of *Fabiola*. Amitys becomes a (purely simulated) transformative heroine. And the final shot echoes *Fabiola*'s concluding image of Constantine's flag and insignia, by turning Amitys into an icon, holding aloft Spartaco's sword in the promise of some future liberation. (*In hoc signo vinces.*) This silly ending belies all the more interesting events and implications that have preceded it, and its absurdity may well have been Freda's revenge for all the interference he experienced in making the film, particularly as he sought to create an even darker vision than that which ultimately reached the screen (Faldini e Fofi: 358). Nonetheless, the underlying darkness does survive, and the impossibility of meaningful social change in the film seems to reflect not only problems within the Italian left and communism in general, but the larger stasis that had already begun to characterize Italian politics and society by 1952.

Having moved from successful revolution—albeit Christianized, monarchized, dematerialized, and deprived of genuine social transformation—in *Fabiola* to a failed and quite hopeless revolution in *Sins of Rome*, we move to an even more conservative political model—restoration—in Mario Camerini's *Ulysses*. Both as a story of restoration and as the only Italian sword-and-sandal film of note between *Sins of Rome* and *Hercules*, *Ulysses* serves as a major harbinger of the peplum. It also seems to presage the *filone* as a turn to the classics or high art and away from anything remotely linked to a national popular, though the peplum's use of the classics will have a distinctively popular culture orientation. *Ulysses* does, though, presage the peplum's escape into a kind of past that is unusable as potential allegory for a revolutionary present or future (in contrast to the historical precedents reworked by *Fabiola* and *Sins of Rome*).

The story is, of course, grounded in Homer's *Odyssey*. Its status as a classic sets it largely apart from the other films under consideration, and for that reason, I deal with it more briefly than with the others.

Despite its remoteness in time and space, the story resonates quite nicely with numerous aspects of Italy's wartime experience, depicting an island (read peninsular) society occupied by strangers (the suitors),[4] in a virtual state of civil war, suffering from a lack of leadership and a consequent void in political authority, and, of course, in desperate need of liberation. Moreover, both *The Odyssey* and *Ulysses* foreground the problem of postwar readjustment, of a soldier and his family having to address the former's return to a domestic peacetime environment.[5]

This latter aspect makes *Ulysses* seem less a political than a more broadly human or personal document: more the return of an individual to his rightful place than the restoration of a king to his rightful throne. Ulysses' ability to serve as a kind of "everyman" is reflected in his playing the beggar upon his return, and remaining undetected as long as he wishes. Nonetheless, it is made clear that the "democratizing" of Ithaca in terms of meritocratic competition among the suitors for the hand of Penelope is an evil that must be remedied through a return to the old monarchy and Ulysses, the once and future king. Moreover, in strong contrast with both *Fabiola* and *Sins of Rome*, there is virtually no representation of the common people. The fact that Ulysses impersonates one only to achieve his royal aims underscores their effacement.

Put another way, Ulysses' commonness, present not just in his disguise but in his representation throughout the film as a kind of "all-American Joe"—affable, adventurous, one-of-the-guys, heroic-but-greatly-flawed—constitutes a kind of strategic ideological contradiction, recalling the kind of impossible conflation of communism and Catholicism at work in *Fabiola*, rearticulating monarchy in the language of commonality rather than imperious royalty to satisfy the democratic tastes of newly republican Italy while still retaining the bases of conservative political authority.

Whereas *Ulysses'* focus on monarchy and restoration might be explained away as the result of the story's ancient origins, *Hercules* establishes the theme of restoration as fundamental to the Italian sword-and-sandal film of the later 1950s and beyond. This first true peplum, *Hercules* (*Le fatiche di Ercole*, 1958), along with its successor *Hercules Unchained* (*Ercole e la regina di Lidia*, Pietro Francisci,

1959) furnishes the template for future pepla, especially those with Hercules as protagonist, and the almost inevitable plot is the enlistment of Hercules to restore a rightful ruler or his or her rightful heirs to a throne. When the peplum moves from Hercules to other musclemen heroes and even when the template begins to dissolve as the *filone* veers into weirdly distorted variants, the vast majority of stories have to do with the restoration of (the old) order following some crisis (normally political or manmade, but occasionally the result of marauding monsters). The ideological work of the peplum then can be summarized as rendering the perpetuation of traditional power relations through some correction to a parenthetical (to use Croce's noted term for Fascism) interruption to a normal political situation.

With *Hercules*, the common people, central to *Fabiola* and *Sins of Rome*, and at least metonymically important through Ulysses-as-beggar in *Ulysses*, are absent as a narrative force. Worse still in *Hercules*, the one notable common man in the film is pure evil: i.e., the assassin hired by the usurper of the throne and present throughout as a dark and menacing force. How far removed we are not only from the first two pepla I have discussed, but also from man-in-the street neorealism.

The gravitation of the 1950s Italian sword-and-sandal film toward stories of restoration and privilege seems much less than incidental in the context of a nation whose sociopolitical motto has been "Things must change so they can remain the same," a slight paraphrase of Prince Don Fabrizio Salina's endlessly cited comment in both Giuseppe Tomasi di Lampedusa's novel (which appeared a year after *Hercules*) and Luchini Visconti's film adaptation *The Leopard (Il gattopardo*, 1963). Italy has been marked by the stubborn reproduction of existing power relations even when change has seemed necessary or even inevitable. The dominant political strategy since the *Risorgimento* (more precisely since 1882 and Agostino Depretis, the head of government at the time) has been *trasformismo*: the reformulation of the status quo and the avoidance of any threat to the existing government via deal-making with the opposition: bringing them into the government, "bribing" them through support on certain issues, and so on. The results of *trasformismo* are seen in the eternal return of individuals and parties to power. DePretis presided over eight governments during a span of 11 years. Giovanni Giolitti was prime minister five times over 29 years (1892–1921).

In the postwar and despite the transformation from monarchy to republic and the seeming opportunity for political alternation offered by full-scale democracy, things got arguably worse. Alcide De Gasperi not only served as last head of government under the monarchy and first of the new republic, he headed up eight governments before leaving power in 1953, while his party, the Christian Democrats, remained dominant from the mid-1940s until 1992. To a large extent, the Christian Democrats represented the re-enfranchisement of pre-war Italian interests and hierarchies particularly in terms of big money and the Church. Pre-war Italy also survived through the so-called "continuity of the state": the legitimization of the king and the existing government in the south of Italy, following the fall of Fascism, which led to "the conservation of state institutions and central bureaucracy which was to prove so fundamental a stumbling-block to any serious reform in postwar Italy" (Ginsborg: 48).

Even Fascism was, in a sense, "restored" following the end of the Second World War and despite the partisan movement. Notwithstanding a brief initiative of *epurazione* or purging, both the structures and functionaries of Fascism remained largely in place during the period of Reconstruction, and as early as June 1946, *epurazione* was effectively ended, signifying not only a continuation of Fascist presence but, in effect, its subtle reestablishment as an acceptable underlying reality of Italian life.[6] (Neo)Fascism even re-emerges as a permanent political force as early as 1953 (Ginsborg: 143).

By the time the peplum emerged, Italy was well settled into political inertia. The Christian Democrats had already been in power for nearly ten years. Amintore Fanfani would return to power five times and head eight governments, embracing 23 years. Giulio Andreotti would be prime minister three times, comprising seven governments and 20 years. This not only belies the notion of Italy as a profoundly unstable democracy, it points to the fact that Italy's unique combination of change (repeatedly reformulated governments) and stasis (always the same ruling party) meant that virtually every new election was, in fact, a "restoration."

One of the principal forces that enabled the Christian Democrats to embark on their long career of self-perpetuation was the United States, rabid in its anti-communism and fear of political and social transformation. Following upon its role in the liberation of Italy, the United States became an ever more powerful economic and cultural force on the peninsula via its Marshall Plan; its meddling in Italian postwar politics; its model of social integration via consumer capitalism; and its transformation of 1950s Rome, as the headquarters of Italian cinema, into "Hollywood on the Tiber" (the apt phrase of the U.S. entertainment press of the time). The Italian sword-and-sandal films strongly reflect this powerful American presence. *Ulysses* was produced not only by Carlo Ponti and Dino De Laurentiis but by William W. Schorr. Three prominent American screen writers, Hugh Gray, Ben Hecht, and Irwin Shaw, were involved in the script. And most visibly, the man who brings Ulysses back not only to Ithaca but to 1950s Italian audiences is Kirk Douglas. The peplum proper is even more *alla Americana*, becoming largely synonymous with the physique of Steve Reeves and owing its success largely and perhaps principally to export to the United States. After *Hercules* enjoyed a significant return on its modest production costs in Italy, the American distributor Joseph E. Levine picked up the rights for next to nothing, mass advertised the film on television, and turned it into a top ten box office success in the United States. He did much the same with *Hercules Unchained*, which also became the largest grossing film in England in 1960. This created the market that made it possible and profitable for the Italian film industry to turn out a seemingly endless supply of spin-offs.

Because it stars not just an American but a bodybuilder (Mr. America, Mr. World, and Mr. Universe), *Hercules* introduces into the sword-and-sandal film the built vs. the natural body: i.e., the "escalation" of the body through a kind of military discipline into a virtual weapon.[7] The clear message "size does matter" also implies that might is right. *Hercules* also introduces the hero as perennial outsider,[8] suggesting that political problems cannot be resolved through mechanisms internal to a society, but only through the importation of power from without.

If we correlate the escalating American body as imported muscle with the role of the U.S. in Europe during the two world wars, and

particularly with its role during the postwar and the Cold War in
Italy and in NATO, the peplum, despite its seemingly resounding
escapism, becomes uncannily allegorical of the very reality that it
seems bent on denying. In most cases, the allegory is unintentional:
the result of fictional narrative paralleling history because it is part of
that history. However, in what I will term the "subversive" pepla, *The
Colossus of Rhodes* and *Hercules and the Captive Women*, the linkage of
peplum hero and American intervention allows for a highly productive reading of the *filone* and of the politics of the time.

The focus on the male body as spectacle in *Hercules* and the peplum
has, obviously, a far more local referent than American intervention-
ist power. As Richard Dyer has demonstrated convincingly (169-76),
the peplum recuperates much of the imagery of Fascism (another
example of "restoration"). And its fundamentally authoritarian vision, evident both in political structure and Fascist iconography, is
expanded to include a religious realm that is arbitrary and intrac-
table. At times the gods exert near total control over the characters in
a manner that defies comprehension or resistance. Read as a model of
religious authoritarianism, *Hercules* (and the pepla in general) accords
with a still deeply Catholic Italy, but also with an America whose
1950s conservatism included a high degree of religious conformity,
reflected in the Hollywood Biblical sword and sandals such as *The
Ten Commandments* (Cecil B. DeMille, 1956) and *Ben-Hur* (William Wyler, 1959). Yet *Hercules* is perhaps most significant as a sign
of its time in its embodiment of the early signs of postmodernism,
or, as Fredric Jameson's terms it, "the cultural logic of late capitalism."
In seeming contradistinction to its emphasis on restrictive social
structure, *Hercules* promotes individualism and self-gratification in
its celebration of the body, sexuality, desire, and spectacle.[9] Though
gratification is to some extent disciplined here and in the peplum in
general by its association with deviance (the Amazon women here,
any number of other similar—and often female—social threats in
other pepla), market appeal easily trumps discipline, as the films'
principal attraction is their sexiness (comic absurdity running not
too far behind). This contests the values of traditional Catholic Italian
culture as well as Puritan/Presbyterian Anglo-American culture.[10] In
terms of *Hercules'* Italian context, the juxtaposition of authoritarian

social forms and heightened individualism captures the paradox of
the 1950s Christian Democrats in their balancing act between the
Church and American materialism: claiming to be the political voice
both of Catholicism and modernization. The emphasis on instant
gratification over coherent and evolving experience begins to evoke
the postmodern when accompanied by hyper seriality and substitut-
ability (all the many Hercules, Ursus's, Macistes, with all the many
actor/body builders who played them and all the many love relationships and at times marriages they enjoy) that unsettle stable identity.
That unsettling is abetted by an annihilation of origins through the
appropriation, disordering, and random reconstruction of the basis
of Western culture: the classics. High culture is transmuted into low
culture or, perhaps more accurately, all boundaries between the two
are dissolved. Through seriality, repetition, and random juxtaposition, conventional Western notions of progress and teleology are
thwarted. Parody, kitsch, and camp, abound, and the homoerotics of
the scantily clad, aesthetically and physically dominant, male body
question traditional modernist Hollywood strategies of gendering of
spectatorship and identity.[11]

The largely American cultural logic of late capitalism is, of course,
a double-edged sword (and slippery sandal). The assault on normativ-
ity and authoritarian social structures can be seen as liberating, subversive, progressive. However, the destabilizing of social and political
identifies can also be seen as radically atomizing and disempowering,
turning (American) democracy into a plurality of unhinged hedo-
nists or, worse still, sociopaths—which is what our last two pepla,
The Colossus of Rhodes and *Hercules and the Captive Women*, in opening the largely conservative peplum out to parody and satire, seem
to imply.

The comic book seriality and spec(tac)ularity of the peplum are
linked to its perceived audience and marketing. Within Italy, the
peplum was directed to a poor and often illiterate audience, often
with rural viewing experiences of the "strongman" à la Zampanò in
Federico Fellini's *La Strada*. In the United States the peplum was
marketed to a growing mass audience that thrived on schlock dou-
ble-bills, the drive-in, and, ultimately, television. The *filone*'s utter
irreverence toward high culture and toward an education system that

Steve Reeves' built male body
challenges norms around
sexual representation
and orientation in the 1950s
in the title role of *Hercules*
(1959).

still promoted high culture, as well as its ability to be read as self-parody, made it ideal fodder for the adolescent mentality of an emergent youth culture. (It was certainly entertaining fodder for me as a 15-year-old growing up in New York City and heading off to cheapo double features every weekend.)

As much of the above would suggest, *Hercules*, in all its widescreen packaging (it is the first widescreen film in my "trajectory"), its action-adventure (non)narrative, its commitment to the body and senses over the mind, and its resounding renunciation of "seriousness," is pure product. It speaks, as its reception in the Anglo-American world made clear, to American consumerism, which is in high gear by the later 1950s. It also helps mark the arrival of the Italian Economic Miracle—the meteoric rise in living standards, American-style capitalism, and individualism—that transpired in Italy through the late 1950s and into the early 1960s. To the extent that the Economic Miracle is equivalent to Americanization, *Hercules* becomes much less a story of restoration than of profound subversion, signaling the overthrow of traditional Italian values in the face of the "American Italian revolution" long prepared for by American interventionism during and after the Second World War.

There is also something subversive in *Hercules'* participation in the birth of a youth consumer culture that brings with it powerful deconstructive tendencies. In fact, the insistent mockery with which it treats everything it represents, from classic literature to heroism to happy heterosexual endings, makes it difficult to take its conservative politics very seriously. In fact, it seems to herald the "irreverent anti-authoritarianism" that Ginsborg saw as characteristic of the Italian student movement of the later 1960s (304), but that also serves as an apt description of much oppositional 1960s Western culture.

Having witnessed the disappearance of potential political transformation or revolution—and with it any meaningful representation of "the people"—as we move from the early Italian postwar sword-and-sandal film to the peplum and from postwar ferment to the conservatism of the 1950s, we now move to the 1960s and the emergence of self-reflexivity in the peplum. *The Colossus of Rhodes* and *Hercules and the Captive Women*, seem to avail themselves of the subversive energy potential within the absurdities and contradictions of *Hercules* and turn it into sustained parody or "irreverent anti-authoritarianism" on the level both of genre and of politics. While part of this involves a dismantling of alternative social formations à la *Sins of Rome*, these films are significantly different from their predecessor. *Sins of Rome*'s vision of the impossibility of revolution and the fallibility of revolutionaries was quite circumscribed in mirroring the exhaustion of Italian postwar aspirations for social, and more precisely socialist, transformation. *The Colossus of Rhodes* and *Hercules and the Captive Women*, inscribe themselves on a much larger canvas, reflecting the internationalism of their historical moment and of the issues they implicitly invoke.

The former, directed by Sergio Leone,[12] was conceived as parody even before the lead actor Rory Calhoun arrived on the set, mistakenly embraced a number of men thinking they were Leone, and fell into a swimming pool before the astonished eyes of the director (Frayling: 102). As one might deduce from Calhoun's social and physical ineptness, much of the film's parody targets the notion of the hero. For one thing, Calhoun/Dario has a supercilious smirk on his face most of the time. For another, Leone dresses him in costumes that seem at times a mix of classic tunic and women's summer outfits of the early 1960s. (Though we may initially fail to realize the absurdity of the costumes, accepting them as historical, a close look reveals them to be, instead, laugh-out-loud ridiculous.)

On the level of character, Dario, virtually duplicates the moral weakness of Spartaco, bringing about a massacre of rebels and the arrest of their leaders by leaving their camp to visit a woman of the

Rory Calhoun, as
Dario, is dressed
in a girlish-looking
tunic in *The Co-
lossus of Rhodes*
(1961).

ruling class, Diala. Worse even than Spartaco, he tells Diala where
the rebels are hiding, oblivious to the fact that she is intimately involved in all the evildoings on Rhodes. He thinks he is acting in the
best interests of Rhodes and of the rebels in visiting Diala, but he is
utterly clued out.

Dario is also the virtual antithesis of the do-all peplum hero à la
Hercules. Unlike the latter, who can move or hurl any object, no
matter its size or weight, Dario cannot even budge a piece of the
Colossus' mechanism that falls on Diala at the film's end. In fact,
he barely even tries. Certainly not a strongman, he is a failed hero
in many other respects. At the very beginning, he gets trapped in
a labyrinth by Diala, who clearly has more smarts than he. He gets
knocked out after about two seconds of fighting with the rebel leader,
Peliocles. He has to be freed by the rebels after he has been arrested
by the leaders of Rhodes for trying to escape in one of their boats.
(At least here he participates with vigor in the fighting, but the scene
occurs less than midway through the film, and he does nothing to
match it for the remainder.) When the rebel leaders have been tossed
into the arena, thanks to Dario's indiscretions with Diala, they free
themselves, while Dario looks on from the sidelines. (His only significant activity is to disable one charioteer and make a speech to the
crowd about the dangers facing Rhodes.) It is thus quite ironic when,
after the arena battle, Peliocles says to Dario: "You've done more than

your share, Dario. Now you'd better think of safety."

The parody gets even stronger when Dario spends the entire rebellion locked up in the Colossus and then has to be spared and untied by Diala. Immediately thereafter, as the earthquake begins, he runs to the back of the room, covering himself rather than helping Diala—failing her on grounds of both chivalry and (since she has just decided to save his life) gratitude. He does not confront or kill Thar, the evil leader of Rhodes, Peliocles' brother Creonte does.

Described in this manner, Dario's failings as a hero seem patent. However, Leone's portrayal (like the costuming) is subtle and not particularly noticeable upon a first viewing of the film,[13] and it is here that much of the brilliance of the film's parody lies. Leone puts his "hero" in heroic situations, gives him heroic poses, and has him treated as a hero ("You've done more than your share Dario") so that we assume he is the hero unless we scrutinize the nature of his (in)activity. (The arena sequence and its aftermath, where Dario's "heroism" consists almost entirely of his words and those of Peliocles, is an excellent example.) In so doing, Leone not only parodies the typical action hero, he critiques audience expectations based on genre, on notions of the "great individual," and on classic Hollywood film.

In fact, Leone admitted to using Alfred Hitchcock's *North By Northwest* (1959) as his inspiration for much of *The Colossus of Rhodes*. He reproduces surface similarities, making Dario's character resemble that of Hitchcock's Roger Thornhill: "a spoiled child, a little tired of it all, who finds himself involved in a series of events he doesn't understand, and has to spend all his time looking for ways to escape from everyone" (Leone quoted in Frayling: 99). More important, he captures the self-reflexive spirit of Hitchcock's movie. *North By Northwest* portrays the creation of a Cold War hero by the CIA, which effectively casts the weak-kneed mama's boy Thornhill in the role of a non-existent "George Kaplan," who by film's end is performing feats that Thornhill never could have. Hitchcock's film is not only about the construction of American heroes (and thus the lack of American identity), in relation to external crises (manufactured or otherwise), it is also, like *The Colossus of Rhodes*, about the movie hero and levels of audience gullibility in relation to it. Hitchcock pushes his protagonist's heroics well beyond anything we could imagine either

Thornhill or Kaplan (or for that matter *any* Cary Grant protagonist) doing: for example, saving himself and the heroine by holding on to her with one hand while dangling by the other from a cliff on Mount Rushmore, while the latter is being crushed by the foot of a trained killer. Yet the audience is forced by the interpellating power of the Hollywood formula film (much as Thornhill is forced by the CIA and the interpellating power of American ideology) to surrender its autonomy and be carried unquestioning to the end. It is precisely this kind of critique that Leone reproduces in his film.

The Colossus of Rhodes appropriates not just the critique of the hero in *North By Northwest* but the film's use of cultural iconography, mimicking the Mount Rushmore scenes with those of tiny human figures scrambling around the surface of the Colossus. The Colossus was meant to suggest not only Mount Rushmore, but an even more fundamental icon of America, the Statue of Liberty. Given the fact that the Colossus is built in Fascist monumental style, the Colossus links Fascism and the United States, and the Statue of Liberty becomes, as Frayling has noted (98) "a symbol of tyranny." Rather than "welcoming the huddled masses," the Colossus pours boiling oil upon them twice. It serves not only as a weapon of mass destruction, but also as a prison and a barracks. Perhaps most tellingly in terms of American military technology, nuclear escalation, and postwar interventionism, the Colossus is a site of technological experimentation gone horribly wrong. It has been used, against the wishes of the inventor and scientific wizard Carete, for world domination.

As should be clear from all I have just said, Leone's film is a critique not just of the hero but of the specifically American hero. Consistent with Hercules before him, Dario comes from outside. Not only is he, yet again, played by an American, but he comes from Athens, a classic symbol of democracy often appropriated by the United States in its endless self-championing as the epitome of democracy: in the wake of Nazism and Fascism, in the rhetoric of the Cold War, and now following 9/11.[14] Dario does not want to get involved at the start, reflecting a longstanding tradition of American isolationism. He is shallow and naïve, extroverted, friendly, and swashbuckling—a compendium of clichés identifiable as "American," particularly from a European perspective.

Leone's *Colossus* (1961) parodies Hitchcock's Mount Rushmore and the
Statue of Liberty, with little creatures battling on the right bicep and
shoulder while others crawl out of the right ear.

Leone's critique of the hero and the need for an outsider to (presumably) clean things up serves as part of a more global critique of
political order(s). At first *The Colossus of Rhodes* seems to hearken
back to the earlier sword-and-sandal films of revolution, in that there
is a rebel group seeking to take power and constantly invoking "the
people" in their declarations of political and military opposition.
However, while those in power are either thoroughly ignorant or
thoroughly corrupt, the rebels have their own significant limitations.
First of all, they are convinced their salvation lies in enlisting the aid
of Dario, whose ineptness we have detailed at length. They too, in
short, are dependent on authority, which recalls the analysis of the
rebels in *Sins of Rome*. And though they enjoy some minor victories
(enough to demonstrate both their marked superiority to Dario and
the absurdity of their reliance on him), they make no real headway
against their Rhodian oppressors until the earthquake, which is pure
deus ex machina, pure Hollywood/peplum cheap trick. It is the earthquake that destroys the Phoenician fleet, central to the evil plans of
the Rhodian leaders. It is the earthquake that sends Thar running out
of the Colossus to his death. And it is the earthquake, not any political revolution, that brings about the death of the old order.

Leone also gives us more pointed clues as to the rebels' limits as leaders of a popular revolt, though much of this is missing from the choppy conclusion to the recent U.S. DVD release of the film. With the earthquake devastating Rhodes, the rebels are happy to fight their enemies but unwilling to stay on and risk their lives to help those caught in the collapsing buildings. There is one exception, Creonte, and only when Dario is summoned by Creonte does he do anything to help. When Creonte is killed by a falling building, the minimal relief work done by the rebels is effectively ended, and Dario and Peliocles seek an escape route from the city. They pause briefly when another collapsing building traps a Rhodian, but they leave him struggling or dead amidst the rubble as soon as another of their group calls out to them. They steal the key to one of the gates of the city from a dead soldier and high-tail it out of Rhodes. The image of Peliocles prying the key loose with a kind of obsessed fury is given prominence and resonates with a number of other images of people plundering or hoarding goods amidst the earthquake. Tellingly, the film cuts back to people still in the city as the rebels leave: a distraught man carrying his dead child, an older child helping a younger child when both get felled by falling beams. Both are images of human solidarity in sharp contrast to the rebels leaving the site of devastation. The earthquake escape sequence confirms what has been suggested throughout the movie: the rebels are an insular group whose sense of solidarity does not extend beyond them or beyond those who, like Dario, are willing to join them. They are defined far more by bellicose homosociality than by any social mission or conscience. The one significant female member of the band, Mirte, who is also Dario's love interest by film's end, is a figure of continual empathy and grieving, but always and only for her own. Having effectively turned their back on their city, this alternative political bunch will hardly be the architects of a glorious new social reconstruction.

It goes pretty much without saying, but the cynicism, apocalypticism, and jaundiced Americanism of *The Colossus of Rhodes* anticipate in various ways Leone's spaghetti westerns.

The final film under consideration in this essay, *Hercules and the Captive Women*, can be read as a companion piece to *The Colossus of Rhodes*, though it is arguably even more ironic and parodic. Perhaps most notable in the context of this essay's trajectory, it dismantles the kind of restoration drama central to *Ulysses* and *Hercules* and places democracy at the center of its political discourse—an interesting challenge given the nature of government in the societies normally represented by the peplum.[15] Its director Vittorio Cottafavi, though never to attain the world-class status of Leone, was a highly accomplished director of postwar melodramas who then came to specialize in pepla during their brief moment of dominance. At times he seemed inclined to renounce its trash tendencies by turning it into art. His final sword-and-sandal film, *Son of El Cid* (1964; *I cento cavalieri*), is highly self-reflexive not just on the level of genre, but on the level of story-telling itself, featuring a self-ironizing narrator who seems to presage Pier Paolo Pasolini's examination of art and the artist in his "Trilogy of Life"—*The Decameron* (*Il Decameron*, 1971), *The Canterbury Tales* (*I racconti di Canterbury*, 1972), and *The Arabian Nights* (*Il fiore delle mille e una notte* 1973). *Son of El Cid* obtained significant critical success, but was such a failure at the box office that Cottafavi decided to renounce film directing in favor of becoming a television director, a role he carried out with enormous distinction at a time when Italian state television produced many high quality telefilms and mini-series. Among his television productions were celebrated adaptations of Sophocles, Euripides, and Aeschylus. Though largely unrecognized in the English-speaking world (where *I cento cavalieri* was released as *Son of El Cid* with 40 minutes and all of its complexity edited out), Cottafavi has been the subject of continuing interest in France and in Italy.[16] It is therefore not surprising to discover that *Hercules and the Captive Women*, the film that immediately precedes *I cento cavalieri* in Cottafavi's filmography, is readable in ways seldom encouraged by other pepla.

The point of departure for *Hercules and the Captive Women*, like that of *The Colossus of Rhodes*, is a parody of the hero. The first time we see Hercules, he is stuffing his face with food and wine and refusing, despite entreaties from his son Hylas and his best friend Androcles, to get involved in a barroom brawl that has broken out around him. Shortly thereafter, aware of a grave threat to the Greek states, Hercules refuses to help Androcles who, as King of Thebes, wishes to discover and destroy the source of the threat. Androcles and Hylas have to drug and kidnap Hercules to get him to come along. Then,

Reg Park's Hercules is a consumer society layabout instead of an action hero for much of *Hercules and the Captive Women* (1961).

when he awakens at sea, he refuses to do any work, choosing instead to loll, pose, and sunbathe on the ship and on the beach. The hyperactive Hercules of earlier pepla, responsive to even the slightest provocation to adventure, has (with *The Colossus of Rhodes* as a segue) been transformed into an anti-hero of the Economic Miracle: indolent, vain, ironically detached and apolitical, and intent only on self-gratification. He is also the re-domesticated male of the 1950s,[17] refusing Androcles' call to arms because he wants to spend more time with his wife and son. The only time he becomes active is when a situation arises that calls for an immediate heroic response. For example, when Androcles' crew mutiny and try to steal Androcle's ship, Hercules single-handedly pulls the entire crew and ship back to shore with a chain. When he comes upon a woman melded to the rocks of the island Atlantis, he frees her by conquering the source of the problem, Proteus. In other words, rather than exercising his powers in support of significant moral principles or long-term projects and goals, Hercules acts principally in the moment. And the only reason he gets involved on Atlantis is for purely personal reasons: his best friend Androcles has disappeared.

Even when he takes more comprehensive action in response to the evil shenanigans on Atlantis, we can see it more as heroic role-playing than any more social-minded commitment. In fact, by going off to destroy the evil stone that transmutes the islanders into clones and slaves, he effectively sacrifices the members of the Resistance whom he has just freed from a concentration camp, for left without leadership and organization, they rush to the city and are immediately massacred.

In the end, Hercules is a consummate embodiment of *la bella figura* and *sprezzatura*: the desire to look cool and to appear to be making absolutely no effort to accomplish his ends. Not only longstanding traits of Italian masculinity, *la bella figura* and *sprezzatura* are also perfect reflections of the new image-conscious male of 1950s capitalism and Italy's Boom.[18]

As we look beyond Cottafavi's critique of the hero to the film's portrayal of politics and society, the latter initially seems rather banal: Queen Antinea, in a quest for world domination, has learned to tamper with nature and clone humans in order to produce a race of identical and seemingly indestructible Aryan warriors. The scene in which these figures, previously covered from head to toe, take their helmets off in unison and reveal themselves to be blond-headed, blond-bearded Nazi ideals is visually impressive (as is the attempted killing of Hercules and Hylas in a gas chamber). However, how many post atom-bomb movies had we had by 1961, preaching against playing god with nature and making the bad guys neo-Nazis (read totalitarians or, in many Cold War films, communists)? When we consider the fact that the material she has used to perform her "violation of nature" was the stone formed from the blood of Uranus—i.e., uranium—things become a bit more interesting, though not truly compelling. In fact, it seems historically inaccurate to align nuclear destruction with Nazi science.

The more closely we look at the film, however, the more complex its sociopolitical critique becomes, and much of that critique is directed toward democracy. Although the film (like all the pepla) is set in times of monarchy, the film labors to introduce democratic mechanisms, such as council meetings, and references to democracy[19] to create a seeming contrast between democracy and totalitarianism that dissolves in such a way as to raise the question: does the former really guarantee better results, in humanistic terms, than the latter?

The opening sequence seems to present us with a socially ideal, interclassist, situation that quickly and emphatically (though quite comically) disintegrates. We begin in a tavern in which rich and poor, kings and common folk, drink together. (This setting is unique in my experience of pepla.) A woman server moves through the two-level space, filling wine vessels in a joyful dance in which she turns work into pleasure and art. The rhythm is set by characters within the scene, beating tables with hands or implements used as drum sticks, implying internal harmony (vs. unity created by extra-diagetic or "imposed" music), reinforcing the seemingly democratic enjoyment of life. It becomes clear, however, that many of the customers are blind drunk, and at a certain point one of the men (we later find out he is Hylas, son of Hercules) grabs the dancer, pulls her down, and kisses her. Another man hits him over the head with the server's wine jug, and the aforementioned brawl breaks out. It goes on and on and on until Hercules, having finished wining and dining, stands up, yells "*basta*," and everything comes to a halt. The implication seems to be that people left to leisure and their own devices (ideals within liberal capitalist democracy) self-destruct. They consume excessively and are fundamentally aggressive, and the only way they can be controlled is through the might of a Hercules. Hercules, in fact, does not appear or "exist" until the fight breaks out, implying that he, the hero, is born out of the aggression and need for order in so-called free society. His radical disengagement from all around him until he exerts his muscle (in itself a rather unhealthy form of engagement) suggests the profound asociality that lies beneath the façade of social harmony within a seemingly democratized world.

The film's critique of democracy is anchored in a scene that follows shortly upon the opening dance-turned-dustup: a meeting of the council of Greek states in which Androcles seeks to organize a response to the threat to Greece. He encounters only self-interest on the part of the other leaders. Not a single "ally" is willing to support him. The one who claims to be most willing, says he must answer to a council of 30 politicians back home, and they can never agree on anything. The council meeting is hilarious in its representation of the petty ambition and infantilism of political leaders, obviously echoing Italian parliamentary democracy, and for that reason, became a cult moment in the history of the peplum (Giordano: 47).

One of the most striking moments in the council meeting occurs when Hercules picks up Androcles' throne and smashes it, saying that, in this way, Androcles need not worry that any of his bickering heirs will occupy it while he is off seeking out and destroying the

"grave threat." Shocking in its mixture of humor and political sug-
gestiveness, it is one of the many elements of *Hercules and the Captive
Women* that set it apart from the ordinary peplum and allow for unexpectedly complex readings. In contrast to Hercules' rather limited
and short-sighted interpretation of his action, we can posit:

a) Hercules or mere muscle is the real power behind the throne,
precisely because more civilized tools of government, such as democratic debate, lead only to stalemate and a void in meaningful
leadership.

b) Hercules' utter self indulgence (confirmed by the irresponsibil-
ity of his action here) means that the political power is ultimately
arbitrary rather than socially grounded.

c) Leadership is destructive rather than creative, inclined toward
breaking apart rather than unifying.

The juxtaposing of imperialist adventure (Androcles and, ultimately, Hercules) and a failure of politics on the home front resonates with the history postwar politics, particularly among the major
players of the Cold War: Russia and the United States.

Not only does no one in the Council support Androcles, his own
Thebans express their free democratic choice[20] by refusing to come
along, and democracy specifically takes the blame in an exchange
between Androcles and Hercules after the latter has awakened on
the former's ship. Hercules makes fun of Androcles for having no
military support and a crew of criminals and lowlifes, willing to come
along only because they are getting pardoned or paid, and Androcles
tries to silence Hercules by saying that this is all the result of the democracy that Hercules is so fond of praising.[21]

The fact that Androcles undertakes the journey with no political
support means that the seemingly positive outcome of the film—the
destruction of "evil," the preservation of Greece and democracy—are
the result of individual actions divorced from any meaningful political process. This is underscored by the fact that the only figure with
a strong political and social sensibility, Androcles, ends up crazed
and powerless the whole time he is on Atlantis (a state induced by
Queen Antinea) while all the salvific action is brought about by the
profoundly dissociated Hercules.

The film lends itself to the conclusion that while totalitarianism breeds vicious leaders, mindless clones, and coerced consensus, democracy breeds ineffective leaders, atomized individuality, the absence of consent, and at best, the arbitrary and individualist pursuit of do-goodism without social sanction. "Doing good," in this respect, is just another form of self-gratification. We can also conclude from this and from much I have said above that, since the underlying principles of democracy are freedom of choice and, particularly, individual freedom, democracy generates not effective political institutions but a consumer society.[22]

While the prevailing political figure of Nazism/Fascism is the "Dictator," the prevailing (a) political figure of democracy is the "Hero," and it is in the effects wrought by the "democratic hero," Hercules, that *Hercules and the Captive Women* opens itself out to sociopolitical analysis on the broadest level. These effects are hinted at by the film's title. Although it is known as either *Hercules and the Captive Women* or *Hercules Conquers Atlantis* (by far the better of the two)[23] in the English-speaking world, the title in Italian, *Ercole alla conquista d'Atlantide*, can be translated as *Hercules to the Conquest of Atlantis*. In this respect, the title undermines the traditional sense of the hero as someone perennially off "to the rescue." The film then seems to equate conquest with annihilation. For in the end, it is not Antinea who harnesses uranium to its most destructive ends, but Hercules, who, in aligning the rays of the sun with the stone of Uranus, unleashes an explosion that destroys the island: not just Antinea and her clones, but an entire civilization, guilty and innocent alike. I hardly need to draw the obvious analogy between Hercules' nuclear feat and those of the United States at the end of the Second World War. Through this analogy, the film resituates the most serious dangers of nuclear experimentation from Nazism to democratic culture.[24]

Hercules' act of mass destruction is strongly ironized by an earlier discussion in which our "hero" castigates the high priest of Uranus for talking only of "death and destruction" and, in the same conversation, boldly announces that "there is nothing to fear, I will defeat Antinea without harming Atlantis or its inhabitants." This suggests that when he finally begins to act, Hercules does so in a state of delusion, ignorant of and unable to control the destructive consequences of his actions. Hercules' ill-fated prediction occurs immediately after an extremely sanctimonious prayer to Zeus, whose aid he invokes in order to perform a test that will convince the high priest to share with him the secret of Uranus. Hercules' belief that he is one with the gods is mythologically accurate: he *was* a demigod. However, in the film, the fact that he makes his one great failed prediction in the presence of the gods undermines his divine origins and turns him into an all-too-mortal hero who misguidedly thinks himself to be an agent of the Divine.

There is a temptation to reduce Hercules as hero solely to the American hero, particularly in the light of my discussion of *The Colossus of Rhodes* and despite the fact he is played by a British (Reg Park) rather than an American actor. (As Dyer notes, the casting of body builders as peplum heroes always had an American signification because the built body at the time was perceived to be an American phenomenon [174].) There are many things that would support such an equation. Like Dario, he is isolationist, charming, rather shallow, complacent, and a representative/proponent of democracy. Though he is inclined to stay above the fray, when he enters he always wins (something that was true of the U.S. at the time but not any longer). His metaphoric association with the atom bomb seems to seal the analogy. The notion of the American hero *alla conquista* can even be expanded to reference the American transmutation of rescue into conquest through strategies such as the Marshall Plan and more overt forms of bribery and coercion as Italy was about to vote in the crucial 1948 elections. And of course with more recent events in the Middle East, coupled with religious fundamentalism in the United States, the hero-on-the-side-of-the-Lord acquires a compelling American resonance.

Certainly *Hercules and the Captive Women* seems part of a growing contemporary response to blind postwar Western faith in democracy, faith that resulted from the horrors that other political systems had perpetrated in World War II and that was fueled by Cold War American rhetoric. This blind faith tended to ignore the fact that Nazism was the product of a democratic society, the Weimar Republic. Nevertheless, I also believe the film is readable beyond an American or democratic context and points toward the weaknesses in all social systems, deriving from the weakness of those that create them. In fact, it is not a matter of deciding which social system is more disposed toward wholesale annihilation. Everyone seems so disposed, as the co-dependency of Americans and Germans, Hercules and Antinea in the production of violence implies. I think that *Hercules and the Captive Women* also demonstrates a particularly Italian degree of disillusionment with politics and society that has roots, extending back at least to Machiavelli, in a long history of colonization, exploitation, and deceit on the Italian peninsula (Ginsborg, Duggan, and Barzini 1964 and 1971). At the same time, taken beyond its Italian context, the film might be seen as part of an existential nihilism that was a prevailing current of postwar European thought and that was to morph into certain forms of leftwing totalizing negativity following the disillusionments of May 1968.

With this in mind, I would like to return briefly to the film's treatment of the Resistance that I noted earlier. When the island's political prisoners are released from the concentration camp, they are so consumed by a sense of victimization and desire for revenge that they cannot act constructively or await Hercules return, as he has requested, before impetuously assaulting the city and meeting instantaneous destruction. In contrast to democracy's leisure-lout, over-consuming common man, totalitarianism produces a populace so scarred by oppression that it ends up being irrational and suicidal. So added to the negative social psychologies of consumer democracy, totalitarian leaders, and "the hero," we have that of potential revolutionaries. Moreover, the inability of the resisters to listen to Hercules, and the fact that their own leader goes off with Hercules while they just annihilate themselves, suggests that social dysfunction has evolved from the more benign versions visible in the opening sequence and in the council meeting to levels of violence and disaggregation that can only end in extermination and apocalypse.

In conclusion, *Hercules and the Captive Women*, along with its "companion piece" (for the sake of this essay), *The Colossus of Rhodes*, has taken us far from the uplifting social harmony of *Fabiola* and the limited social critique implicit in *Sins of Rome*, both of which speak to issues and possibilities emerging from the Second World War and persisting through the end of the 1940s and, very briefly, into the 1950s. These two later pepla also move us well beyond the restoration comedies of *Ulysses* and *Hercules*, and the conservative 1950s society and politics they bespeak. *The Colossus of Rhodes* apocalyptically destroys a society without offering substantive promise of a positive new one to take its place. *Hercules and the Captive Women* reveals the dark side of cultural or national "preservation," i.e., the annihilation of one society in order to sustain another that is arguably as problematic. In their implicit and at times explicit critique of leisure, consumerism, politics, the social, and themselves-as-spectacle—particularly in light of Italy's Economic Miracle and the prosperity of 1950s Western democracies in general—*The Colossus of Rhodes* and *Hercules and the Captive Women* are in perfect alignment with the far more highly prized "art films" of the period: e.g., Michelangelo Antonioni's *L'avventura* (*L'avventura,* 1959), Fellini's *La Dolce Vita* (*La Dolce Vita,* 1960), and Luchino Visconti's *Rocco and His Brothers* (*Rocco e i suoi fratelli,* 1960). In terms of genre film, and Sergio Leone is clearly the pivotal figure here, these two surprising and complex films move the peplum far beyond the expressive limits of the peplum *filone* and toward the far more exhaustively explored terrain of the spaghetti western, whose subversive, sardonic, cynical, self-reflexive, and often violent vision would come to serve as harsh illumination of a 1960s in grave turmoil. But most important in terms of the parameters of this essay, *The Colossus of Rhodes* and *Hercules and the Captive Women,* in conjunction with the four other sword-and-sandal films under consideration, illustrate the strong interrelation of society, politics, and popular culture and the way in which a genre or even a sub-genre intended for the most part (and at times entirely) for entertainment can speak to us eloquently of the worlds from which it has emerged.

NOTES

1 "*Legata alla sinistra.*" Capussotti is making a comparison with another production company, Film Costellazione, which she designates as closer to the Church "(*legato*) *al mondo cattolico*" (32).

2 The "evil seductress" as counterforce to the "good wife or lover" is, of course, a staple of the genre and will reappear in one form

or another in the remaining four films I will be discussing. It is generally much more about male fantasies of polygamy, often justified through narrative stratagems such as amnesia or drugging, than about anything more serious. Here, however, it is a strong indicator of failed leadership.

3   Wyke claims, "In Freda's *Sins of Rome*, the historical narration most closely addresses (and perhaps attempts to justify) the recent marginalization of the (Italian Communist Party) in Italy's political life where it represents operational differences between the commanders of the slave army. ... Such rifts between the slave leaders resemble those lately reported between the leader of the post-war PCI" (56). Actually, the Italian left has always been victim of major disempowering rifts, beginning with the communist secession from the socialist party in 1921. However, I do not think that Freda was consciously "addressing" specific contemporary conflicts within the left. Nonetheless, I think he picks up on certain fundamental problems in the Italian political situation, postwar and even earlier, which motivates the films rather "dark" (see the body of my argument) perspective.

4   Actually, in the poem, the suitors are not all strangers; many are from Ithaca. But in the movie, Penelope asserts, "You are all strangers on this island," bringing the film into closer alignment with the Italian wartime occupation experience.

5   I have written an extensive analysis of *Ulysses* and post re-domestication. See Burke.

6   As Paul Ginsborg notes, not only did much of the bureaucracy inherited from Fascism remain unchanged, but so did the entire judiciary, while numerous Fascist leaders were acquitted of their crimes for ludicrous reasons (92). "In 1960 it was calculated that 62 out of 64 prefects (the central government's principal representatives in the provinces) had been functionaries under Fascism. So too had all 135 police chiefs and their 139 deputies. Only five of these last had contributed in any way to the Resistance" (ibid.).

7   For a fine discussion of the peplum hero, the built body, and masculinity, see Günsberg.

8   *Hercules Unchained* does take him back to his homeland, Thebes,

but far more often than not Hercules, like other peplum heroes such as Maciste and Ursus, is summoned to or happens upon a distant society in political crisis.

9   Jameson and many others would argue, of course, that consumer-driven late capitalist individualism is depoliticizing precisely in such a way as to promote the rise and dominance of conservative social structures.

10 This kind of contestation was prefigured even in *Fabiola*, where the heroine was highly sexualized through much of the movie and where the scenes of persecution included women's breasts bared by Roman soldiers in quite titillating ways for the times. And it has always been a part of the sword-and-sandal film, hearkening back to the days of silent cinema.

11 Of course much of what I have just said is true of other cultural forms that arose in modernity and persevered into postmodernity. Serialization begins in the nineteenth century. The comic book, which is a fundamental precursor to the Hercules *filone*, begins well before the *filone* itself. Spectacle was fundamental to the origins of narrative cinema, and nowhere more so than in Italy. What I want to emphasize is particular conjunctions that occur in relation to the peplum—conjunctions that signal the emergence of a postmodern sensibility.

12 The story of *The Colossus of Rhodes* is loosely based on the erection, then destruction by earthquake, of a statue of Apollo at Rhodes in the third century B.C.

13 While the film's subtlety is mostly intentional, I also think that some of the subtleties take time to discover because the film contains a reasonable amount of unassimilated material that at times conflicts with the underlying parody: moments for example when Dario acts heroically without parody being in any way implied. This was the result of the speed with which Leone had to mount the production. He complained that "with two months' extra preparation … I could have made a much more personal film" (in Frayling: 100).

14 And more recently of course in the so-called "War on Terror."

15 Another sword-and-sandal film of the same period that also creates parallels with contemporary democratic societies is Jacque

Tourneur and Mario Bava's *The Giant of Marathon* (1959). See Lagny.

16 François Truffaut was a great admirer of Cottafavi's 1950s work. French critic Michel Mourlet considered Cottafavi, along with Losey, Lang, and Preminger, "the great of the great" (Catalog, Il Cinema Ritrovato 188). His pepla received significant attention in France at the time of their release. Bernard Tavernier has given testimony to his work on several occasions in the past 40 years, most notably in the beautiful French DVD version of *Hercules and the Captive Women* (*Hercule à la conquête de L'Atlantide*). In Italy, Cottafavi merited a book-length study (Rondolini) in 1980 and extensive tributes when he died in 1998. He has enjoyed numerous retrospectives, most recently at the 23rd edition of *Il Cinema Ritrovato* (Bologna, June 27-July 4, 2009). A recent (2007) issue of *Bianco e Nero* was dedicated to the filmmaker and his work. I refer the reader to this issue and to the catalog of *Il Cinema Ritrovato* (available online) for further information on Cottafavi's importance in France and Italy. *Bianco e Nero* includes numerous writings celebrating the director by both French and Italian cineastes.

17 For thorough discussions of 1950s re-domestication of the male, particularly in an American context, see Cohan, May, and Burke. The last addresses re-domestication in relation to *Ulysses*. Although I analyze the film in terms of American re-domestication, citing the extent to which the film was an American as well as an Italian production, I think the film's success in Italy suggests that the theme resonated within a postwar Italian as well as American context.

18 Both are forms of individualism and social alienation resulting from the hard-earned cynicism of centuries of invasion and exploitation, coupled with the experience of national and local politics and bureaucracy that aid the few and neglect the many. For the "Italian experience" that produces these kinds of defense mechanisms, see Ginsborg and Barzini (1964,1971).

19 Surprisingly, given its analysis of democracy, the film substitutes Thebes for Athens as the origin of "resistance" to Atlantis. In the Platonic myth of Atlantis, Athens organizes a coalition that falls

apart and ends up fighting Atlantis on its own, ending up victorious. Then Atlantis is destroyed by earthquakes and floods (we might assume tsunamis, in the light of contemporary knowledge) before the Athenians can even return home. Aside from the Theban substitution, there are clear parallels between the myth and *Hercules and the Captive Women*.

20 Turning Thebes into a democracy involves a bit of historical legerdemain on the part of Cottafavi, especially since Androcles is king. We must assume that, at best, we have a limited monarchy with a democratically elected parliament.

21 Because of the crypticness of the conversation, one has to extrapolate the meaning, and mere quotation doesn't work. Androcles lists all the people who were against him—the priests, the old people, commanders of the fleet—and then says sneeringly to Hercules, "And isn't it you who is always saying 'but that's democracy'?" What he is saying, in effect, is that Hercules' beloved democracy has gotten him into the very mess that Hercules is mocking him for, so he (Hercules) should be quiet.

22 Androcles is much more closely aligned to the democracy championed by Hercules than to the totalitarianism of Queen Antinea. He is a monarch constrained by democracy who would appreciate more authority to carry out his interests. However, he is a product of a society presented in the film as largely democratic, and his critique of democracy is clearly a defensive reaction to Hercules' mockery, not a serious endorsement of authoritarianism.

23 The first does not make sense, because there is only one captive woman.

24 Dyer has a slightly different take on the Fascist-democratic hero relationship, but one that dovetails, I think, quite nicely, with my argument. He notes (176) that while the story of *Hercules and the Captive Women* seems to pit Hercules against the Nazi-Fascist regime and ideals of Queen Antinea, his muscular body reincarnates the very image of Fascism.

2

HORROR CINEMA

The Emancipation of Women and Urban Anxiety

Andrea Bini

The subject of this chapter is the evolution of the horror genre in Italian cinema in terms of its portrayal of women vis-à-vis the process of modernization and urbanization in Italy. The status of women was not a principal theme of postwar Italian cinema, either in the films of notable directors (Visconti, Rossellini, De Sica, Fellini) or in those considered less artistic. Even the Italian-style comedy, which duly captured the changing dynamics of Italian culture, rarely brought up the issue of women's emancipation (although there were a few exceptions, such as the films of Antonio Pietrangeli). This did not happen by accident. This neglect often disguised a deep-rooted misogyny on the part of directors and screenwriters, all of whom, with very few exceptions, were male. It was instead the horror genre that both implicitly and explicitly addressed the issue of women's gradual emancipation within Italian society and exposed male fears surrounding female sexuality. These phobias arose with the changes in Italian culture that were a consequence of the new consumerist society of the late 1950s. They finally exploded during the sexual revolution of the late 1960s and 1970s, along with the post-1968 social turmoil and the resulting urban angst.

Italian horror can be divided into three periods, each lasting about ten years and corresponding to three different phases of Italian society. The first period, the so-called "Italian gothic" (1956–66), followed the revival of Dracula movies and is characterized by romantic nineteenth-century settings. These films, although original and interesting, did not achieve any success with the general public and disappeared in the late 1960s, to be replaced by mystery films with modern settings—the *giallo* (1967–77). The *giallo* became very popular with the Italian public, particularly in the years 1970–75, and established itself as one of the mainstream genres of Italian cinema for about a decade. This second period was gradually replaced by a third one characterized by excessive and gratuitous gore—a sort of radicalization of elements that were already present in the first two— during which time (1978–86) Italian horror slowly returned to being a minor genre. This study will focus on the first two periods, since it is during these that the central theme and the true originality of Italian horror are found, that is, the woman as the motivating force of the storyline. In both the Gothic and the Italian mystery (*giallo*) sub-genres, the central character is female. The woman's pivotal role reflected the ongoing cultural changes and the growing male angst and insecurity in the face of women's emancipation.

Italian Gothic: 1956–1966

Italian horror was officially inaugurated in 1956 with a film that was produced quite by chance: *Lust of the Vampire* (*I vampiri*), directed by Riccardo Freda 1909–1999, one of the most eclectic and underrated directors of Italian cinema.[1] Eugenio Testa's then forgotten *The Monster of Frankenstein* (*Il mostro di Frankenstein*, 1920) is one of the very few examples of Italian horror films that appeared before *Lust of the Vampire*. During the Fascist era (1922–1945), it would have been impossible to produce a horror film. Still, director Alessandro Blasetti created two interesting melodramas, *The Haller Case* (*Il Caso Haller*, 1933) and *The Dinner of Mockers* (*La cena delle beffe*, 1941), which foreshadowed the cloudy and noxious atmospheres that would be characteristic of the Gothic horror. There is no doubt that Italian Gothic horror owes much to the melodrama, especially in its emphasis on female characters and use of sexual connotations, as can be observed in Mario Soldati's *Marina of Malombra* (*Malombra*, 1942), which is the second filmic adaptation of Antonio Fogazzaro's

1881 romantic novel (the first version was produced by director Carmine Gallone in 1917). Soldati's *Marina of Malombra* is full of the elements that will characterize the future Gothic horror: foggy locations, the castle, the woman. Although the classic melodrama is usually concerned with the rescue of a young woman overcome by evil forces which endanger her virginity and her life, it must be recalled that the D'Annunzian-Symbolist melodrama of the early twentieth century established in Italian opera, plays and films the figure of the wicked *femme fatale* who has the power to bring about the destruction of men.[2] Still, we can only speak of the birth of the Italian horror genre when Freda's film was made, more than a decade after the end of the Second World War.

Lust of the Vampire is set in Paris and tells the story of an assassin who kills young women in order to extract their blood. This culprit is not a vampire. He is simply a doctor who kills not in order to satisfy a perverted desire but to keep his succubus, the diabolical 100-year-old Duchess Giselle Du Grand, young and seductive. This film, which had no success in its homeland, included the most original elements of Italian horror, foremost, the rejection of the supernatural monsters found in Anglo-Saxon films in favor of a more realistic approach (the film is in fact similar to *film noir*) in which the source of evil is internal or psychological. This was not an innovation in itself, since it had already been used in German expressionist cinema. The true novelty of the genre lay in placing women as the focus of the films' overall themes. As Paolo Frazzini writes:

> ... Bypassing Dracula and the werewolves and ghosts of Anglo-Saxon cinema, Italian films promote the female as their central figure, the only true protagonist of the genre who, from vampire to witch, from femme fatale to madwoman, becomes the driving force behind all of the sinister events. (2004, 59)[3]

Italian horror uses the patterns of melodrama by making the wicked woman the focal point of the film. She is the true protagonist, neither merely a victim whose fate is to suffer nor some secondary, anonymous character destined to be eclipsed by the hero. In particular, the sexually active woman is depicted as an ambiguous and dangerous character. Evil lurks in her and is unleashed through her or for her. Even when the assassins are male—like the mad doctors typical of Italian horror—they carry out their hideous deeds because they are under the spell of a woman. Years before its time in terms of thematic evolution, *Lust of the Vampire,* portrays evil arising from a woman's desperate attempt to remain young and seductive. This theme is linked to another characteristic of Italian horror, the duplicity and ambiguity of women. In effect, the sinister Duchess Du Grand and her young niece, the fascinating Marguerite, are actually one and the same person. Marguerite is a voluptuous *femme fatale* who wants to manipulate men through her powers of seduction (the girls are killed only because their blood is a necessary ingredient for the doctor's treatment).

Although *Lust of the Vampire* fared better in foreign markets, especially in France and the United States, the fact that it had no success with audiences in Italy justified Italian producers' mistrust of this cinematic genre. In fact, between 1958 and 1959, only one horror film was made in Italy: *Caltiki, the Immortal Monster* (*Caltiki, il mostro immortale,* 1959). This science-fiction horror film, which was also entrusted to Freda,[4] followed the release of the American film *The Blob* (1958). Italian productions started to appear regularly only after 1960, prompted by the international rebirth of the Gothic horror genre following the success of Terence Fisher's 1958 remake of *Dracula* by Hammer, the British film company. During the same year, four films were produced in Italy, the first of which was Mario Bava's renowned *Black Sunday* (*La maschera del demonio,* 1960). With this film, Bava made his debut as a director after a successful career as cinematographer and visual effects specialist (among his works are *Lust of the Vampire* and *Caltiki*). He became the undisputed master of the Gothic horror genre throughout the 1960s.[5]

With *Black Sunday* Bava created his first genuine masterpiece and set the standards for the definition of "Italian Gothic." Like the Anglo-Saxon tradition revived by Hammer, the Italian Gothic is set vaguely somewhere in the 1800s; in a world filled with castles, carriages, villages and forests. Bava, however, branched out, going in search of themes and atmospheres more closely linked with Italian traditions. As Bava himself loved to point out, vampires and other

Asa, the vampire-witch played by Barbara Steele, beckons her (male) victim in *Black Sunday* (1960). Only her face and claw-like hand are completely illuminated in this scene, emphasizing the power of feminine beauty to charm and to grasp.

supernatural monsters do not exist in Italian folklore. Instead there are the *fattucchiere* or powerful witches. Although *fattucchiere* are not necessarily malevolent, they represent an alternative culture and are therefore a menace to a patriarchal society whose values are symbolized above all by the Catholic Church (the male institution *par excellence*).

Black Sunday—loosely based on Nikolaj Gogol's short novel *The Vij*—is the tale of a female vampire who returns to life to seek vengeance. Here, evil is clearly represented by a woman who resembles a witch much more than a "normal" vampire. The cross (the most recognizable symbol of the Church) is still effective against her and other vampires, but a mask of spikes replaces the stake which is normally used to pierce vampires in the heart, and the only way to destroy them for all time is to burn them.

Most importantly, the witch-vampire Asa's power does not stem from physical strength, but lies wholly in her ability to enchant and to captivate the men around her. It was her perverse sexual activity (which had contaminated her family and the entire village) that rendered her unacceptable to the patriarchal community and condemned her to the torment of the mask. Throughout the film, Asa remains immobile in her glass coffin, attracting her male prey with seductiveness, snaring them in her web like a black widow. The shots above and below show that although Asa's face is disfigured by the mask's spikes, she is still stunningly beautiful as she gasps provocatively and invites her victim, Professor Kruvajan, to kiss her. The bite on the neck is not necessary. A kiss alone brings about the man's total subjugation and vampirization. For the first time in the history of horror cinema, Asa can be considered a "Vamp" in the truest sense of the word. In American and British movies, Dracula's seductive look hypnotizes his female victims and reduces them to somnambulistic slaves, but in Italian horror, the woman's gaze triggers the same effect on men.[6]

In this film, we are clearly confronted with the legacy of the Italian patriarchal Catholic culture which views female sexuality as a mysterious force always drawing men toward temptation and damnation. In such a culture, a woman is accepted only as a virgin or a mother. Even though the mother figure is fundamental in Italian society, the legitimacy of that role is not recognized unless the woman represses her own sexuality and limits her sphere of power to the domain of the family. It is no accident that at the beginning of the film, the judge who sentences the rebellious Asa to the torture of the spiked mask is her own older brother. When Asa returns from the dead to seek revenge, the family she attacks is her own. From then on, Italian horror cinema often portrayed the female figure as subverter of the patriarchal social order by virtue of her irresistible provocative sexuality. The fact that the man who brings Asa back to life is a doctor shows that not only are science and reason useless before the power of feminine allure, but they are destined to be its first victims. In fact, whereas in Anglo-Saxon horror cinema, we find characters such as Doctor Van Helsing, who is the very incarnation of rationality and socially recognized knowledge, and, therefore, a worthy adversary for Dracula, from Freda's *Lust of the Vampire* onwards, Italian horror cinema is characterized by the figure of the mad doctor—a man of reason totally under the control of the female figure. As Maggie Günsberg points out, in Italian horrors, "female vampirism is the key concern of (these) films. The female vampire is either the initial and dominating vampirizing force (…) or takes over the narrative trajectory and/or dominates visually in terms of camera time, then in a way sexually exploitative of the female body" (2005, 154). The primary theme of these films, therefore, is the morbid fascination with evil, which is distinctly feminine and sexual in nature.

It is not by chance that, while horror movies in the United States were generally destined for a young audience, in Italy horror was a genre *per adulti* (for adults). From the beginning, eroticism and horror, both associated with graphic exposition of the human body, were intertwined in Italian films. This is well exemplified in Gualtiero Jacopetti's notorious pseudo-documentary *Mondo cane* (1963), the precursor of the *mondo movies* sub-genre, which exploited viewers' attraction to the prohibited and the lurid for some 20 years. Among the Gothic films, this is particularly evident in the production of the minor director Renato Polselli. From his very first film, *The Vampire's Lover* (*L'amante del vampiro*, 1960), Polselli continually emphasized the bond between horror and sexuality. In this film, the vampire is a man, but his victims are not undefiled young women typical of a repressed puritanical society. They are uninhibited girls from a modern dance group whose sexuality is so robust that they almost seem eager to become the monster's prey.[7] Here, the vampire has a companion vampiress (a countess) with whom he has a unique sadomasochistic relationship: He bites the girls and she, in turn, bites him.

Therefore, there are great differences between these films and those of the Anglo-Saxon tradition. Although Dracula represents pure evil, he is still the personification of the patriarchal society, and therefore is the absolute ruler of his three wives as well as of the other women he bites. On the contrary, in Polselli's *The Vampire's Lover* it is difficult to discern who is master and who is slave. The vampire and the countess seem more like a couple dealing with a crisis in their relationship, perhaps brought on by their long period of cohabitation. Despite his constant infidelity with the girls he bites, he still loves the countess, while she can no longer abide him and would like to do away with him. They do not trust each other, nor does he trust the other women he vampirizes. He impales his victims when they become vampires, shouting, "I alone must be the master of my world!" He is clearly jealous of his power and almost frightened by the idea that the female vampires, over whom he evidently has no control, could increase in number and strength.[8]

Riccardo Freda, Mario Bava, Antonio Margheriti and the directors who followed them were recording and displaying—perhaps more subconsciously than intentionally—what was happening in

In her ambiguous first appearance in *Black Sunday*, Katia (also played by Barbara Steele) is dressed in black with two large, black dogs on a leash. Angel or demon? Here again, the only part of the scene that is illuminated is her face.

Italy during that era. Italian horror cinema came into being and was nourished by the sense of excitement that arose from the well-being Italians began to experience after 1957–1958. With the spreading of more wealth, the impulse to disobey rules and assume behaviors that had been prohibited in the past took root and grew among both men and women. One of the most significant changes was certainly that of women's role in society. Despite having won the right to vote and to have access to parliament in 1946, women remained subordinate until the end of the 1950s when they finally began to break free of the ties that had bound them to their traditional roles, gaining rights previously denied them.[9] During those years, the most notable changes in social mores occurred as a consequence, in some measure, of the death of Pope Pius XII in 1958, after which the strength of the Catholic Church's control over Italian society began to diminish. Furthermore, with the economic boom and the advent of a consumer society, even women were able to get a taste of the new more liberal lifestyle and felt the urge to rebel against the traditional rules. In those years, Brigitte Bardot was the sexual icon of the modern, open-minded woman. She was a focal point for male fantasies, but she also drew the attention of many young women who were gaining new independence and self-awareness in the area of sexuality.

There were two principal consequences of this new attitude: On the one hand, it showed how irresistible feminine sexuality could be; on the other, it made people uneasy and had an enormous impact on a culture in which sex and sin were considered one and the same. This is why the *theme of the double* often appears in Italian horror films, contrasting the perverse, "sexualized" woman with the traditional, "virginal" one. Antonio Tentori writes: "One of the most interesting aspects of the figure of the female-monster is her duality; her division into two forms, one normal, the other cruel. Often the cruel personality tries to take possession of the body and mind of the other, and entirely replace her" (1997, 89).

In Bava's *Black Sunday*, for example, we find Katia, a beautiful young descendant of the witch Asa. Asa desires to steal Katia's beauty and lifeblood in order to return from the dad once and for all. Katia is the exact opposite of Asa in that she is virginal and "pure," that is, not yet contaminated by evil. The unnerving aspect is that, despite this, Asa and Katia are identical in every way, including the black dress they both wear. In fact, they are played by the same actress, the then-unknown Barbara Steele. When Katia appears on screen for the first time, with her black cape and aloof behavior, the audience easily mistakes her for the film's villain (see picture). The consequence of this is that a male viewer can no longer be certain of the nature of the woman in front of him, especially when she is beautiful and seductive as the gorgeous Barbara Steele.[10]

It should be pointed out that in Italian horror, even when a woman is the victim (unless she is a virgin), she is represented as the bearer of what was considered a perverted or sick sexuality (nymphomania, lesbianism, or sadomasochism).[11] For example, in *The Whip and the Body* (*La frusta e il corpo*, 1963), Bava dared to film a story completely based on sadomasochistic passion, which was well ahead of its time. As the title suggests, the female protagonist enjoys being whipped by her lover (played by Christopher Lee) and her sexual obsession endures long after the mysterious death of her partner. In the end we discover that she is not at all a victim of the series of events, but instead is actually the one who killed him. It is significant that in this film Lee, who at that time was identified with the Dracula character, is eliminated almost immediately by the beautiful Daliah Lavi, even though he returns as a ghostly reflection of her perverse desire.[12]

As I said before, horror films remained a very marginal genre in Italian cinema until the end of the 1960s, constituting about 1 percent of the total number of films produced in Italy each year. The production of horror films and other B-movies was possible because the national cinematic industry produced enough pictures in this period (300-400 per year) to allow the marketing even of minor genres that often had uncertain box-office returns. At that time, ticket sales in Italy were inferior only to those of the United States—a fact that seems incredible today. Another contributing factor was the lack of competition, since Italian television had non-commercial TV networks and broadcast only two films a week—usually 20-year-old films shown on the least popular days of the week. Consequently, at the time, there was room to accomodate a large number of production and distribution houses and many low-budget (and extremely low-budget) films were made. These films often sold well in foreign markets and were considered good investments even if they brought in next to nothing in Italy. For this reason, directors such as Bava, Freda, and Margheriti are well-known and held in high regard in countries like France and the United States.

But why did Italian Gothic horror not become popular like the peplum (or sword-and-sandal) genre and the spaghetti western? These films were unsuccessful commercially, although they mirrored in a very original way the changes that were occurring in Italian society. One reason may be the sense of realism inherent in Italians, which would explain their limited interest in the supernatural, the fantastic, and the decadent settings of the Anglo-Saxon school that characterized Gothic horror. A second reason is that Italians, at that time, had not yet developed the many fears that other contemporary and more developed urban societies were harboring. In Italy, which is historically an agricultural country, fear was associated mostly with poverty. During the years in which they began to experience economic prosperity for the first time, Italians were far from thinking that their mass-industrialized society could be a source of fear and anguish. Therefore, although they lived in a period of great modernization and urbanization in the 1960s, the majority of the public was still unaware of how violent and dangerous their society was becoming.

Initially, even the new independence of women within society did not arouse enough apprehension in the male public to guarantee the popularity of this genre. The emancipation of women was not yet seen as a threat to male power or to the partiarchal society. Thus the horror genre remained on the fringe of the Italian market for many years. Italian audiences avoided works produced in their homeland (another reason why Italian writers and actors hid behind Anglicized names), but they were fascinated by foreign films. Italian men were attracted by the sex between the vampires and ghosts in Hammer's horror films, which defined the genre as one for adults rather than for teenagers. Dardano Sacchetti (one of the most important scriptwriters of the horror genre in the 1970s and '80s) comments:

> The Italian public was never aware of the fact that the objective of these films was to cause fear. Even when the first English films produced by Hammer began to arrive—with their ghosts and haunted castles—people went to see them because you could get a peek at the actresses' breasts as Dracula attacked them! (he laughs) (quoted in Fazzini 2004, 124).[13]

In fact, there was also an entirely commercial explanation for the strong bond between evil and eroticism (associated with the ideas of sin and the forbidden) which characterized Italian horror. From the very beginning, Italian horror films used scenes of violence as an excuse to show, along with the gore and splatter, all those things that were considered too scandalous for "normal" cinema.

The Italian *Giallo*: 1967–1977

Its "forbidden" content notwithstanding, Gothic horror soon saw its demise, because of commercial failure, in 1966 and gave way to the so-called Italian *giallo*, characterized by modern settings and driven content. This evolution was possible thanks to the relaxing of censorship restrictions, which allowed films to be produced that were even more violent and sexually explicit. Filmmakers eventually realized that their gothic settings had become too out-of-date. The castles, carriages and noblewomen in rich nineteenth-century dresses no longer allowed the audience to actively participate in the stories or identify with the characters. The years between 1967 and 1969 represented a transition period during which Antonio Margheriti's *gialli* were produced, *Naked You Die* (*Nude… si muore*) and *Screams in the Night* (*Contronatura*). The same period also witnessed the release of two of Umberto Lenzi's *gialli* featuring a torrid Carroll Baker, *Paranoia* (*Orgasmo*, 1969) and *So Sweet… So Perverse* (*Così dolce così perversa*, 1969). However, these first attempts to produce a modern thriller full of sexual implications did not capture the attention of the Italian moviegoers, who were still unimpressed by the representations of fear and violence typical of the genre. During the 1960s, comic books like *Diabolik* and other violence-based pulp fiction steadily gained popularity among young people, but even this did not consolidate a large enough audience to assure success for the Italian *gialli*.[14] This genre became profitable only after the release of Dario Argento's first two films, *The Bird with the Crystal Plumage* (*L'uccello dalle piume di cristallo*, 1970) and *The Cat o' Nine Tails* (*Il gatto a nove code*, 1971).[15]

At this point we may wonder why Argento's thrillers succeeded, while the preceding horror films remained on the margins. Argento's unexpected and resounding success, and that of the Italian *giallo* in general, was due to the fact that the repercussions of the cultural changes and escalating disorder in the country could no longer be ignored. The years 1968 and 1969 witnessed the beginning of a tempestuous period in Italy. In 1968, student protests erupted and there was widespread opposition to the sociopolitical system.[16] Students joined the cause of the trade unions, whose strike action had been increasing since the mid-1960s, and by the fall of 1969, the number of striking workers reached 5 million. In December of 1969, the Piazza Fontana massacre (in which a bomb placed at a bank in Milan killed 16 and injured 90) launched the so-called *strategia della tensione* (strategy of tension) and the period of turmoil called *anni di piombo*, or "years of lead" (1969–1982), the darkest period of Italian postwar history.[17] Suddenly, people no longer felt truly safe.

Argento seized on and skillfully exploited this widespread sense of fear. Although his films have no explicit political content—unlike, for instance, the new American horror cinema of George A. Romero,

Wes Craven, and Tobe Hooper—he was the first filmmaker to situate his stories in an undeniably Italian urban context. He set his films in cities that were unmistakably Italian, but depicted them as nightmarish and terrifying places. Therefore, despite continuing to shoot in English and using English-speaking actors as protagonists, Argento's great insight was to show how undefined fear and irrational violence had become two crucial elements of Italian daily life.[18] His films are a perfect representation of 1970s urban angst.[19] Argento's films portray the fears of Italians whose cities and communities had undergone such rapid growth and change that they had become unfamiliar and threatening places. In fact, in a mass consumer society, the individual seems free from the oppression and social conditioning of the past, but in such a society he ultimately loses his true identity. Violence and murder are no longer viewed as the exception in the modern world, but as the rule, and therefore, anyone can become a victim at any time.[20] The serial killer—a faceless maniac who kills randomly and without reason—is a manifestation of that fear. It must be observed that the death of Argento's assassins does not lead to a happy ending. Their death is in no way redeeming—see, for example, the final shot in *Deep Red* (*Profondo rosso*, 1975)—nor does it eliminate the spectator's feeling that evil and violence are escalating and that we are powerless to fight them.

At the same time, Argento and the Italian *giallo* take us back to Gothic horror in that he portrays evil as basically feminine in origin. His success is not due only to the fact that he gave voice to the urban fears experienced by Italians, who were finally becoming aware of the more unnerving aspects of modern society. His films, like all Italian *gialli*, also depicted distinctly masculine fears, which steadily grew stronger after the end of the 1960s, as a consequence of the major changes in sexual mores during the late 1960s and the early 1970s. The first men's magazines were published in those years (*Men* came out in 1966, and *Playmen* in 1967). The first erotic comics appeared with their anti-heroines Satanik and Valentina. The first birth control pill was put on the market, followed by the Church's official condemnation of contraception in Pope Paul VI's 1968 encyclical *Humanae Vitae*. The liberation of women, especially with regard to sex, became a major topic of discussion. All of this gave rise to a sense of insecurity and anxiety in relationships between the sexes that had been unknown to most before 1968.

In 1968, a new feminist movement arose which was more radical than previous ones. Earlier feminist movements had developed within established political parties (chiefly the Italian Communist Party and the Italian Socialist Party). Still, when women presented their demands in those parties, they often met with resistance from their male colleagues. Even the leftist parties were afraid of offending the Church and jeopardizing their alliance with the Christian Democratic Party by initiating reforms that were not considered priorities in their political agenda.[21] Things changed in 1968 when, along with the student protests, a new extra-parliamentary feminism was born that was much more aggressive in its demands and methods. For feminist organizations like the *Movimento Liberazione delle Donne* (created in 1969), but especially for the more radical *Fronte Italiano Liberazione Femminile* and *Rivolta Femminile* (both born in 1970), men came to be viewed, without compromise, as the enemies who needed to be eliminated in order to attain emancipation. Men unquestionably became the enemy who stood in the way of the path to liberation and needed to be defeated. The divorce law of 1970 (and the following 1974 referendum) was seen by left-wing feminists as a step towards abolition of the institution of marriage, perceived as the pillar of patriarchy and the foundation of bourgeois society. The most resounding taunts from the feminism of those years and slogans such as "the witches are back" have remained more vivid in the collective memory than many feminist issues of the time. Without a doubt, for many conventional thinkers, the witches really were back. They had certainly returned to invade popular subculture. In addition to horror cinema, pulp publications like the erotic comics of the early 1970s are full of witch-vampires and other sexually aggressive anti-heroines like Zora, Lucifera and Sukia.

Argento and the directors who followed him were demonstrating that in modern society even male-female relationships had became ambiguous and dangerous. This was achieved not only by associating female sexuality with perversion, but above all by displaying the hatred harbored by women towards men after centuries of subjugation. In Argento's films the assassin is often a woman and the murders usually result from an unbalanced relationship between the sexes. These assassins are women whose resentment and need for revenge drive them to get rid of the men in their lives. The feminist aspect of his films can be seen in the abnormal reaction of the female killers to traditional male oppression. For example, in his third film, *Four Flies on Grey Velvet (Quattro mosche di velluto grigio*, 1972), the protagonist is threatened by a killer who is later revealed to be his wife (portrayed by the androgynous actress Mimsy Farmer). The speech she gives at the end of the film, after she has killed her husband and declares her hatred towards him and all men in general, is worth quoting in its entirety:

> Are you suffering now? I've suffered for years and years. That swine of a father of mine wanted a son. He was a military officer and couldn't stand the idea of having had a daughter. He made me dress like a little boy and he would beat me so I could learn to take it like a man. Then he'd say I was crazy like my mother who died in a nursing home and he had me locked up in a mental hospital. The doctors were men, *men everywhere*. But I knew how to wait. That swine of a father of mine died before I could kill him. When you arrived, you were like a miracle to me, you looked exactly like him. *You are my father!*[22]

However, all the justification for women's resentment and aggressiveness towards men—such as the rape in *The Bird with the Crystal Plumage* or the paternal violence in *Four Flies on Grey Velvet*—does not assuage, but only serves to intensify the deep-seated anxiety that Argento's films inspire in the audience; namely, the feeling that any woman, even (and in particular) one's own companion, could suddenly turn out to be a deadly threat.[23]

With Argento this ambivalence is always present. From a rational point of view, women are seen in a positive light, as a being superior to men, but for this very reason, there is a subconscious sense of terror towards them. If the men in Argento's films seem to have accepted the power of the opposite sex and appear fragile and almost effeminate in the wake of the hybridization of roles that is characteristic of the post-1968 sexual revolution, they nonetheless live with the subconscious fear of eventually being disposed of by the women in their lives. The inability of Argento's male characters to fight back in any substantial way corresponds to the masculine nightmares of impotence and castration—in fact, they never appear eager to go to bed with with their partners. In essence, Argento's films show the decline of male supremacy and the establishment of a new female leadership, which may be either beneficial or detrimental to males. This female power is seen by the director as both new and very old, and is represented with Jungian-like symbolism. Argento's characters passively endure the world around them, and are often literally swallowed up by objects that symbolize submersion into a feminine-type element (houses, tunnels, water).[24] Quite interestingly, Argento does not emphasize a woman's sexuality, but rather her casting off of traditonal roles to the extent that she ultimately consumes the man in her life, whether he be lover, husband or son. In his films, as opposed to the majority of Italian *gialli*, eroticism is not in the foreground and is totally sublimated into the violence.[25]

In *Deep Red* (1975), all of Argento's themes work in perfect synthesis. Marcus, an English jazz pianist who teaches at an Italian conservatory, witnesses a crime which he is unable to prevent. He sets out to investigate the crime together with Gianna, a resourceful journalist with whom he squabbles constantly. Gianna is sweet and pretty, but she is also the typical liberated woman of her day: stubborn and independent (she lives alone). She also has some male mannerisms, for example she smokes little cigars. The scenes featuring the two characters often take on the tone of a romantic comedy, much like the sophisticated American comedies from the 1930s to the 1950s, in which the main theme was the war between the sexes and the weakness of men when confronted with enterprising modern women (the films of Howard Hawks come to mind). In Argento's films, however, these scenes alternate with ones of such suspense and violence that one begins to believe this battle between the sexes has gone on for so long that it cannot be resolved without bloodshed.

Throughout the movie, the audience will wonder if Gianna herself is not the maniac who committed the terrible crimes. The fact that she is not the assassin is of secondary importance after all. Gianna, who was played by Daria Nicolodi (the director's new companion at the

In *Deep Red* (1975), Gianna (Daria Nicolodi), filmed in profile, slowly puffs a cigar while the protagonist (and the audience) watch with a certain amount of discomfort.

time), is a very disconcerting character. She drives Marcus around in her old Fiat 500, in which he is forced to sit on the floor because the passenger seat is broken. The real discomfort arises from the awareness that Gianna is the dominant figure in their relationship. This becomes clear in the scene in which she beats Marcus at arm wrestling. At the end of the film, the true culprit is revealed to be the mother of a gay alcoholic pianist who is a colleague and friend of Marcus. A flashback shows the audience events that occurred years earlier. The mother, played by the now elderly diva of 1930s and 1940s Italian cinema, Clara Calamai—the wicked protagonist of Luchino Visconti's *Obsession* (*Ossessione*, 1943)—is a former actress who had been forced to give up her career in order to care for her family. Afterwards, she shows clear signs of insanity, and her husband wants to have her institutionalized. She kills him in front of her young son. The audience is presented with this woman who has become an emasculating witch, rebelling against an already vulnerable male authority. Her obsessive overprotectiveness leaves her son incapable of becoming independent and epitomizes the negative aspects of the prevailing Italian *mammismo* ("momism").

It is therefore evident that, for Argento, sexually active women are not the only threat. It is not only sexually active women, but also young girls (like the watchman's malicious daughter in *Deep Red*) and post-menopausal women who take on a menacing aspect in his films. In a very brief scene (without dialogue) from *Deep Red*, the camera leaves the protagonist for a moment and lingers on a room that looks out onto the street, thus giving viewers information about a homi-

An old custodian in her "cavern" in a scene from *Deep Red.* Her gown and air of nonchalance seem to give her an air of superiority with respect to the news being broadcast on the television in the background.

cide which appears on the television news program in the background (see picture above). In the foreground is a strange-looking elderly lady smoking a cigar, filmed in profile; in a pose very similar to that of Gianna in the preceding photograph (Page 69). This woman, who is probably a custodian, is dressed in a bizarre fashion, wearing an odd-looking toga that lends her an almost noble air. Even in this scene, apparently of little importance, the contrast between the woman and the banality of her surroundings has the effect of creating uneasiness in the viewer. It seems as though Argento wants to suggest to his audience that a witch may be hiding anywhere, even within the most ordinary of women.[26]

In his next films, *Dario Argento's Suspiria* (*Suspiria,* 1977) and *Dario Argento's Inferno* (*Inferno,* 1980), Argento developed the theme of woman-as-threat to such an extent that he virtually abandoned the Italian *giallo* structure and returned to the fantasy atmospheres typical of the earlier Gothic horror genre. In these films, danger does not come from one woman, but from an all-female powerhouse which is seizing control of the world, leaving no possibility for escape. *Suspiria* and *Inferno* are part of a trilogy (unfinished at the time), whose theme is the myth of the "three mothers."[27] Although they are called "mothers," these witches no longer reflect robust sexuality. On the contrary, they are the embodiment of sterility. Their power seems stronger because they have lost (perhaps intentionally) the ability to procreate. As opposed to the vampire-mantis of Gothic horror in the previous decade, Argento's witches, much like the more radical feminists, seem to have rejected their own sexuality. Perhaps it is for this reason that they present a threat not only to the men, but also to the exuberant college girls in *Suspiria* (1977). It is significant that in this film, as well as in the subsequent films *Creepers* (*Phenomena*, 1985), *Terror at the Opera* (*Opera*, 1987), and *Dario Argento's Trauma* (*Trauma*, 1992), the protagonist is a virgin. The young women of these films discover horrifying incidents and risk being consumed by evil since they are bearers of another deviance—a hidden repulsion toward sex.[28]

Argento's films, along with the most markedly "horror" of horror pictures—such as those of the diabolic subgenre (clearly a spinoff of William Friedkin's *The Exorcist*): *The Antichrist* (*L'anticristo*, Alberto De Martino, 1974), *The Devil Obsession* (*L'ossessa*, Mario Gariazzo, 1974), *The Malicious Whore* (*Malabimba*, Andrea Bianchi, 1979)— remained linked to the preceding genre, the Italian gothic, by portraying sexually active women as deadly and dangerous beings. In the Italian *gialli* of the 1970s, however, women were more often depicted as victims than as executioners. Following the example of Bava's prototype *Blood and Black Lace* (*Sei donne per l'assassino*, 1964) the recurring theme in these films is the sadistic violence inflicted upon the bodies of women by psychopathic men. In Paolo Cavara's *Black Belly of the Tarantula* (*La tarantola dal ventre nero*, 1971), a maniac kills young clients of a beauty salon. He begins by piercing his victims' necks with a hatpin in order to leave them paralyzed but conscious and then lets loose his rage on their entire bodies. At the end of the film, the audience discovers that the assassin is the institute's masseur (pretending to be blind) who had gone insane after becoming impotent and then being betrayed by his wife.

These films clearly display the frustrations of men as woman's sexual liberation reached its peak. Women were considered at fault for experiencing their sexuality freely and consciously—a sexuality in the face of which men felt inadequate. The *giallo* expressed the idea of sexually active women as beings with deviant and pathological behaviors, an idea that was already present in Gothic horror. Lesbians and nymphomaniacs are the norm in these films, and it is these types of behavior that condemn women to becoming the victims of a raging maniac. Therefore there is no real difference between the woman-as-witch and the woman-as-victim roles in the Italian *gialli*, in the sense that both figures embody, although in different ways, the male fears which had emerged during the most turbulent years of the

The assassin in *Black Belly of the Tarantula* (1971) ravages the naked bodies of beautiful young women after paralyzing them with a hatpin and leaving them conscious but defenseless.

sexual revolution and feminism.

The Decline of the Italian *Giallo* and Extreme Horror (1978–1986)
In the mid-1970s, after five years of great success, the Italian *giallo* went into a slump. This was due first of all to a glut of similar films swamping the market, as often happened in Italian cinema once a genre had become popular. Another contributing factor was the worsening social situation in Italy. The economic crisis and the "years of lead" gave Italians many other reasons to be afraid. The classic Italian *giallo* with its serial killer, although rich in powerful scenes, was no longer able to keep pace with a society that by that time was exhausted and prey to widespread and seemingly uncontrollable violence. Even Argento's films following *Deep Red, Suspiria* and *Inferno* did not attain as much success in Italy as had been expected.[29] Argento paid a heavy price for departing from the original *giallo* style which had made him famous. It was, in fact, the supernatural, almost fairytale-like elements of his last two films that drove the Italian viewing public away, as they had always been wary of the fantastic and farfetched. In fact, with *Unsane (Tenebre*, 1982), he returned to the original formula of the Italian *giallo* and once again achieved success.

In general, after the success of George A. Romero's *Dawn of the*

Dead (1978, co-produced by Argento), Italian horror headed ever further in the direction of the typical slasher film. While Argento decided to remain more or less faithful to the themes that had made him famous and that his fans expected of him, directors like Lucio Fulci, Aristide Massacesi, Ruggero Deodato, Umberto Lenzi, and Lamberto Bava (son of Mario) opted for exaggerated and visceral solutions like those found in zombie movies, cannibal movies, and *mondo* movies. These directors took the violence and sadism already present in Italian *giallo* to the extreme. Above all, the exploitation of blood and gore, as well as graphic, gratuitous, and excessive violence, seemed the only way to represent the fears Italians experienced during the years of lead, as well as a means to recapture an audience that was growing less and less fond of the genre. In fact, in the 1980s, these films had to compete against the new commercial television channels, whose audiences were gradually growing accustomed to the news and violent images that were broadcast in ever-increasing numbers (this was the topic of Ruggero Deodato's much-disputed *Cannibal Holocaust*).[30] A main consequence is that, in light of the general crisis in Italian cinema, these films were produced mainly for foreign markets, something which had already happened with films of the Gothic horror period.

In this new breed of horror films, the female figure lost her position of importance. With the years of lead getting worse in the late 1970s, the anxieties caused by the sexual revolution were put aside as other problems replaced them in unsettling and alarming Italians. In 1978, Aldo Moro, the leader of the Christian Democratic Party and the most important Italian politician of the time, was kidnapped and murdered by the extreme left-wing terrorist organization the Red Brigades (*Brigate Rosse*). In addition, toward the late 1970s the more radical, non-parliamentary feminism lost part of its power. The more moderate and "institutional" feminist groups that worked within the party structure took up political initiatives and demonstrated their efficiency and expertise with a series of important social reforms.[31] This does not mean that male fears concerning the opposite sex were completely suppressed, but only that they no longer aroused such intense feelings of apprehension and were exorcised in other ways, primarily through laughter. At first glance, it might seem a paradox, but from this point of view the coarse comedy of the 1970s and early 1980s was, in fact, the ideal continuation of the *giallo*. These comedies were heavily criticized by feminists, but often for the wrong reasons. In many ways they portrayed, with a certain degree of honesty, the difficulties men experienced when confronted with the modern, liberated woman. The male characters are depicted as mediocre and ridiculous, intimidated by women who, in contrast, appear completely comfortable in traditionally masculine roles (parking attendants, police officers, teachers, doctors, etc.) and totally self-confident about their own sexuality.[32]

In the 1980s Italian cinema as a whole found itself in a steady decline, shoved aside by the ever-increasing predominance of commercial television. Furthermore, with the official end of the years of lead in 1982 and the beginning of the so-called *riflusso* (reflux)—a period dominated by a general feeling of political disengagement and rejection of the troubles of the previous 15 years—Italians no longer viewed the urban environment as hostile, but as an place for entertainment in the wake of the second economic boom, which was exemplified by the slogan "*Milano da bere*" ("Milan to drink"). Consequently, Italian horror again became a genre that was appreciated by only a very few, and slowly disappeared from Italian cinema.[33] Of all the cinematic genres, only the comedy, represented by Carlo Verdone, Massimo Troisi, Francesco Nuti, Nanni Moretti and Gabriele Salvatores, survived commercially. Nevertheless, while urban anxiety may have disappeared in the 1980s, men's concerns about women's independence still existed, so even in the comedies by these young directors, women were often regarded as disturbing beings whose presence had the power to upset the self-confidence, life and friendships of Italian men.

As has been demonstrated, in the first two decades of their existence, Italian horror films focused on women. From the beginning, the directors of the Gothic period, who were producing low-budget films on commission and without commercial success, distanced themselves from the themes typical of Anglo-American cinema. Viewing these films, together with the subsequent Italian *giallo*, one can understand the growing discomfort men experienced during the 20 years from the end of the 1950s until the end of the 1970s, with the steady advance of women's liberation, especially when it came to sex. In effect, it was only after 1968, during the most intense period of the sexual revolution and social upheaval, that this genre saw any kind of popular success in the form of the Italian *giallo* characterized mostly by urban settings.

At this point one must ask: Was Italian horror misogynistic? Italian horror's correlation of female sexuality with perversion leads one to conclude, perhaps too easily, that it was to a large extent a misogynistic genre, although an unequivocal answer cannot be given. There is no doubt that much of Italian cinema can be regarded as fundamentally misogynistic, but it should also be noted that Italian horror lacks genuine heroes with whom one can identify, since the male characters are often weak and ineffective. As a consequence, there is no Van Helsing figure in Italian horror. The doctors, who should be among the strongest representatives of the patriarchal establishment, are often the first to succumb to women's powers of seduction, and their authority is never restored at the conclusion of the movie. They are usually destroyed by the female protagonists. In many cases the ultimate defeat of the evil female(s) does not reestablish the previous social order, thus revealing an essential weakness and breakdown that is the cause, and not the effect, of women taking of power. The fear of feminine sexuality and independence lies within men who have acknowledged, but not consciously accepted, that the time in which their supremacy over women could be taken for granted has ended. We must also recall that in the Italian *giallo* women are often the victims, and not the culprits, of brutal murders perpetrated by men who are unable to stand the former's "perversion."

The conclusions of many Dario Argento films show this ambivalence in Italian horror: The threat of an evil matriarchy is ultimately avoided, and yet in the final scene the mood is not triumphant but negative and pessimistic. In other words, blatant misogyny may be read as an open confession of a crisis of the masculine psyche, and not necessarily as a defense of the old patriarchal society. Argento was the only Italian director of horror films ever to consider himself (and be considered) an *auteur*, and to achieve longstanding success with the public and the critics. His works clearly show that through this genre (and the ensuing romantic comedies of the 1980s), filmmakers and the public tried to cope with their *own* sexual and cultural crises brought on by the liberation of women and the inevitable decline of the old cultural-social models. How well they succeeded is, of course, a topic that warrants further discussion.

NOTES

1   Freda bet some producers that he could produce a film in fewer than two weeks. He won the bet—the film was finished within 12 days— even though he left the set prior to the end of filming due to his disagreements with the producers. Despite its modest budget, the film was enriched by the collaboration of such talents as set designer Beni Montresor, composer Roman Vlad, and director of photography Mario Bava (who finished shooting the film after Freda's departure). They all contributed to creating the decadent atmosphere in the most beautiful scenes of the film.

2   The figure of the *femme fatale* became very popular in Italian films of the war years, such as Carmine Gallone's version of *Marina of Malombra* (1917), Augusto Genina's *Femmina* (1918), and Romolo Bacchini's *La tigre vendicatrice* (1918). According to Lucia Re, the reason is quite similar to that which will explain the rise and success of the horror genre many decades later: "These strangely retrograde D'Annunzian films represent the anxiety of a moment in Italian history when traditional gender roles were being questioned to the point of crisis, and when women, who had entered the public sphere *en masse* (notably in the production of arms and armaments, to substitute for the men who were fighting at the front), seemed to have lost their femininity and to resemble men in an increasingly 'unnatural' manner" (2008: 147).

3   "*Oltrepassando Dracula, i licantropi e i fantasmi del cinema anglosassone, le pellicole italiane promuovono come figura centrale la donna, unica vera protagonista del genere, che, da vampira a strega, da femmina fatale a femmina folle, diventa il motore di tutte le tenebrose vicende presentate*" (the translations are mine, as are all other quotations from Italian books).

4   Still, it is interesting to compare the two films. In *The Blob*, the gelatinous monster is an alien organism that comes from outer space in a meteorite. In the Italian film, the monster is awakened when an archeological expedition discovers an old temple dedicated to the Mayan *goddess* Caltiki. Furthermore, before becoming a huge blob-like mass in the final scenes, it takes the body and then the mind of a *male* member of the expedition who eventually goes insane.

5   Mario Bava (1914–1980) was born into an artistic family. His father Eu-
    genio was a cinematographer—he worked as special effects technician in
    Enrico Guazzoni's *Quo Vadis* (1912), Giovanni Pastrone's *Cabiria* (1914),
    and photographed *Cenere* (Febo Mari, 1916)—as well as a painter and
    sculptor. He also made a few movies as a director before becoming the
    director of special visual effects of the newly formed LUCE institute in
    1926. Mario Bava began his professional career as a director of photog-
    raphy during the Second World War (his first works were Rossellini's
    "home-made" documentaries). After the war and throughout the 1950s
    he was extremely sought-after, above all by Italian peplum and epic pro-
    ductions, for his ability to create visual effects and his magic-like touch
    to make even a modest-budget film take on a look of richness far sur-
    passing its financial restrictions. To get a taste of his talent, one needs
    only to look at the splendid scenes at the beginning of *Caltiki*, a film
    attributed to Freda, but filmed in large part by Bava.

6   I have previously observed the connection between the figure of the evil
    woman of the Gothic horror and the *femme fatale* of the earlier melo-
    drama. In particular the similarities between Asa the Vampire-witch in
    Black Sunday and the hypnotic Queen Sofonisba in *Scipio the African*
    (*Scipione l'africano*, 1937) are worth noting. The latter embodies the
    quintessential sexual temptress (in one scene she is dressed in a gown
    decorated with serpents). Sofonisba's make-up recalls that of the Hol-
    lywood stars due to the fact that Francesca Braggiotti, the actress who
    played the role, lived and worked in Hollywood, thus establishing an
    interesting connection between female sexuality and Americanization
    of customs. We find many examples of the evil queen/femme fatale as
    opposed to the pure woman/virgin to be saved in the second cycle of the
    peplum from the late 1950s and early 1960s, for instance, *The Last Days
    of Pompeii* (*Gli ultimi giorni di Pompei*, 1959) or *Hercules Unchained*
    (*Ercole e la regina di Lidia*,1959). Without any doubt, the Gothic hor-
    ror genre shares this equation (female sexuality=witchcraft) and other
    similarities with the peplum, of more or less the same era, as well as the
    talent of director/cinematographer Mario Bava. However, the peplum
    is a reassuring celebration of the quintessential masculine power, repre-
    sented by the body, whereas in the Gothic horror male superiority and
    traditional social bonds are not reestablished at the end.

7   A recurrent theme in Italian horror is that of a group of provocative
    dancers (or models) as victims. It can be seen, for example, in Polselli's
    next film, *The Vampire of the Opera* (*Il mostro dell'opera*, 1961, released
    in 1964). In the 1970s, Polselli included in his films erotic scenes that
    increasingly went beyond the accepted boundaries until they reached
    the level of explicit hardcore.

8   Likewise, in Roberto Mauri's *Curse of the Blood Ghouls* (*La strage dei*

vampiri, 1962) the male vampire has problems controlling the women he vampirizes.

9   In 1958, law No. 75 was passed under pressure from the socialist Senator Lina Merlin. It abolished brothels, and thus the state's exploitation of prostitution, and returned full civil rights to prostitutes. In 1959, a female police force was established, (at first having duties relating only to women and minors), and in 1961, women finally gained access to careers in the judicial system and diplomatic corps.

10 In Freda's *The Ghost* (*Lo Spettro*, 1963), Barbara Steele is an adulterous wife who pressures her lover into killing her paralyzed husband (Dr. Hichcock) for his inheritance and then, in turn, butchers the lover. Another filmmaker commited to this genre, Antonio Margheriti, directed *The Long Hair of Death* (*I lunghi capelli della morte*, 1964), in which a witch's daughter seduces and drives mad the men who condemned her mother to the stake.

11 In his historical comedy *For Love and Gold* (*L'armata Brancaleone*, 1966), director Mario Monicelli makes an ironic point about these themes when he has Steele—who was by then an undisputed icon of Italian horror—seduce and then literally whip poor Vittorio Gassman.

12 In the same year Daliah Lavi also acted in Brunello Rondi's *The Demon* (*Il demonio*, 1963). In a small isolated village in Lucania, Purificata, a young girl, shows signs of madness when the man she is in love with prefers another. Her behavior is such that she is declared possessed by the devil and kept locked up at her parent's house. Her inability to repress her feelings leads to her being murdered by the man she loves. This is an ambivalent film since on the one hand, it is consistent with Italian horror films in condemning female sexual desire; yet on the other hand it portrays the woman as the predestined victim of a superstitious and archaic patriarchal society. This unusual film owes more to Viscontian Neorealism—with clear parallels with Giovanni Verga's novel *La lupa*—than to the horror genre, and it is probably for this reason that it never found its audience. An analogous theme recurs ten years later in one of director Lucio Fulci's first *gialli*, *Don't Torture a Duckling* (*Non si sevizia un paperino*, 1972), also set in Puglia. Here, the real assassin of the boys in the village turns out not to be the local *fattucchiera* (witch), but the local priest. He kills because he is obsessed with his mission to keep them pure and untainted by the temptations of modern society. The truth does not come out until after the villagers have beaten the innocent woman to death with iron bars.

13 *"Il pubblico italiano non ha mai avuto coscienza del fatto che erano film che avevano come obbiettivo quello di far paura. Anche quando iniziarono ad arrivare i primi film inglesi prodotti dalla Hammer, con fantasmi e castelli stregati, li andavamo a vedere perché si intravedevano le tette delle attrici*

che venivano aggredite da Dracula! (ride)"

14 Mario Bava himself directed the film *Diabolik* (*Danger: Diabolik*) in 1968 at the request of producer Dino De Laurentiis. In effect, Bava should be also considered a precursor of the Italian *giallo* with two films: *The Evil Eye* (*La ragazza che sapeva troppo*, 1962) and *Blood and Black Lace* (*Sei donne per l'assassino*, 1964).

15 Particularly with *Blood and Black Lace*, he anticipated Dario Argento's baroque representation of violence and death. In this modern Gothic, significantly set in a fashion house, the true protagonist is the *mise-en-scène* of brilliant and unnatural colors, while the characters are only puppets ready to be converted into corpse-like mannequins. The six women referred to in the title are all young models who are murdered in the most horrible fashions (one is pushed face first onto a scorching hot stove) by a faceless assassin clad in a raincoat, gloves and a black hat (these articles of clothing would become typical of the serial killer in many subsequent Italian *gialli*). The identity of the assassin is not important—there are two: the owner of the fashion house and her lover, who kill each other at the end—since the real intent is to depict on screen the sadistic pleasure of causing death (to young women in particular) in a way that would thereafter characterize many Italian and American slasher movies. Although the audience is invited to uncover the assassin's identity and his/her motives for having killed the women, the logic behind these crimes is, so to say, purely esthetic.

16 It is worth recalling that, when *The Bird with the Crystal Plumage* was released in 1970, it was—with few exceptions—a commercial failure. The head of Titanus, producer Goffredo Lombardo, did not believe in the project and was persuaded to finance a second picture only thanks to the unexpected success of the film in the United States, where it was distributed in the New York area under the title *The Gallery Murders*. This explains the decision to give a decidedly American flavor to Argento's subsequent film, *The Cat o' Nine Tails* (*Il gatto a nove code*, 1971), in both subject matter (with a rather science fiction feel) and cast (the actors James Franciscus and Karl Malden). The success of *The Cat o' Nine Tails* in Italy prompted Lombardo to release *The Bird with the Crystal Plumage* for a second time and the film was eventually a hit.

17 On March 1, 1968, a large student protest march took place in Valle Giulia in Rome, near the College of Architecture and, for the first time, overran the police blockade.

18 The term *anni di piombo* usually refers to the whole period from 1969 through to the early 1980s. It came to be known as the "years of lead" because of the waves of bombing, shootings, general violence and threats attributed to actions of the far-right, far-left and secret services. Its darkest years (1977–80) were marked by an escalation of violence attributed

to both right-wing and left-wing extremism.

19 With Gothic horror films, Italian directors were forced to change their names and set their films in foreign locations in order to try to sell their products as Anglo-Saxon in the Italian market. It is true that even in the 1970s many Italian *gialli* are set in European cities like London, Paris, Munich and Madrid. In this case, however, the decision was made mainly to increase the sales of these films—all of which were co-produced with foreign companies—in *foreign* markets.

20 Argento adopted (and took to the extreme) a theme that was already characteristic of Michelangelo Antonioni's films such as *Eclipse* (*L'eclisse*, 1962), *Red Desert* (*Deserto rosso*,1964) and *Blow Up* (*Blow-Up*, 1966). Antonioni was probably the first director to represent Italian (but also foreign) landscapes as hostile environments which the characters passively endured until they disappeared into them. *Deep Red* can be regarded as essentially a remake of *Blow Up*, with the same actor in the protagonist role.

21 From this point of view, the themes of Italian mystery (*giallo*) are analogous to those of the so-called *poliziottesco*, an Italian action-crime genre that became very popular during the same period (the first of these was Fernando di Leo's *Caliber 9* (*Milano calibro 9*) in 1971).

22 The coming together of the Christian Democratic Party and the Italian Socialist Party had already begun after the 1958 political elections and the death of Pius XII. The first center-left governments became possible in 1962–63, concurrent with the Second Vatican Council (1962–65), which signaled a new openness on the part of the Church towards the needs of a secularized society.

23 "*Soffri adesso? Io ho sofferto per anni ed anni. Quel porco di mio padre voleva un maschio. Era un militare, non sopportava l'idea di aver avuto una femmina. Mi faceva vestire da ragazzo e mi picchiava perché imparassi a reagire come un uomo. Poi disse che ero pazza come mia madre, che era morta in una casa di cura e mi fece rinchiudere in manicomio. I medici erano maschi, dappertutto maschi. Ma io ho saputo aspettare. Quel maiale di mio padre morì prima che potessi ucciderlo. Quando arrivasti tu, mi parve un miracolo, gli assomigliavi come una goccia d'acqua. Tu sei mio padre!*"

24 The previous film, *The Cat o' Nine Tails* (1971), is exceptional in Argento's creative output given that it is one of his few films featuring a male assassin. He is a scientist who slays in order to hide the fact that he possesses a presumed rare triple chromosome XYY, which might be—according to a top-secret research conducted in the medical institute where he works—the cause of criminal behavior. In this case, aggressive behavior is depicted as a male aberration due to the extra Y chromosome (women have only double X chromosomes). I already observed in another footnote that the producer wanted this film, after the

American success of *The Bird with the Crystal Plumage*, to have a specifically American flavor—this is due to the screenwriter Dardano Sacchetti,
while Argento stated on many occasions that he did not like the fact
that this film looked like an American mystery. In general, Argento's
males, whether they be lovers, husbands or sons, are driven to kill or to
aid female assassins because they are under female subjugation. In *Terror at the Opera* (*Opera*, 1987), for instance, the assassin is male, but has
become insane because his lover forced him to torture and kill for her
own personal excitement.

25 Used by Argento as a source of inspiration, the Jungian symbol of the
archetypal mother depicts her as both nurturer and devourer.

26 This was possible because Dario was the son of Salvatore Argento, with
whom he co-produced his films. From the beginning, he enjoyed a certain freedom from the production constraints that were imposed on
other directors of this genre. It is important to note that the 1970s were
a time when not only producers of *gialli* and commercial cinema, but
also highly respected directors like Pasolini, Antonioni, Visconti, Bertolucci and Fellini, indulged quite freely in representations of sex.

27 The two women murdered in *Deep Red* are "good" witches: a German
medium and an author of legends and esoteric subject matters.

28 The idea of the three mothers was drawn from Thomas De Quincey's
book *Suspiria de Profundis*. It was suggested to Argento by his companion, the actress Daria Nicolodi, who was a devotee of the occult.

29 In *Creepers* the protagonist is a sleepwalker (who is also able to communicate with insects); in *Opera* she is frigid and austere; and in *Trauma*
she is anorexic. In the subsequent *The Stendhal Syndrome* (*La sindrome
di Stendhal*, 1992), the protagonist is a police officer who suffers from
the syndrome featured in the film's title and, after having been raped
twice by a maniac, goes on to become an assassin. In other Italian *gialli*,
such as *All the Colors of the Dark* (*Tutti i colori del buio*, 1972, Sergio
Martino) and *Autopsy* (*Macchie solari*, 1975, by Armando Crispino), the
female protagonists suffer from psychological blocks which leave them
incapable of sexual relationships.

30 *Suspiria*'s success outside Italy (where it has become one of his bet-
ter-known films) allowed Argento to continue the trilogy with *Inferno*
(1980). *Inferno* was supported by American financing and distributed
by Twentieth Century Fox, but after its commercial failure—Twentieth Century Fox did not like the film, and hardly distributed it in the
American market—the "mother trilogy" was left unfinished. Argento
has recently completed it with a film entitled *Mother of Tears* (*La terza
madre*, 2007), in which he explicated the idea of a war between good
and evil witches vying to rule the world.

31 This is the plot line of the 1979 film (then repeated in *The Blair Witch*

Project, which also allowed the viewing public to believe that it was a real documentary). Four television reporters disappear while on location in the Amazon. Their film canisters are found and the films are then viewed. It is obvious that the reporters had found nothing of interest, but that they themselves had inflicted brutal acts of violence against the indigenous peoples, thus provoking the latter to seek a terrible revenge on the reporters.

32 Among the most important: the new Family Rights parliamentary legislation of 1975 which finally gave husband and wife equal status; law no. 903 of 1977 that imposed "equality in the treatment of men and women in the workplace" and finally the abortion law of 1978.

33 While the period of the extreme horror came to an end in the mid-1980s, Italian horror as a genre did not survive much longer. A major reason for its demise—with the exception of Dario Argento, who still has the advantage of a sufficient number of fans and a worldwide reputation—was the new 1990 law that regulated television broadcasting (the so-called *Legge Mammì*). After a 15-year period of anarchy in which the newly created private channels operated without any specific regulation (1976–90), the new law reaffirmed the old prohibition (Censorship Law No. 161 of 1962) on the broadcasting of all films rated PG-18, whereby PG-14 films cannot be shown on prime time but only after 10:30 p.m. (in Italy there were two restrictions until 2007: forbidden under the age of 18 and under the age of 14. In 2007 a new rating was added for children under the age of 10). That is, not only was the prohibition explicitly extended to private television, but a film that was originally rated PG-18 could not be re-cut in order to be shown on television (as is common, for instance, in the United States). Since at that time, Italian public and private television networks (RAI and Silvio Berlusconi's Fininvest-Mediaset) were already the most important producers and acquirers of Italian films, this law had the effect of eliminating any controversial films and film genres from national filmmaking from that time on.

3

DOLLARS, BULLETS AND SUCCESS

The Spaghetti Western Phenomenon

Flavia Brizio-Skov

In August 1964, Sergio Leone's *A Fistful of Dollars* (*Per un pugno di dollari*) was released on the Italian cinema circuit. The film was an Italian-Spanish-German co-production which cost only 120 million lire to make; between 1964 and 1968, the film made more than $4.5 million in Italy and, in the United States, where it was not released until 1967 due to the legal dispute with Kurosawa,[1] it made $3.5 million. Leone's second film, *For a Few Dollars More* (*Per qualche dollaro in più*, 1965), also an Italian-Spanish-German co-production, earned $5 million in Italy between 1965 and 1968 and the same amount again in the United States. *The Good, the Bad, and the Ugly* (*Il buono, il brutto, e il cattivo*, 1966), the third film of the so-called Leone trilogy, an exclusively Italian production, earned more than $4 million in Italy between 1966 and 1968 and $6 million in the United States.[2] The enormous success of *A Fistful of Dollars* unleashed the spaghetti western phenomenon: 462 films in a decade, with an average of more than 70 per year in 1967 and 1968 and more than 45 per year in 1971 and 1972, all with respectable box-office takings.[3] Between 1976 and 1977, the production regressed to three spaghetti westerns per year and decreased even further to two in 1978. The "phenomenon" can be considered finished by the second half of the

1970s despite a few sporadic later appearances, such as Enzo Castellari's *Django rides again* (*Keoma,* 1976), Lucio Fulci's *They Died with their Boots on* (*Stella d'argento,* 1978), and *Jonathan of the Bears* (*Jonathan degli orsi,* 1995) by Enzo Castellari.[4]

The spaghetti westerns, thanks to both their popularity and earnings, constitute an unprecedented event in the history of Italian cinema. Many critics attributed this success to economic factors: In the 1960s, cinema was still one of the most popular forms of entertainment with annual sales of 700 million tickets and a national production in Italy of about 300 films. The 1950s and 1960s were undoubtedly the Golden Age of Italian cinema. Toward the end of the 1960s, Italy produced more films than Hollywood, a situation that had previously occurred only in the period preceding 1915, when Italy was one of the major global exporters of silent films.[5] Unfortunately, the *dolce vita* of Italian cinema ended in the 1970s: The Americans withdrew funding, private television began to grow more and more, and, consequently, TV surpassed cinema as the most popular form of entertainment. At the end of the 1970s, Italian cinematic production decreased to around 100 films per year, and ticket sales to 100 million lire, with 80 percent of takings going to American-made films.[6]

Since it is now impossible to conduct empirical research on the sociology of the audience of the time, we can only form some hypotheses based on the existing data. If, as Spinazzola maintains, in 1964, there were 10,517 movie theaters in Italy, among which 20 percent had prices of less than 100 lire (16 cents), 57.8 percent between 100 and 200 lire, 14.3 percent between 200 and 300 lire, 6.9 percent between 300 and 1,000 lire, and only 0.2 percent sold tickets for more than 1,000 lire, it seems obvious, given the majority of the low-priced movie theaters and the high profits earned by the spaghetti westerns, that we are dealing with an authentic popular success. On the other hand, the assertion that the monetary success of the Italian western was, above all, a phenomenon linked to the second and third-run theaters and to a certain type of audience is negated by the box-office earnings from first showings, which saw *A Fistful of Dollars,* less than a year after its distribution on the national circuit (1964-65 season), in fourth place at the box office with 642,551,000 lire (more than half a million dollars).[7] From this data, it is clear that the old claim, according to which the spaghetti western obtained success primarily via secondary theaters or, in other words, in rural or suburban areas or parts of Southern Italy, i.e. areas with an audience comprised mostly of working class or uneducated people, cannot be considered valid.[8] The distinction between cinema *engagé* for the intellectual/urban classes and commercial cinema for the inferior/rural/southern classes, or, as some say, between "high and low culture," is an untenable model in the 1960s. The Italian western shattered the barrier between popular cinema and *élite* cinema; the genre was appreciated by all, by the bourgeois of the cities as well as by the proletarians of the suburbs, by women as well as by men. We are facing a mass phenomenon.[9]

There is no doubt that a growing cinema industry and a flourishing market were the indispensable conditions for the prosperous development of the Italian western; however, if we assume that cinema is an industry that lives off profits in addition to being a form of "cultural consumption" or a "*bene culturale commestibile*," if we wish to understand the spaghetti western phenomenon, we must examine some key factors. Firstly, what kind of pleasure did the audience derive from watching these films? Secondly, what did a diversified and heterogeneous mass of people find so fascinating in the spaghetti western? Thirdly, why did people, for more than a decade, flood theaters to watch films that were not always very well put together? And finally, what type of relationship did these films have with the reality of the time, if any?[10]

We are perfectly aware of the fact that the study of film reception, as cultural studies dictate, is considered problematic by many due to the difficulty of empirical research based on the gender, age, class, etc., of the audience.[11] However, in the case of the spaghetti western, given the abundance of sociological, historical and economic studies on the 1960s and the copious data on the cinema industry of the period, we believe that it is possible to formulate *a posteriori* some theoretical hypotheses on film reception, especially considering the fact that, starting from Christopher Frayling's 1981 seminal study, precisely titled *Spaghetti Westerns*, to the present day, there exists an abundance of solid critical texts, both Italian and from other countries, which analyze the Italian western and a great part (if not all) of the filmic production of the decade in question.[12]

We all know that the filmic text addresses the spectator and, in doing so, elicits a certain response. Naturally, at the moment of reception other elements come into play because the "message" is filtered by the subject through a variety of factors, such as age, class, gender, ideology, ethnic group, culture, etc. In short, there is a notable gap between the ideal viewer that the filmic text implies or, at the theoretical level, presupposes (the one who would fully identify with the message) and the real spectator who, seated in the theater, receives the message. The ideal spectator as a passive subject, or as a container into which the project of dominant ideology, designed to homogenize and dominate the masses, is poured, no longer seems sustainable. On the other hand, the subject that rebels and totally refuses the hegemonic message also seems to be a chimera. Our goal is, therefore, to reconstruct the type of filmic messages that the spaghetti western directed toward the various kinds of viewers of the time, retrospectively discussing the processes of both *identification with* and *refusal of* the figure of the protagonist, without which the films' success would be impossible.[13]

Unlike the classic American western in which the hero is a pure, fearless knight, such as, for example, in George Stevens' *Shane* (1953), the hero of the Italian western is driven by personal motives that oscillate between vendetta and the acquisition of money.[14] The hero is a bounty hunter, a stranger with no name, or an outlaw who, in the course of events, striving to achieve a certain goal, commits some good deeds, not for the good of society, but only because he hates those who are arrogant and pushy. In the Italian western we are dealing with an anti-hero. Shane, in the film of the same name, like the true hero he is, does not think of personal interest and defends a community of vulnerable farmers against overbearing cattlemen, so that one day a city may rise in the prairie where everyone can live in peace and where law can reign; Shane sacrifices himself so that the West may become "civilized." The anti-heroes of the spaghetti western operate in a way that recalls the Far West, but only as a cinematic myth, an echo of far-away things. The American cinematic myth was affected by the theorization of Frederick Jackson Turner's Frontier, by Henry Nash Smith's idea of the "virgin land," by the archetypes produced by an impressive output of novels, which, in their turn, found inspiration in the epic conquest of the West, completed long ago in 1890. Therefore, even if a time gap existed, the ideals were still present in the American imagination. The spaghetti western deals instead with the "myth of the myth" that by now has nothing to do with the historical events that occurred in the Far West and, as a consequence, does not show any preoccupation with historical verisimilitude, nor does it share the same initial ideals.[15] In the spaghetti western there are no cities to build, nor communities to save; the future, like the past, is out of the frame, only the present exists.

These anti-heroes, like the heroes of the classic western, come from an unknown place and are going toward a place just as unknown; they do not have a home, family or ties, but, unlike Shane, they are not seeking justice, only gold. We could hypothesize that at the end of the film, with the money obtained, they will buy a ranch as far as possible from every kind of civilization, because the society in which they exist does not seem to be an exemplary model of civilized living. In this world, sheriffs are corrupt, power is in the hands of violent clans, and the citizens are divided into victims and executioners; in brief, the law of the strongest reigns. It is clear that, in order to survive in such a world, one needs quickness of hand and mind, determination, a big dose of cruelty and a good knowledge of weapons.

It becomes clear, at this point, that the hegemonic message the spectators would need to absorb in order to fully identify with the filmic anti-hero, is one of celebration of ruthless individualism. After the economic boom of 1958-63, Italy became an industrialized country. The idea of an individual who achieves success through skillfulness and cold determination is a celebration of the new professional. He has to be a person capable of standing out in a capitalist society, who can depend on his own resources in order to survive in a world in which technological knowledge and intelligence must be used "to overpower in order to not be overpowered," and in which money equals power. The new "capital market law" is the law of survival of the fittest. In short, the difference between peons and gunmen can be compared to the difference between salaried workers and successful managers, those who are victims of economic power and those who use it to their advantage. The merchants who amass wealth in the boom years, the small industries that become big industries, the lower class that becomes the middle class (i.e., those benefitting from the economic betterment caused by the boom throughout the country) see Italy's transformation from an almost rural country to an industrial power as a positive event. In the eyes of the spectators, who have in various ways been positively affected by the economic wellbeing of the period, the western hero appears as a reconfirmation of the values of professionalism, wealth, individualism and tenacity in which they firmly believe. Similarly, we can understand how all—those who have succeeded in the system and those who have not—fall under the spell of the protagonist. Both groups, identifying with the *pistolero*, feel successful; he who is already successful in life gains further confirmation, and he who is not vicariously lives the exhilarating experience of being a winner in the film's 90 minutes.

On the other hand, the spectator who, for ideological reasons, judges the arrival of the new industrialized society negatively, does not see monetary gain as the ultimate aim of every action, and sees in consumerism the foundation of many social evils would, as a consequence, naturally be led to refuse identification with the anti-hero as a symbol of capitalism—we are thinking in particular of the young people and workers who a few years later will take to the streets and demonstrate their discontent in the 1968 uprising—nevertheless, even he ends up succumbing to the charms of the spaghetti western's protagonist. In fact, the anti-hero arrives, destabilizes society, kills the bad guys and, having achieved his goal, goes away, assuming that it will be someone else's job to eventually re-establish "law and order," if it ever happens. The anti-hero, in his position on the margins of society, is able to destroy a system that does not work, and in doing so, performs an act of rebellion. The *pistolero* shows with his acts that he detests society because it is unjust; his attitude implies that in a world such as this suffering and injustice are everywhere, and for this reason violence becomes the only possible response, a temporary response though it may be. For those who, in the mid-1960s, began to rebel against "the fathers" and denounce the hypocrisy of the political system and the corruption of the Christian Democrats, the extreme violence of the anti-hero could not help but appear as an additional confirmation of their revolutionary convictions. Unlike the heroes of the sword-and-sandal films or pepla, the *pistolero* does not aim to restore anyone to the throne, not even the good rulers; hence, it is the anti-hero's anarchic position that obtains success among the youth audience, something missing in characters such as Hercules, Macistes and Ursuses in the sword-and-sandal epics.

It has been said many times that the Italian western is a masculine universe, even an excessively masculine universe, in which women hardly exist and when they do appear, are usually sexual objects to be used and forgotten. Consequently, it was assumed that these films principally attracted a male audience. However, if, as some critics argue, identification with the protagonist is fundamental to the success of a film, that does not mean that within this process there is no possibility of identifications arising which surpass the gender identity of the viewer.[16] Had it not been true that several "positions" or "views" were possible when receiving the film, then the female spectators of the time, who a few years later would take to the streets for the first feminist battles for equality, divorce, and abortion rights, would have perhaps abstained from watching this film genre, when in fact it is obvious, given the earnings and number of tickets sold, that the genre also captivated the female audience.

On the other hand, although there is no doubt that in the spaghetti western violence is perpetrated against women, it is also true that such violence usually comes from the bad guys.

Many have pointed out that there are no positive female characters, but this is not totally true, a few prominent female characters do exist: Think, for example, of the widow McBain in *Once Upon a Time in the West* (*C'era una volta il West,* 1968) and Adelita in *A Bullet for the General* (*El Chuncho, quien Sabe?* 1966); the former a redeemed prostitute and the latter a warrior of liberal customs, but both independent, courageous, militant women able to go head to head with the men, both good and bad, who gravitate around them. Furthermore, the female audience of the time could not help but notice that the anti-hero of the Italian western, in his position of outsider, as a man who has no ties and wants no ties, in his refusal of family and, therefore, of domestic life—viewed by him as an obstruction to his search for adventure, since the domestic is the realm of the preservation of the species, of security—breaks with patriarchal rules and

Claudia Cardinale as the widow McBain in *Once Upon a Time in the West* (1968); the film revolves around her character.

rebels against the ideals on which the Italian Catholic society of the time rested. Furthermore, the *pistolero* is a free being, also sexually; he does not want ties, he does not look for them, and he does not favor them. His friendships are temporary and, usually, with men like him. He is rather misogynistic, but at the same time anti-patriarchal; he does not need to force his authority onto a wife and children or hand down his name because he loves his freedom.

Many female viewers of the time were raised in a postwar society that still viewed women according to the dictates of the Fascist era, which maintained that a woman's place was the fireside and wanted to marginalize females in the home so as to impede their emancipation, because if such emancipation were to take place, starting from the sexual arena, it would rapidly extend to other areas of life, such as politics and labor. The outcome would be sexual and economic independence, and this freedom would end up unhinging the patriarchy's solid rules, which were enforced to keep at least part of the population—women—in a state of subordination and servitude in order to guarantee that the conservative Christian Democrats remained in power. It was precisely these oppressed female spectators who had to admire the *pistolero*. As chauvinist as the protagonist was, these female spectators, by identifying with him, enjoyed in short moments on screen the benefits that such a position of power entailed: absolute independence, courage, tenacity, sexual freedom ... conditions that were obviously denied to them in everyday life, but offered to them in the filmic text.

Finally, the majority of viewers in the 1960s were part of the work-force that had made the economic miracle possible. However, indus-trialization, with the consequent internal migration and urbanization of the country, had come at a price; working life ran at a stressful pace and created tension and frustration. From a psychological point of view, it would have certainly been liberating for those who were part of the new working world, that is to say the majority of the audi-ence of the time, to identify with the *pistolero* and dream of "killing the bosses" in real life with a nice pistol shot. In this way, as if by a miracle, the department heads, the office heads, and all those who held power would be eliminated in an instant. And ultimately, iden-tification with the protagonist offered all viewers, female and male, the possibility of shifting, through fantasy, to a world much more exciting than the real one, a world far away from the drabness and routine of daily life.

We cannot forget, though, that there are other factors that also contributed to the Italian western phenomenon. The success of both the peplum films between 1957 and 1963 and the spaghetti westerns —let us not forget that pepla also earned enormous sums at the box office for a five-year period before being dethroned by the spaghet-tis—is due to the fact that both these filmic genres could be exported without problems, while the *commedia all'italiana*, although a suc-cessful genre in Italy, due to its culture context did not enjoy the same fortune elsewhere.

In addition, in a cinematic market such as the Italian one in which from 1916 until 1950 the film diet offered to the audience was, out-side the parentheses of the war years, almost completely made in Hollywood, the fact that the spaghetti dressed itself in "Anglophone clothing" was a determining factor. In fact, American actors, even if they were not yet famous, often appeared in the main roles (e.g. Clint Eastwood). In addition, the directors, cinematographers, pho-tographers, musicians and all the crew members, even if they were Italian, appeared in the credits under English pseudonyms. This had a double advantage: It made Italians want to see the films by enticing them with the "appeal of the exotic," sending the viewer back to the classic American western world created by men like Ford, Hawks, Mann, John Wayne, etc., and, at the same time, it supported sales in

Harmonica (Charles Bronson) plays a tune instead of answering Cheyenne (Jason Robards) in *Once Upon a Time in the West*. Ennio Morricone wrote the film's famous music.

the major foreign market of the time, the USA, where the presence of some American actors also captivated the audience. Naturally, Leone's films are the exception to the rule, as Leone uses both American "stars" who were still little-known such as Eastwood or Lee Van Cleef as well as already famous actors like Henry Fonda, James Coburn, Rod Steiger and others.

Between 1961 and 1965, the number of Italian films shown in Italy surpassed the number of American ones. Obviously, at the time there was a flourishing market whose audience levels still were not threatened by television. But one must also keep in mind that this is the decade in which popular cinema has the lion's share of Italian screens. With alternating luck, the peplum films, the spaghettis, the *commedia all'italiana*, the thrillers/horror films, the homemade spy movies (in the vein of the English James Bond films), and the cycle of exotic-sexy pseudo-documentaries like *Mondo cane* and *Mondo di notte*, filled the screens. This is the season of utmost splendor for mass cinema. Certainly, we could argue that the influx of audiences brought with it enormous earnings and, therefore, triggered the proliferation of film genres, but at the same time we could rebut by stating that the production of this type of film contributed to the public success. Trying to find an answer would lead us to the old brain-teaser of the chicken or the egg; therefore, we find it more productive to focus on the fact that the success of the popular genres and of the Italian western in particular must have had something to do with the

Clint Eastwood as the mysterious unshaven stranger with big hat, cigarillo and poncho in *A Fistful of Dollars* (1964)

socio-political reality of the time. These popular genres must have touched some nerves relating to the great change which was occurring in the Italian society of the time.

Without going into the merits of such a change, it is sufficient to remember that "the 1960s mark the end of *Italietta* (the provincial, old fashioned, narrow-minded Italy of the Fascist period)," and it is in this decade that "the passage from a reality tied to outdated forms of development to one that attempts to grasp the idea ... of *modernity*" occurs.[17]

These are the years in which Italy moves from the heavy political, ideological and cultural burden inherited from the Fascist regime into a chaotic period which will later be defined as the "crisis of the ideologies." In short, cinema finds itself immersed in an era of transition in which everything that concerns both the public and private spheres is called into question. The cinema of these years, therefore, records, comments on and exposes these changes using the tools at hand.

To take stock of the situation, we can therefore say that the success of the spaghetti western must be attributed to the plurality of messages it could transmit to the audience. As we have shown, the filmic text is open to multiple interpretations, from the hegemonic (celebration of the capitalist individual) to the revolutionary (use of violence to strike an unjust society), from the quasi-feminist (refusal of the patriarchy) to the escapist (fleeing from daily life into a fantastic and exciting world). The Italian western at its best is by nature a "hybrid," a form that encompasses multiple messages. It is exactly this possibility of numerous interpretations that made it a genre of great flexibility, consumption and success. On the other hand, the spaghetti western, although it was the heir of the classic American western, shows itself to be, not only at content level (filmic message),

Clint Eastwood rides into San Miguel at the beginning of *A Fistful of Dollars*. The bare and arid countryside is the landscape of Almeria, Spain, where the film was shot.

but also at a stylistic level, the product of a new era.

Let us examine, for example, Leone, who gives birth to the spaghetti phenomenon with his *A Fistful of Dollars* and gives rise to a long line of films, which are at times, as he himself used to say, "perverted offspring."[18] Leone creates the figure of the *pistolero*, far removed from the classic cowboy. His anti-hero rides a mule, wears a poncho, moves around an inhospitable setting (often a desert-like place), and his endeavors usually take place in small cities that often resemble ghost towns. Thus the groomed and immaculate hero of the classic western is replaced with an anti-hero who seems to never shave and bathes very infrequently. This disheveled, unkempt *pistolero* is shown in a series of extreme close-ups that concentrate on the details of his figure: his eyes emerging from the rim of the cowboy hat, his hand clasping the pistol, his belt buckle, his spurs, his cigar, the type of weapons he uses, etc. The insistence of the camera on these minor details emphasises the fact that he is an outsider, a man who lives outside the law. His attire and his actions are underlined also by the soundtrack, which, thanks to the skill of Ennio Morricone, Bruno Nicolai, and others, ceases to be a generic accompaniment to the film (as in the classic western) and becomes a commentary. From the opening credits, even before the film begins, the music creates a sense of amazement in the viewer with its unusual arrangements of electric guitars, trumpet solos, organs, singers, and classical music mixed with

Clint Eastwood, the "man with no name," is about to draw his gun and kill four "baddies" in an opening scene of *A Fistful of* Dollars.

other noises, animal cries, squeaks, spurs clinking, Winchester shots, cannon fire, whistles, chimes, harmonicas, etc. Every musical note moves in unison with the protagonists and underlines their every act and movement. The music and iconography allow Leone to reduce to a minimum the dialogue in his films, and, though it is true that the heroes of the classic western did not talk a lot either, in the spaghetti, the dialogues are reduced to a few stony phrases. After all, thanks to the unusual use of the camera shots, the iconography, the music and the inclusion of flashbacks, a method which usually belongs to the thriller/horror genre, but which Leone successfully inserted into his films to give psychological depth to the characters, Leone's *pistoleri* do not need to say much to make themselves understood.

In 1964, those who went to see Leone's first western expecting to see an entirely good hero who sacrifices himself for justice, who respects the law and never fires first, instead found themselves faced with a type of hero who not only does not operate according to the rules of the classic western, but who does not even dress or act like a "hero." The prairies, herds, Indians and good sheriffs have all disappeared; there remains an off-center world, where the church is not the center of the community, but often the den of the "baddies," where families are criminal clans and violence and death are part of daily life. The setting of these films also acts as a corollary to the displacement of this society: decaying towns in desert areas, treeless countrysides burned by the sun, characters who move in a world in which just surviving would be difficult even without injustice and violence. In this filmic universe history enters through the back door, and when we encounter the American Civil War, the Mexican Revolution, or the arrival of the railways, the great history seems to be nothing but a continuous series of massacres.

The iconoclastic impact of the filmic style together with the versatility of the filmic message makes the spaghetti western a typical product of the confusion and ideological turmoil of the 1960s. After Auschwitz, after the various small wars (not least the Vietnam War), after the assassinations of John F. Kennedy, Martin Luther King and Che Guevara, after the various revolutions against imperialism and colonialism fought in the so-called Third World, after the Cold War's grimmest years, after the tough years of the reconstruction of postwar Italy, it was no longer possible to believe in the ideals displayed by the classic American western of the 1940s and 1950s. The violence, the injustice present in the world could no longer be ignored, values had changed; they were controversial and ambiguous like the *pistoleri*. The *pistolero*'s shocking violence, if measured against the "legal" violence of history, became a trifle, his "dishonesty" (if one wants to call stealing from dishonest people dishonesty) a venial sin. Even the American western, influenced by the spaghetti western, would never be the same. Let us think, for example, of Peckinpah's *The Wild Bunch*, which was released in 1969, and of all the other wonderful westerns produced afterward (today called "post-westerns" to distinguish them from the classic American westerns). These films show a diversity that would not have been possible without the films of Leone and his "savage heap" of followers.

The iconography, the music, the virtuosity of the shots, the "pluralism" of the filmic message, in brief, all the novelties brought to the western genre by the Italians, were noted by the audience who came in huge numbers to see these films, but they were never understood by the Italian film critics. Various factors contributed to this disinterest. First of all, due to the Cold War, Italy since 1947 had become politically polarized into two distinct and combative fronts that reflected the country's division between the Communist Party and the Christian Democrats. The economic-political division of the world between East and West had a notable impact on the country due to its strategic position in the center of the Mediterranean. Italy became an area of NATO interest and received enormous economic aid from the United States during the postwar reconstruction years, becoming a major sphere of American influence. Within the country, the existence of a strong Communist Party further complicated the Italian situation and because of this historical and political climate a deeper cultural and social split divided the nation; even the intellectuals fell for the political dichotomy of the country. The *intelligentsia* divided itself between Marxists and Catholic conservatives, between those who would have liked to prolong the great neorealist season forever and those who aspired to the conservation of the old values of the Fascist period. All the cultural production of these years, from literature to cinema, was assessed under fixed parameters. Here we do not wish by any means underestimate the great artistic achievements of neorealism; however, the leftist critics failed to realize that Italian society in the 1960s was not heading toward a "more just world" as the neorealist ideals would have liked, but toward an "economic miracle" and a wealthier society that wanted to forget about the heroic years of the Resistance and the difficult ones of the reconstruction as quickly as possible and, as a consequence, was also trying to jettison neorealism. In this period critics on both the right and the left studied only those cultural products that fitted into the political-ideological canons they upheld.

Unfortunately, all popular cinema, and I refer in particular to the genre cinema of the 1960s, was victimized by the critics' myopia. The genre cinema of the time was accused by the Marxists of being a "cinema of evasion" which, by hiding in myth, in the Far West, in the horror castles, attempted to keep the plebs in ignorance, or rather, keep them far away from the intentions of social change that were implicit in neorealism. Genre cinema was branded by the Marxists as "hegemonic-conservative cinema." On the other hand, rightwing critics, horrified by the violence and immorality of the Italian western and by the social satire of the *commedia all'italiana*, shocked by the iconoclastic assault on old Catholic patriarchal moral values, launched an attack against this popular cinema without analyzing it fully, simply defining it as "edible cinema for the masses." We can deduce from this that extreme parochialism impeded the critics from analyzing the works in relation to the social reality of the time, creating a void and a deep incomprehension that, especially in the case of the Italian western, was difficult to bridge even in the years that followed.

Vittorio Spinazzola, in his important 1974 volume, *Cinema e pubblico: lo spettacolo filmico in Italia 1945-65*, laments that from 1960 onward "the possibility of actively intervening, via film, in life in general" disappears, and even if he praises directors such as Leone and Tessari, he claims that "falling back on western folklore implicates a distancing not only from daily reality, but also from the Italian historical-cultural tradition." However, he adds that in the Italian western "cynicism is also a form of self-consciousness … through a metaphor exaggerated to the level of the grotesque, our westerns intend to represent in essence the bourgeois capitalist mentality: The law of free competition is equated with that of the jungle…"[19] Spinazzola recognizes in the Italian western two opposing attitudes in regard to the myth of monetary gain: On the one hand, a sort of romanticism, in the sense that the anti-hero, though inserted into a world of brutal economic rules, is able to accomplish some good deeds (see the "heroes" of Sergio Leone's films); on the other hand, a sort of irony (films à la Tessari) in which the superiority of the protagonist does not translate into a moral superiority, but into a form of unflappable skepticism, like saying "the world is what it is, so let's enjoy ourselves," with the result that the "hero" in this case becomes a cunning, easy-going supporter of a sort of "intellectual anarchism deriving from the certainty that strength, craftiness and duplicity are worth quite a bit more than being right."[20] The critic concludes by saying:

> After the pinnacle of the great neorealist chronicles we saw the advent of popular neorealism … then there was the age of the idyllic comedy, the 'pink' neorealism; then we found ourselves facing a neorealist rebirth at the supershow level. Now the most diverse types of spectators find themselves enchanted in front of the same screen, following the events of the infallible gunmen, irreverent messengers of a simplified justice understood only

as overpowering the powerful. The lights go out, the massacre begins. At the end of the screening, among the many victims, we could also count Italian neorealism.[21]

There is no doubt that Spinazzola laments the demise of neorealism as the end of great Italian cinema and is unable to see the Italian western as a product which, through its multitude of messages, reflected the socio-political and ideological changes of the time and marked the beginning of that crisis of values that would lead to the 1968 revolution and, later, to the "years of lead" (*anni di piombo*) dominated by terrorism.

Although, in his study entitled *Cinema italiano: gli anni Sessanta e oltre,* edited in its first edition in 1975, Lino Micciché laments the lack of an overall and thorough study of the spectacular archetypes and sociological implications of the Italian western, he does not come across as being very warm toward it. The critic isolates as salient elements of the genre "the ultra-violence and the absolute immorality, both far removed from the model of the American classic western in which violence is always, or almost always, the epic representation of a *bellum justum contra injustum* [a just war against injustice] ...,"[22] The critic, however, affirms that the classic western wants "to create an epic image of the past so as to exorcise the present of the *American way of life* and glorify the USA's role of armed guard: attributing to the Tom Mix of yesterday and to the Johnsons, or Nixons of today a similar role of violent flag-bearers ... of the *pax americana* against the 'bad Indians' of yesterday and today."[23] Micciché praises Leone as "the most gifted and the cleverest" director among the group of those "often pathetic imitators from the Italian province" that followed him. He claims that Leone is a first-class "cinematographic animal" and that his films should stand out from the "purely gastronomic" production of the other westerns.[24] The characteristics that the critic praises in Leone—great linguistic ability, shrewd dosage of narrative elements, knowledgeable distribution of suspense mechanisms, extraordinary rhythmic continuity, and violence dressed with irony— are certainly undeniable qualities of the director. Although he praises Leone, Micciché does not, however, seem to notice the existence of a large number of excellent films such as those by Corbucci, Damiani,

Tessari, etc. The critic admits that the Italian western reflects "some psychological traits and some inclinations" of 1960s Italian society, and that it mirrors the ideological and moral confusion of a society seized in the moment of transition from regressive cultural, political and social values to the "modern" ones of an industrialized country.[25] However, for him, the western reflects above all "a shared space of the everyday behavioral psychology of the average Italian: that of over-powering (or participating in the common abuse of power) in order not to be overpowered."[26] He concludes by saying: "The popular cin-ema of those years (be it 'sexy' or 'western'), in its ... mercenary cyni-cism ... reaches one of the lowest levels of the postwar years."[27]

All things considered, it seems that Miccichè did not know how to evaluate the spaghetti phenomenon without being contaminated by certain prejudices. If it is true that he does not openly wish for a return to a cinema *engagé,* when we read between the lines his disap-proval of the popular genre cinema becomes clear.

To see a different kind of attention paid toward the Italian western by film historiography we need to wait about 20 years. In 1991, in his book *Cent'anni di cinema italiano: dal 1945 ai giorni nostri* Gian Piero Brunetta does not make clear-cut judgments. He recognizes in Leone the maestro of the genre, but he also mentions other directors like Tessari, Corbucci, Damiani, Lizzani, etc., as his worthy follow-ers. The critic claims that the Italian western set the standards for and contributed to changing the American western, and, above all, praises the "political spaghetti," a sub-genre of the Italian western that usually takes place "south of the Rio Grande" and is therefore connected to the Mexican Revolution. According to Brunetta, this type of western became the vehicle in which one deposits

> ... the lofty revolutionary ideals of the screenwriters and direc-tors who are no longer able, because of old age, to join the 1968 student demonstrations in the *piazzas.* The Mexican Revolution and third-world ideology of many of the films written by Fran-co Solinas (*The Big Gundown, A Professional Gun, Face to Face, Quien sabe?:* "Don't buy bread, boy, buy dynamite!") become one of the final vanishing points of the intellectual revolution before the terrorist pistols and machine guns silence this game

of constructing possible worlds. With few exceptions and important results, they revitalize the genre, they once again create on the screen untarnished horsemen as protagonists, defenders of the weak in a playful fairy tale with an happy ending, sophisticated, and brimming with cinematic and cultural cross-references ...[28]

In short, we are facing, even in the few brief pages dedicated to the western genre, a judgment that leans toward a more balanced assessment of the genre in question.

On the American front, however, Peter Bondanella in his 1983 *Italian Cinema: From Neorealism to the Present*, had already dedicated an entire chapter to the spaghetti western and, though he gives more space to Leone's films, he does not forget to also mention the films made by his followers.[29] It is interesting to note that the critic asserts more than once the importance of the Italian western, specifying that films such as Sam Peckinpah's *The Wild Bunch* (1969), Don Siegel's *Coogan's Bluff* (1968) and Ted Post's *Hang 'Em High* would not have been possible if the spaghetti western phenomenon had not existed.

Having examined these diverse histories of Italian cinema and affirmed that today a few excellent critical works, from both Italy and elsewhere, exist on the spaghetti western, it still seems that justice has not yet been done to the genre. There are far too many instances in which these films are treated with indifference, and with the exception of Leone, who is by now recognized as one of the great directors of Italian cinema, the western genre continues to suffer from a "Cinderella complex." We would therefore like to conclude by mentioning the proverb of the "bird, the cow, and the coyote," told by the protagonist of Tonino Valerii's film *My Name Is Nobody* (*Il mio nome é nessuno,* 1973), which, if paraphrased, would go something like this: "People who seem to want to help you, do not always really want to, and those who seem to wish you ill, don't always really wish it." A proverb emblematic of the moral ambiguity of the western genre *all'italiana*, in which "Good" and "Bad" often coexist within the same character, in which "Good" is not always perfect, life is not black and white, but characterized by a large gray area, where the *pistoleri* show weaknesses and virtues common to all of us, and where, despite what the great history teaches, the "bad men" are not always punished. The spaghetti western is therefore a genre which revealed itself at an ideological level to be much more realistic and prophetic than the critics thought, a genre that has, at least in its better examples, deserved the wide popularity and success it achieved.

NOTES

1   Kurosawa's *Yojimbo* (1961) was released in Italy under the title *La sfida del samurai*. Leone saw the film and used the story for his first western. Nevertheless, later, when copyright issues were raised, he claimed that the inspiration for the film was provided by an eighteenth-century comedy by Goldoni, *Arlecchino servo di due padroni*. Kurosawa, for his part, claimed that Dashiell Hammett's *Red Harvest* (1929) was the source of inspiration for his own film. At any rate, at the end of the legal dispute, Kurosawa was given the distribution rights for *A Fistful of Dollars* in Japan, Taiwan and South Korea, and 15 percent of the worldwide profits. See Frayling, Christopher (2000) *Something to Do with Death* (London, Faber and Faber): 148-150.

2   For information on box-office takings, see Christopher Frayling, *Something to Do with Death* (London, Faber and Faber, 2000): 130, 168, 186, and 203, and C. Frayling, *Spaghetti Westerns* (London, I.B.Tauris, 1998): 287; Frayling notes that *Once Upon a Time in the West* (1968), an Italian-American production directed by Leone, earned almost $4 million in Italy and $1 million in the United States between 1968 and 1970. For this fourth western by Leone, there was a drop in earnings in the USA, because the distributor Paramount reduced the original film of 180 minutes to little more than 120 minutes, cutting fundamental scenes and making it impossible to understand the story. Naturally, other spaghetti westerns also earned as much as Leone's *Django, Trinity Is Still My name, Day of Anger, A Professional Gun*, etc. (C. Frayling, *Spaghetti Westerns*: 62)

3   Before the release of *A Fistful of Dollars* in August 1964, there had been a revival of the western in Europe. In 1962, *Treasure of Silver Lake* (1962, directed by Harald Reinl), a German-Yugoslavian production, had started a series of adventures based on the warrior Winnetou, adapted from the novel by the German writer, Karl May. These films had achieved great popularity and this helped convince the Cinecittà producers that the "return of the western" was possible. For an accurate discussion of the "Winnetou cycle," see C. Frayling, *Something to Do with Death*: 120-128, and, by the same author, "Karl May and the Noble Savage" in *Spaghetti Westerns*: 103-117.

4   See Luca Beatrice, *Al cuore, Ramon, al cuore!* (Florence, Tarab Edizioni/
     Dies Irae Records, 1996): 9-10 and 183-249; according to Christopher
     Wagstaff, there are only 450 films [see "Cinema" in *Italian Cultural
     Studies*, David Forgacs and Robert Lumley eds. (New York, Oxford UP,
     1996): 224].

5   See C. Wagstaff, "Cinema," 218-229.

6   See C. Wagstaff, ibidem: 219. Until 1915, Italy produced 562 films,
     but in 1930, production decreased to 12 films per year. After the First
     World War, the American industry reorganized itself and aggressively
     distributed its products on both the national and international mar-
     kets.

7   See Vittorio Spinazzola, *Cinema e pubblico—Lo spettacolo filmico in Ita-
     lia 1945-65* (Milano, Bompiani, 1974): 337-347. Naturally, one does
     not wish to deny the fact that the incredible earnings of *A Fistful of Dol-
     lars* and other Italian westerns came also from second- and third-runs,
     because all films that follow the normal distribution circuit eventually
     pass from the first-run theaters, to the second and third runs, then to
     the provincial theaters, etc., remaining in circulation for years and con-
     tinuing to earn. In fact, on June 30, 1966, *A Fistful of Dollars* appeared
     in first place with 2,556,430,000 lire obtained on the entire national
     market, and *A Pistol for Ringo* by Duccio Tessari appeared in fifth place
     with 1,071,412,000 lire, a success that included first-, second-, and
     third-run theaters (Ibidem, 339).

8   See note 2.

9   Spinazzola, in his above-cited volume, *Cinema e pubblico*, distinguishes
     popular cinema from cinema of the masses by asserting: "The films
     made for the exclusive consumption of the lower classes can be called
     popular cinema; mass cinema, on the other hand, is programmed with
     the desire of merging together the bourgeois and proletarian audience,
     and is, therefore, anti-class division." (*"Al cinema popolare appartengo-
     no le opere destinate al consumo esclusivo delle classi subalterne; il cinema
     di massa è invece programmato in vista di una unificazione del pubblico,
     borghese e proletario, e appare perciò dotato di una valenza interclassista."*)
     (348) The translation is mine.

10   For a discussion of reception problems, see *Viewing Positions: Ways of
     Seeing Films*, edited by Linda Williams (New Brunswick, Rutgers UP,
     1994), especially the sections entitled "Vision and the Apparatus" and
     "Viewing Antitheses," 23-58 and 155-230.

11   See *Viewing Positions*, 11-13 and 170-183.

12   On the classic American western, great critical works exist, see John G.
     Cawelti, *The Six-Gun Mystique Sequel* (Bowling Green, Ohio, Bowling
     Green University Press, 1999); Jane Tompkins, *West of Everything* (New
     York, Oxford, 1992); R. Philip Loy, *Westerns in a Changing America*

(Jefferson, North Carolina, McFarland, 2004); Edward Buscombe and Roberta E. Pearson (editors), *Back in the Saddle Again* (London, British Film Institute, 1998); Richard Aquila (editor), *Wanted Dead or Alive* (Urbana, University of Illinois Press, 1996); Philip French, *Westerns: Aspects of a Movie Genre* (New York, Oxford, 1977); Rita Parks, *The Western Hero in Film and Television* (Ann Arbor, Michigan, UMI Press, 1982); Jeffrey Wallmann, *The Western* (Lubbock, Texas, Texas Tech UP, 1999); Alf H. Walle, *The Cowboy Hero and Its Audience: Popular Culture as Market Derived Art* (Bowling Green, Ohio, Bowling Green UP, 2000); Richard Slotkin, *Gunfighter Nation: the Myth of the Frontier in 20th Century America* (New York, Harper and Collins, 1993).

13   See *Prima della Rivoluzione: Schermi italiani 1960-69*, edited by Claver Salizzato (Venezia, Marsilio, 1989): 203.

14   I have based my analysis of the spaghetti phenomenon on a vast number of films made by directors such as: Sergio Leone, Sergio Corbucci, Damiano Damiani, Carlo Lizzani, Giulio Questi, Domenico Paolella, Sergio Sollima, Duccio Tessari, Tonino Valerii, Enzo Barboni.

15   The Italian western feeds upon the cinematic myth created by the American classic western from 1939 onward. Leone knew Ford's films and the American western genre very well, and the abundance of "references" in his films is self-revealing, but we need to bear in mind that his films are born from a myth twice removed from the reality that originally triggered these stories.

16   In this regard, see the essays by Maggie Günsberg, *Italian Cinema* (New York, Palgrave Macmillan, 2005), Hughes Howard, *Once Upon a Time in the Italian West* (London, I.B.Tauris, 2004), and Robert C. Cumbow, *Once Upon the Time: The Films of Sergio Leone* (Lanham, Maryland, Scarecrow, 1987).

17   See *Tutto il cinema di Sergio Leone* by Marcello Garofalo (Milano, Baldini e Castoldi 1999: 113). The translation is mine; "*…gli anni sessanta mettono fine alla storia dell'"Italietta'… il passaggio da una realtà legata a forme di sviluppo arretrate ad una che tenta l'aggancio all'idea … di modernità.*"

18   Cfr. Ibidem, 115. The translation is mine; "*figli snaturati.*"

19   Cfr. Vittorio Spinazzola, *Cinema e pubblico: lo spettacolo filmico in Italia 1945–1965*: 342 and 345. The translation is mine; "*il ricorso al folclore western implica un allontanamento non solo dalla realtà odierna, ma anche dalla tradizione storico-culturale italiana;… il cinismo è pure una forma di autocoscienza… attraverso una metafora esasperata sino al grottesco, i nostri western intendono rappresentare al nudo la mentalità borghese capitalistica: la legge della libera concorrenza viene a identificarsi con quella della giungla…*"

20   Ibidem, 337-339. The translation is mine; "*il mondo è quello che è quin-*

di divertiamoci…; …anarchismo intellettuale derivante dalla certezza che la forza, l'astuzia, e la doppiezza valgono assai più del diritto."

21 Ibidem, 347. The translation is mine; *"Alle alte intenzioni drammatiche del grande cronachismo neorealista vedemmo succedere l'era del neorealismo popolare… poi fu la volta della commedia idillica, il neorealismo rosa; quindi ci trovammo di fronte a una rinascita neorealistica a livello di superspettacolo. Ora, i più diversi tipi di spettatori si ritrovano incantati davanti allo stesso schermo, a seguire le vicende degli infallibili pistoleri apostoli irridenti di una giustizia concepita soltanto come sopraffazione dei sopraffattori. Le luci si spengono, comincia la strage. Alla fine della proiezione, tra le tante vittime potremo contare anche il neorealismo italiano."*

22 Micciché, *Cinema italiano: gli anni 1960 e oltre* (Venezia, Marsilio, 2002): 139. The translation is mine; *" …la violenza parossistica e l'assoluta amoralità, ambedue estremamente differenzianti rispetto al classico 'western' americano dove la violenza è sempre, o quasi sempre, la rappresentazione epica di un bellum justum contra injustum…"*

23 Ibidem, 140. The translation is mine; *"…costruire un'immagine epica del passato tale da esorcizzare il presente della* American way of life *e da rendere gloriosa scelta di civiltà, il ruolo di sentinella armata… degli* USA: *attribuendo ai* Tom Mix *di ieri e ai* Johnson, *o* Nixon, *di oggi un assimilabile ruolo di portabandiera violenti… della pax Americana contro gli 'indiani cattivi' di ieri e di oggi."*

24 Ibidem, 141.

25 Ibidem, 141. The translation is mine: *"…alcuni dati psicologici, alcuni stati d'animo…"*

26 Ibidem, 141. The translation is mine: *"un luogo comune della psicologia comportamentistica quotidiana dell'italiano medio: quello del sopraffare (o del partecipare alla commune sopraffazione) per non essere sopraffatti."*

27 Ibidem, 141. The translation is mine; *"Il cinema popolare di quegli anni ('sexy' o 'western' che fosse), nel suo … cinismo mercenario… raggiunge uno dei più bassi livelli postbellici."*

28 Cfr. Gian Piero Brunetta, *Cent'anni di cinema italiano: dal 1945 ai giorni nostri* (Bari, Laterza, 1991): 337–338. The translation is mine; *" …le pulsioni rivoluzionarie ideali di sceneggiatori e registi non più in grado, per ragioni anagrafiche, di scendere in piazza accanto alla protesta studentesca [sessantottesca]. La rivoluzione messicana e l'ideologia terzomondista di molti film scritti da Franco Solinas (La resa dei conti, Il mercenario, Faccia a faccia, Quien Sabe?: 'Non comprare pane, ragazzo, compra dinamite!') diventano uno degli ultimi punti di fuga della rivoluzione intellettuale prima che le pistole e i mitra del terrorismo facciano tacere questo gioco di costruzione di mondi possibili. Con poche eccezioni e risultati di tutto rilievo, che ridanno fiato al genere, restituiscono ai protagonisti i caratteri di cavalieri senza macchia, difensori dei deboli in una dimensione ludica…*

a lieto fine, sofisticata, ricca di rimandi culturali e cinematografici…" Brunetta, in one of his earlier works, *Storia del cinema italiano: dal 1945 agli anni ottanta,* of 1982 gives an accurate and positive judgment of Leone's cinema: "Leone makes a name for himself, from a *A Fistful of Dollars* (1964) onward, for his decisive anti-realistic way of filming, for turning fundamental values upside-down, for deconstructing the western, for increasing the attention to detail, suspense and extreme close-ups, for emphasizing the point of view of the characters, for accelerating and stretching aspects of the action on screen, for using irony to distance the viewer from the events. He chooses to reduce, from the very beginning, the space around his characters: space is no longer filled with men and objects, but with weapons…; (*"Leone si impone, fin da Per un pugno di dollari (1964), per la decisa scelta antirealistica, il rovesciamento dei valori fondanti, la scomposizione della struttura, la moltiplicazione delle fasi di tensione, l'abnorme quantità di dettagli e primissimi piani, l'assunzione decisa del punto di vista dei personaggi, la concentrazione e distensione degli aspetti dell'azione, la componente ironica che consente di produrre immediati meccanismi di distanziamento. Egli sceglie da subito di ridurre gli elementi dello spazio attorno ai suoi protagonisti: unità di misura non sono più le cose e gli uomini, ma le armi…"*) [Gian Piero Brunetta, *Storia del cinema italiano: dal 1945 agli anni ottanta* (Roma, Editori Riuniti 1982: 778].

29 Peter Bondanella, *Italian Cinema: from Neorealism to the Present* (New York, Continuum, 2001): 253-54.

4

THE BIRTH OF COMEDY ITALIAN STYLE

Andrea Bini

The purpose of this study is to analyze the *commedia all'italiana* (comedy Italian style) as a distinct film genre, and to unearth its origins in postwar Italian cinema.[1] Critics and film scholars attribute the birth of the *commedia all'italiana* to the immense success of Mario Monicelli's *Big Deal on Madonna Street* (*I soliti ignoti,* 1958), which supposedly set the standard for the entire genre. In effect, this genre flourished and came to dominate Italian cinema between the late 1950s and the early 1960s, coinciding with the rise of what has been termed the Italian economic miracle (or "boom"), during which the country underwent an intense process of industrialization and urbanization. After the commercial and critical success of *Big Deal on Madonna Street* (*I soliti ignoti*), which also received an Oscar nomination, producer Dino De Laurentiis supported Monicelli's new project, a big-budget and controversial comedy-drama set during the First World War: *The Great War* (*La grande guerra,* 1959). The movie turned out to be a triumph and won the Golden Lion prize at the 1959 Venice Film Festival; thus it demonstrated the genre's great artistic and commercial potential for Italian mainstream cinema.

However, in order to decide whether a film such as *Big Deal on Madonna Street* can truly be considered the first mature example of the new genre, we must investigate its prehistory in the postwar years (1945–58), and trace its evolution and eventual derivation and differentiation from previous film genres. The *commedia all'italiana* is usually associated with the earlier and extremely popular genre called *neorealismo rosa* (rosy neorealism), considered to be its direct forerunner. In my opinion, however, the themes and features of the *commedia all'italiana* are quite different to those of rosy neorealism, whose social optimism and celebration of traditional values can hardly be found in the former. Quite the opposite, I believe that the themes and characters of rosy neorealism are much closer to those of other successful comedies of the 1950s, such as the *Don Camillo* series. As I will try to demonstrate, the *commedia all'italiana*'s predecessors must be found in other more satirical and less successful films. I refer in particular to those directed by Roberto Rossellini and Federico Fellini, and especially to the two films featuring the young comedian Alberto Sordi, *The White Sheik* (*Lo sceicco bianco*) and *I vitelloni* (no English title available). Furthermore, after the two comedies directed by Fellini, Sordi was also the protagonist of other comedies throughout the 1950s that developed the future genre's main themes. Because of their scathing critique of Italian society and social mores, they must be considered not only more pivotal than the contemporaneous rosy neorealism, but also than Monicelli's *Big Deal on Madonna Street*.

The *commedia all'italiana* as a Film Genre: A Satirical Chronicle of Italy

In order to find the forerunners of the *commedia all'italiana* we must first establish its main features and themes. Regardless of the varying opinions about the genre's "prehistory" between 1945 and 1958, the definition of periods of the genre's development after 1958, in relation to Italy's social changes, is usually undisputed. Enrico Giacovelli, in his important monograph *La commedia all'italiana* (published in 1990), divides this period into three main eras: the "boom comedy" (1958–64), the "post-boom comedy" (1964–71), and finally the period of the nostalgic, melancholic comedy (1971–80), which might be regarded as a meditation upon Italian postwar history as well as the whole genre.[2] Without much doubt, this genre's lasting success in Italian mainstream film production is due to the fact that its evolution closely followed the country's socio-economic events: "The extraordinary longevity of the *commedia all'italiana* …

can be explained by the fact that over the course of the years it was able to keep in close touch with the evolution of the customs and the society which it intended to reflect and will continue to in part for a long time, like a mirror which is more or less distorted and distorting" (Viganò 2001: 240). This genre claims to be a chronicle of the nation, and to faithfully describe and criticize the ongoing changes during the frantic process of modernization in postwar Italy, that is, of its traumatic transition from an impoverished rural country to a consumerist urban one.

Typical of the *commedia all'italiana* are the presence of drama and the absence of romance and a happy ending, in contrast to, for instance, the classic American comedy. Pietro Pintus defines the *commedia all'italiana* as a genre characterized by

> a mixture of the comic and the dramatic, a fondness for the portrayal of completely negative protagonists, a vivid attention to the present, if not the absolutely up-to-date and an often ambiguous plot of satire, moral criticism, and derisive caricature devoid of genuine ethical depth (1985: 18).[3]

It must be observed that this certain blend between comedy and drama was not a novelty in Italian postwar cinema, since it can also be found in some neorealist films, particularly those directed by Rossellini and De Sica. Rossellini's war dramas *Open City* (*Roma città aperta,* 1945) and *Paisan* (*Paisà,* 1946), or De Sica's *Bicycle Thieves* (*Ladri di biciclette,* 1948) contain several characters and scenes that belong to comedy. The very fact that two popular comedians from Roman *vaudeville*, Anna Magnani and Aldo Fabrizi, are the protagonists of *Open City* sets the pattern of the future *commedia all'italiana*, that is, a genre featuring a comic actor playing the protagonist of a drama (this would be the model for the films starring Alberto Sordi and Ugo Tognazzi). But—and this is one of the principal merits of Monicelli's *Big Deal on Madonna Street*—the dialectic between drama and comedy also works in reverse when a dramatic actor becomes the protagonist of a comedy (as in the films featuring Vittorio Gassman).

Therefore it is not surprising to see that already in the postwar years many successful comedies followed this pattern, such as those directed by Luigi Zampa in 1947 starring the two actors of *Open City*: *Angelina, Member of Parliament* (*L'onorevole Angelina,* with Anna Magnani) and *To Live in Peace* (*Vivere in pace*)—at the end of which, just as in Rossellini's film, the peasant played by Aldo Fabrizi is shot by the Germans. These "dramatic comedies" usually have working-class people as their protagonists, following the example of neorealist humanitarianism, and lack the predilection for negative middle-class male characters which will be characteristic of the *commedia all'italiana*. In fact, even in Monicelli's two films which allegedly established the new genre in the late 1950s, *Big Deal on Madonna Street* and *The Great War*, the protagonists are poor people still associated with the neorealist idea of *italiani brava gente* (good people, the Italians). A much more negative character is the swindler who collaborates with the Nazis during the German occupation of Rome in Rossellini's drama *General Della Rovere* (*Il generale Della Rovere,*1959), which Peter Bondanella claims to be one of the *commedia all'italiana*'s first mature examples:

> Rossellini begins a long process in the Italian cinema with *Il generale Della Rovere* that transforms the treatment of war, Resistance, fascism, and other typical neorealist subjects from an obligatory and completely tragic perspective to one tempered by the subtle laughter of the traditional Italian comic film, the *commedia all'italiana* (1993: 116).

Its male protagonist (played by director-actor Vittorio De Sica) is not a character in the neorealist tradition, but one of the typical middle-class, rather Pirandellian, anti-heroes which will fill this genre. His final redemptive sacrifice, in which he agrees to be executed with some partisans, parallels that of the two protagonists of Monicelli's historical comedy *The Great War*. Bondanella may exaggerate the contribution of *General Della Rovere* to the *commedia all'italiana*, but without a doubt this film, along with *The Great War*—the co-winners of the 1959 Venice Film Festival—were the forerunners of a series of Italian-style "historical comedies" produced in the early 1960s.

The fact that the *commedia all'italiana*'s definitive success came with a series of historical films produced between 1959 and 1961 should come as no surprise. In fact, *General Della Rovere*, *The Great War*, *Everybody Go Home* (*Tutti a casa*, Comencini, 1960) and *A Difficult Life* (*Una vita difficile*, Risi, 1961) (Alberto Sordi acted in the latter three films and they made him a star) establish once and for all the genre's most important themes and elements, that is, the ineptitude and self-indulgence of the Italian male in the backdrop of a dramatic story with no happy ending. This dialectic between comedy and drama is the result of a larger opposition between the "comic" story of an individual and the dramatic history of a country. That is why Maurizio Grande calls the *commedia all'italiana* "epic comedy" (*commedia epica*), based on "the 'anomalous' relationship established between the *tragic backdrop* of civilized society and the *comic proscenium* of individual life" (2008: 223).

It is not difficult to realize that this moral commitment to rendering an accurate narration of the country through the stories of individuals makes the *commedia all'italiana* an important part of the neorealist legacy. In fact, the strong influence of neorealism on the *commedia all'italiana* lies not only in some filmic elements (naturalistic lighting, real locations, use of spoken language and dialect), but also in its main theme, that is, "the discourse-denouncement of the evils of contemporary society" (D'Amico 2008: 127), based on the narration of seemingly insignificant aspects of everyday life in their relation to the "big" historical events.[4] Furthermore, and most importantly, the tragic destiny of the individual in the *commedia all'italiana* is due to the fact that he no longer appears able to find his place in society. This breakdown of societal bonds and cultural values was already present in the neorealist films, but their overt rejection of a set framework, in view of the dissolution of the traditional constituents of Italian society was, in my opinion, one of their greatest innovations. In the neorealist films, "postwar Italy" no longer constitutes a fixed framework, a set system of values, but an empty space that must be re-established on a new basis. Italy's institutions—the state, the family and the Church—are either portrayed negatively or are simply absent, and ordinary individuals are left to face their day-to-day problems on their own. From this stance comes what we might call the neorealist "pessimism of the intellect" (the need to show a destroyed country without embellishment) that must necessarily precede its "optimism of the will" (the commitment to reconstructing the country, the hope for a better future and a new society in a moral and not simply a material sense).

Likewise, the *commedia all'italiana*'s connection to the neorealist commitment to giving an accurate narration of the country makes it an essential part of a larger narration. Along with other film genres and *auteur films* of the same period, it constitutes what we might call the "discourse on the new nation." This is a sort of a collective narration that begins with neorealism and makes Italian cinema of the 1950s and 1960s a seamless, unfolding text. In other words, as Gian Piero Brunetta writes, Italian postwar cinema represents a unique space of narration in which the most important directors, authors and genres meet each other and their audience in order to describe and comment on the evolution of Italian society and its discontent:

> Postwar cinema, in a completely new step compared to the past, describes the dynamics and the transformations in Italians' lives, in their behavior and mentality, in a kind of "public diary" in which real events and fantasies of possible worlds overlap and are condensed without a break, different ideological waves follow each other, and other ways of perception and representation of the diversity of the country are arranged in open order ... *a diary written by a collective I*, a record and a book of stories in which are noted the profits and losses, the useless squandering of energy, and the difficulties and severity of the obstacles to be overcome, the pain and resignation together with the will to start over (2000: 29, my italics).[5]

For this reason, in my opinion, it would be a mistake to look for the forerunners that influenced the *commedia all'italiana* in other comedies and sub-genres. The genre's predecessors within this "diary of Italy" represented by Italian cinema may be found in any movie, whether comedy or drama, and particularly in those dealing with the advent of modernity and of new lifestyle models in Italian society.[6]

I stated above that the *commedia all'italiana*, in contrast to the majority of the comedies of the postwar decade (1945–54) whose protagonists are still "neorealist" characters dealing with postwar hardship, cannot be imagined before the late 1950s. It is in this period that, along with the first signs of economic development, the first affirmation of a mass culture and a consumerist society eventually took place in Italy. During the so-called "economic miracle" of the 1950s, Italy's national income doubled and, especially through the great spread of mass media (movie theaters, portable radios, juke-boxes, television, advertising), a new way of life based on prosperity emerged. Two key years were 1957 and 1958. The year 1957 saw the first widespread ownership of television sets, followed by the success of the TV game show *Lascia o Raddoppia?* and of the first TV-advertising show *Carosello* (which began on February 3).

The economic boom was represented by the appearance of status symbols such as the car and the modern apartment fully equipped with bathroom, refrigerator, television set and all the other "indispensable" domestic appliances. Everything seemed to lead to a new society less bound by the traditions of the past and more concerned with international tastes (especially American). When the singer Domenico Modugno won the "Italian Song Award" at the 1958 Sanremo Festival (which still holds an important song competition), his cry of "*Volare*" (Flying) gave loud voice to the newly colored dreams and hopes—the title of the song was *Nel blu dipinto di blu* ("In Blue Painted Blue")—of an entire country that was eager to enjoy its new prosperity after the long postwar reconstruction. These widespread expectations were reinforced by the new pope, John XXIII (1958–63), who moderated the traditional reactionary politics of the Vatican and decided to open the Church to modernity and to some left-wing social causes in the epoch-making Second Vatican Council (1962–65).

Therefore, in the late 1950s, people became convinced that Italy had a splendid future ahead, without paying attention to the inevitable costs of this rapid and unbalanced growth. The public did not seem aware of the high social cost of this frantic process of modernization and industrialization, or even to have considered whether it was a price they were willing to pay. Still there was another, darker side of the boom. For example, salaries were increasing too slowly in relation to the expansion of the national income, and especially in relation to the lures of consumerism that were introduced to the masses as being easy attainable. Moreover, a new experience, represented by the migration from the south to the north of Italy, brought about social tensions and accentuated the economic, cultural, and socio-historical differences between the two halves of the country. The rapid urbanization of Italy, in particular the uneven growth of the cities, created new unbalances, not to mention the building trade speculation. Finally, the new economy, the fear of communists, and the traditional lack of civic morality in Italian society brought about the great phenomenon of tax evasion. In brief, the promise of material gratification introduced by the economic boom was not for everybody, but only for those who could be quick and cunning enough to acquire the money that the new, advertised lifestyle required.

But if, on the one hand, the majority of the Italians seemed unable to do without this dream of modern life, on the other hand, they accepted its representation as a nightmare in the satire of the *commedia all'italiana*. Moreover, not only does this genre show that this dream is inaccessible for the majority of people, but that there is an irresolvable conflict between the need for new moral values and the desire for social success in a modern society. As Giorgio De Vincenti points out, these films show

> the impossibility for the common man to adhere to the "grotesque social parade of ideological values and standards" which the Italy of the economic boom spreads out before Italians in order to drag them away from the shameful "little Italy" of Fascism toward the new republic of development and modernization (2001: 14).[7]

In other words, this failure is twofold: On the one side it is the failed project of the country's moral and civil reconstruction as the premise for any other transformation that was the core of the neorealist films in the early postwar years. On the other side it is, in Grande's words, a great "epic of loss" (*un'epopea dello scacco*) that speaks about the inability of the new Italian middle-class man to cope with the absence of values in the consumerist boom society. In fact, his failure is not caused by external factors, but by his substantial lack of principles, of a set of cultural and moral coordinates that would enable him to find his own way in the new society. This inability to succeed is a consequence of the inveterate *vitellonismo* of a whole generation of Italian males, that is, their inability to accept responsibility and to decide who they really are and what they want from life. By describing and denouncing this failure, the authors of the comedy Italian style call for new values that are compatible with—rather than opposed to—the expectations of prosperity that we are all to share in a capitalist country.

The Postwar Comedies and Rosy Neorealism

Having established the *commedia all'italiana*'s main features, we can now determine its forerunners in the postwar period. Given its connections with neorealism, it seems logical to find them among the many comedies produced in the postwar years which featured neorealist elements. But we should not forget that neorealist elements can also be found in many other successful films that have nothing to do with the *commedia all'italiana*, such as the overly sentimental melodramas of Antonio Matarazzo.[8] Even some of the slapstick farces starring the famous comedian Totò (Antonio De Curtis 1898–1967) soon display the influence of neorealism, such as, for instance, *Romulus and the Sabines* (*Il ratto delle sabine,* Mario Bonnard, 1945) or Monicelli/Steno's first film *Totò Looks for an Apartment* (*Totò cerca casa,* 1949). In general, the neorealist influence was strong and can be seen in a large part of Italian postwar cinematography as a whole. This trend accelerates in the 1950s, after the definitive demise of neorealism, when its style and themes spread to other film genres, comedy included.

As I have said, the gap between the demise of neorealism (1950–52) and the "official" birth of the new comedy Italian style is usually filled with the comedies of rosy neorealism. One reason is that the latter is probably the most successful comedic sub-genre of the 1950s. However, although we have seen that the former has strong links with neorealism, the majority of critics acknowledge that rosy neorealism merely exploited some superficial neorealist elements for comic and potentially reassuring purposes. At the same time, they recognize the relationship between rosy neorealism and the future *commedia all'italiana* as they apply the generic formula of the *comme-dia di costume* (comedy of manners) to both. For example, Giacovelli writes that

> from the ashes of neorealism, the comedy of manners gradually developed, keeping in mind certain guidelines, however: An al-most morbid attention to reality, the use of dialect, an extreme boldness in alternating and blending the comic and the tragic, the ability to synthesize an entire social situation in a single phrase or sketch. The *commedia all'italiana* will not represent a betrayal, but rather a spectacular evolution of neorealism; how-ever, if one wished to educate the great public, it was necessary to educate them with films that they would go to see, not those that they would not go to see (how many people saw *La terra trema* or *Umberto D.?*). Marco Ferreri [a director of grotesque and exaggerated comedies Italian style] is right when he states that "*comedy is neorealism revised and corrected in order to send people to the movie theaters*" (1995: 21, my italics).[9]

Even director and screenwriter Ettore Scola, while underlining the absence of satire in the latter, speaks of a blood relationship between the *commedia all'italiana* and rosy neorealism:

> Neorealism tried to bring back the dramatic and authentic face of the Italy of those years, while the "*commedia all'italiana*," with the opposite, only deceptive, intent, tried to construct a picture of Italy as compliant, provincial, Doncamillesque, of "bread" and "love." Thus, the "*commedia all'italiana*" began in a rather false way. Little by little, it grew, it began to follow the path of society more closely and more critically. It recorded the changes, the illusions, the realities, from the "boom" to the "bust"; it contributed to the erosion of some of those taboos to which Catholic Italy is prey: taboos regarding the family, sex, the establishment (Monicelli, 1979: 139).[10]

Here, for the 1950s Scola uses the term *commedia all'italiana* in the very broad sense which was employed by many film critics throughout the years (Camerini 1986). But this approach does not help us to formulate a precise history and evolution of the elements that contribute to the creation of this genre and the great difference between it and rosy neorealism that Scola himself explains so well.

In effect, how can the light and optimistic rosy neorealism be the real progenitor of the *commedia all'italiana* once we recognize that the latter "lays bare an undercurrent of social malaise and the powerful contradictions of a culture in rapid transformation … [that] the sometimes facile and optimistic humanitarianism typical of neorealist comedy is replaced by a darker, more ironic and cynical vision of Italian life" (Bondanella 2007: 145)? The noted screenwriter Furio Scarpelli makes an interesting point:

> With neorealism as father and popular farce as mother, the comedy of manners was able to enter the houses of the people when, during the postwar period, the proletariat and the petit bourgeois were struggling for bread. *The comedy of manners was born as the comic and satirical underside of neorealism* (in Salizzato e Zagarrio 1985: 210, my italics).[11]

Scarpelli is clearly referring to the fact that the *commedia all'italiana* is rooted in the farcical *commedia dell'arte*, in which we find the oldest tradition of Italian satire. Without a doubt, the way in which some postwar comedies mix satirical farce and neorealist drama makes them early examples of the "comedy of manners," thus anticipating the future *commedia all'italiana*. On the contrary, it is difficult to say that the *commedia all'italiana* evolves from rosy neorealism once we compare the romantic optimism of the former with the bleak satire of the latter. As I will try to demonstrate, neither rosy neorealism nor the other more successful comedies of the 1950s should be considered real forerunners of the future comedy Italian style.

Ferreri's statement that "the *commedia all'italiana* is neorealism revised and corrected in order to send the people to the movie theaters" is certainly correct if referring to rosy neorealism and the other realist comedies of the 1950s. But it is no longer true if we think of other less light comedies which, for their bitter sarcasm, as I will show, should be better regarded as the true predecessors and early examples of the nascent *commedia all'italiana*. Quite meaningfully, their commercial outcome could not be compared to that of other, much lighter comedies such as those of rosy neorealism or the Don Camillo series, and sometimes they had no success at all. Therefore we must ask: Where should we find the antecedents and the source of *commedia all'italiana* in the postwar decade until the advent of its first "official" film, *Big Deal on Madonna Street* (1958)? Which films are its real predecessors? Can we really say, as Millicent Marcus does, that "perhaps the most illustrious offshoot of rosy realism is the *commedia all'italiana*" (1986: 122)? What is the relationship between *commedia all'italiana*, the postwar comedies, and rosy neorealism?

Rosy Neorealism: The Optimism of a Nation

In terms of commercial fame, the 1950s belonged to the immensely successful rosy neorealism, heralded by films like Renato Castellani's *Under the Sun of Rome* (*Sotto il sole di Roma*, 1948) and *Two Cents Worth of Hope* (*Due soldi di speranza*, 1951), or Luciano Emmer's *Sunday in August* (*Domenica d'agosto*, 1950). With the partial exception of *Sunday in August*—a bittersweet description, strongly influenced by neorealism, of the first collective desire for well-being and lightheartedness in postwar Italy—and unlike the future *commedia all'italiana*, satire is absent in these comedies or reduced to an inoffensive gag that does not sadden the story's outcome and the idealistic representation of the community. As Marcus points out, rosy

Neorealism goes on vacation at the Roman lido: *Sunday in August* (1950).

neorealism takes the most superficial aspects of neorealism and turns them into an innocuous and eventually conservative spectacle: "a pseudo-version of [neorealism] ... mimicked the external trappings of the neorealist model without any of the attendant commitment to social analysis and consequent corrective action" (1986: 28).

This is quite clear if we analyze the first popular rosy neorealist series that began with Luigi Comencini's *Bread, Love and Dreams* (*Pane, amore e fantasia*, 1953). The characters of these films belong to the working class, but here, as opposed to neorealism, the sentimental plot has become predominant and, along with the harmony of the community, it overpowers any potential drama related to the people's adversities. Even though these movies still seem to address some social and economic issues in the wake of neorealism, their approach is optimistic and reassuring. In other words, instead of showing the idealistic commitment of neorealism—the need but also the opportunity for a moral reconstruction of the country as a precondition for the material one—they neutralize it by turning it into a sort of rural version of the social romanticism that characterized the Italian comedies of the 1930s (romance representing the possibility of social fulfillment for the individual). As Spinazzola points out:

> It was neither a matter of giving life to a cinema of regime nor of dismissing *tout court* the legacy of the school which had given prestige to Italian cinema throughout the world, but only of allowing those who were reconstructing Italy to work in peace, to not get mixed up in the political squabbles which were poisoning public life and to assure the cinematographic industry of respectable and attractive products, capable of yielding solid box-office profits without giving up formal decorum. It goes without saying that this meant returning to the only national tradition which was definitely acceptable on the same level as the extremely well-made films: the brilliant pre-war comedy (1965: 108).[12]

The extraordinary success of rosy neorealism demonstrated that the audience of the 1950s accepted overt neorealist elements (realistic settings, working class characters), but only insofar as the original neorealist "pessimism of the intellect" and social criticism gave way to a tale of romance in which the individual is allowed to find harmony and happiness within the social framework.

The problem is not the love story per se but that, unlike neorealism, rosy neorealism reinforced the traditional institutions and values of Italian society. These institutions are the small town community and the family, as celebrated by the fireworks during the final scene of Comencini's *Bread, Love and Dreams* (the box-office winner of 1954), in which the small town commemorates its holiday. The good-hearted protagonist of the *Pane, amore* series (played by Vittorio De Sica) is not a fellow villager, but a middle-aged *carabiniere* who represents authority in a poor town. These films do not completely hide the hardships of the peasants—that would have been impossible after neorealism—but simply turn them into an almost idyllic representation of country life. For this reason, Ernesto G. Laura points out that *Bread, Love and Dreams* is a "comedy of character where the Italian (and especially southern Italian) landscape plays a decisive role in defining characters and situations, portraying in a deliberately optimistic light a certain rustic and provincial reality" (1980: 28). Likewise, Spinazzola observes that these comedies never question traditional Italian values, but ultimately support them:

> The habits, the practices, the conventional traditions of the Italian petit bourgeois and the working class were the subject of polite criticism … The irony and satire were sympathetic and cordial: They were not looking to attack the fundamental institutions, the cornerstones of ethics and civilized life; at the end of the story, the protagonists had to quite rightly become members of the established order, which had never rejected them, just as they had never seriously questioned it (1965: 118).[13]

In the *Pane, amore* series, the major Italian institutions, namely the state, the family, and the Church, are accepted as they are, as the main sources of social cohesion.

Whereas the presence of love stories, social harmony, and happy endings make rosy neorealism quite different from the *commedia all'italiana*, these aspects reveal similarities between the former and other successful comedies of the 1950s. In particular, this depiction of a country made up of villages and small communities that somehow survived the war and Fascism and is even able to overcome the postwar divisions can be found, for example, in the popular *Don Camillo* series (based on Giuseppe Guareschi's much loved books). The first *Don Camillo* was released in 1952 (by the French director Julien Duvivier), and became the box-office hit of the year. As in Guareschi's novels, the "battle" between the priest Don Camillo and the Communist mayor Peppone is more apparent than real, as their common concern is the town's happiness and its protection against external threats, whether human or natural. In theory they belong to opposing factions and ideologies (the Roman Catholic Church and the Communist Party), but this does not really matter to them, since these are remote institutions that do not represent much for the local community. The politics that officially divides Don Camillo and Peppone at a national (and international) level is merely a pretext for skirmishes that follow the pattern of the buddy movie genre. They may use politics as an excuse to unleash their personal idiosyncrasies, but at the same time their similar stubborn characters show how much they share the same roots.

This is quite evident in *The Return of Don Camillo* (*Il ritorno di Don Camillo*, 1953), and in *Don Camillo's Last Round* (*Don Camillo e l'onorevole Peppone*, 1955). During the flood episode of the former (inspired by a real event which occurred in Polesine in 1951), Don Camillo and Peppone together organize the rescue of the local people in the apparent absence of national assistance. In the latter, Don Camillo first helps Peppone to get the elementary school degree he needs to run for the national elections. This is clearly a great opportunity for Don Camillo to finally get rid of his rival. But at the very end he convinces Peppone not to leave, or rather not to "betray" the town by going to the Roman parliament, and to remain mayor of the village instead. The celebration of the local community with a slightly anti-nationalist and anti-urban message contained in the *Bread, Love and Dreams* and in the *Don Camillo* series was in these movies the most important legacy of what director Carlo Lizzani called the neorealist *ideologia della terra* ("ideology of the land"). He observed that the definitive demise of neorealism coincides with the departure from the rural image of the Italian community:

> Neorealism disappeared with the disappearance of the society that was characterized—still in the first postwar years—by the predominance of rural problems and all that came with them, that is, the events of mass migration to the large cities as a consequence of the war and the postwar era, of refugees who came to the metropolitan areas, not because of the industrial miracle yet to come, but in order to find housing or jobs in the service sector, or to work in the black market [...] The fundamental element remains the countryside, where the city is still seen as uprooting, or an instrument of destruction, a confusing conglomeration of human beings removed from nature (1975: 98-99).[14]

Albeit slightly conservative compared to the neorealist films, the *Don Camillo* and *Pane, amore* movies upheld genuine rural and local values against what Pasolini called "the uprooting" (*sradicamento*) produced by modernization and urbanization.

On the contrary, the *Poor, but handsome* (*Poveri ma belli*) series, which in the late 1950s took over the success of the *Pane, amore* films, introduced some major innovations to rosy neorealism in the direction of the *commedia all'italiana* (not surprisingly, the first installment of *Poveri ma belli*, which became one of the box-office hits of 1956–57, was directed by the future master of the *commedia all'italiana*, Dino Risi). I refer in particular to urban settings and to the younger generations, who are the series' absolute and unique protagonists. More importantly, these two elements are united in a third one: Perhaps for the first time an Italian comedy depicts the changes in Italian society toward a new one, different from the traditional background of the fathers. Viviana Lapertosa points out that although the younger protagonists of *Poveri ma belli* belong to the proletarian class, they have begun to look at the oncoming mass culture and consumerist society represented by the city's open spaces in opposition to the closed and restricted context of the family—a trend shown for the first time in Luciano Emmer's *Sunday in August*, set on the beaches of Ostia near Rome: "These young people go to bars, beaches, dance halls, they drink Campari and Coca Cola, they eat ice cream, we witness an out-and-out exodus from the kitchens and dining rooms of the home toward external places, more suitable for giving oneself a modern appearance" (2002: 82).

At the same time we can see analogies between the *Poveri ma belli* and the previous *Pane, amore* series. This is demonstrated by the fact that the boys and girls in these films, albeit attracted by the first lures of consumerism in an urban environment that appears full of new possibilities, never challenge their parents or the values they represent. Indeed, as Giacovelli correctly observes, there is still a continuity between the countryside, the village of the *Pane, amore* films, and the city of *Poveri ma belli*: "The city is still all in the neighborhoods and outlying areas, where the habits and customs of the nearby countryside survive, although certainly confronted with the first consumerist attractions presented by the mass media" (1995: 26). Their young dynamism notwithstanding, the environment and ambitions of the protagonists of *Poveri ma belli* remain predetermined by traditional family values.

Another novelty is the preeminence of female characters in the *Poveri ma belli* series, whose call for women's independence was certainly breaking down the traditional role of the woman in Italian society. However, the female protagonists of these films—embodied by the curvy actress Marisa Allasio above all—are imbued with traditional values, with the middle-class dream of a good marriage still foremost in their minds. Spinazzola observes that, although she shows some proto-feminist aspects:

Allasio's character was lacking in controversial intentions and, quite the contrary, was perfectly integrated into her social milieu, the family, the little world of her neighborhood, which promised her a future rich with household appliances, modular furniture and a lovely Fiat 600, even a shiny new *millecento* (1965: 131).[15]

In Matarazzo's melodramas, where the woman is the central character, she represents society's predestined victim, trapped between traditional values and the dangers of modernization. The cheerful female protagonist of the *Poveri ma belli* series embodies the possibility of harmony, still centered on the familiar institutions, between the old social customs and the new opportunities offered by modernization.

In general, the clash between (rural) tradition and (urban) modernization that lurks in the *Don Camillo* and *Pane, amore* series is absent from the *Poveri ma belli* series. But even in the latter, rosy neorealism's social optimism overrules any attempt to make a satire of urban life in the way that will characterize the *commedia all'italiana*. Consequently, how can we speak of rosy neorealism as neorealism "revised and corrected" in order to send people to the cinema? Although one of the directors of the *Poveri ma belli* series was Dino Risi—one of the most important authors of the future *commedia all'italiana*—the continuity between the two is more apparent than real. In the *commedia all'italiana*, the neorealist moral commitment to a better country and the frothy optimism of rosy neorealism give way to pessimistic bitterness and sarcasm. As I have already said, the *commedia all'italiana* tells of the progressive forsaking of neorealist moral commitments, along with the vanishing of rosy neorealism's hope for the improvement of economic conditions in the process of modernization of the postwar country.

For this reason, we must look elsewhere for the forerunners of the *commedia all'italiana*, in other comedies of manners that contain at least a certain amount of social critique, following the example of the popular satirical magazines published during the Fascist and Postwar years, such as the Milanese *Bertoldo* (1936–43) and the Roman *Marc'Aurelio* (1931–55) where many future authors of the *commedia all'italiana* worked.[16] Accordingly, Brunetta describes the genre's prehistory in this way:

Once the causes and characters which were considered dangerous were weeded out and the themes linked to the Resistance and to the battle for freedom were set aside indefinitely, the green light was given either to those who follow in the footsteps of an Italy of late-Giolittian functionaries, morally upright, but doomed to extinction, or to those who sing in a bittersweet tone of the post-Fascist little Italy, borrowed from the little scenes and caricatures of "*Marc'Aurelio*," bereft of ideals, opportunistic, apathetic, who are pulled along by the development, invent fraudulent jobs ... and move with suspicion, unable to look beyond their own personal "particulars" toward the new political prospects proposed by the government (1991: 324-25).[17]

In these early examples of satirical comedies, the characters "condemned to extinction" in postwar Italy are usually played by experienced comedians coming from the *rivista* (vaudeville) such as Fabrizi, Totò, Macario, Renato Rascel, and Nino Taranto. Good examples are two films directed by Zampa in collaboration with the famous Sicilian writer Vitaliano Brancati and Sergio Amidei (one of Rossellini's closest collaborators): *Difficult Years (Anni difficili,* 1948) and *Easy Years (Anni facili,* 1953). In any case, I believe that Brunetta judges some characters belonging to the second category too severely, such as those played by Totò. As I will explain later, the true negative opportunist, the new breed of ultra-conformist Italian coming out in the postwar years will be embodied instead by the young Alberto Sordi. As a matter of fact, we might say that the difference between the characters played by Totò (and the other old-fashioned comedians) and those played by Sordi makes the difference between the postwar realist satire and the future *commedia all'italiana.*

The Totò phenomenon

Totò became the most successful Italian comedian in the postwar era, particularly in the years 1947–53. His mask is derived from the tradition of the old *commedia dell'arte,* and is similar to Charlie Chaplin's Tramp, not least for his ability to make us laugh about the most serious aspects of real life (hunger, poverty, injustice). Totò's early films reflect his penchant for a more farcical and surreal comedy style that does not fit in well with neorealism. Despite that, he soon adapted to a more realistic and dramatic approach, especially thanks to three films directed by Mario Monicelli: *Guardie e ladri* (1950–51; no English title available), *Totò and the King of Rome (Totò e i re di Roma* (1951), and *Totò and Carolina (Totò e Carolina,* 1954). *Guardie e ladri* is the story of a guard (Aldo Fabrizi) who, after trying to arrest the petty thief Totò, eventually befriends him and his family, to the great outrage of the censors (the film could not be released until 1951, one year after his production). In *Totò and Carolina*, Totò plays a guard who must return to her home a girl who tried to commit suicide because she was pregnant. His trust in the law and in the institutions he proudly represents leads him to zealotry. Throughout the film he seems unable to understand her misery, caused by social indifference, and the fact that her status as an outsider is not a crime but a curse brought on by people's prudishness, which condemned her to a life of solitude not dissimilar to his own. Only at the end, since no one wants her back, does he decide to take her with him and (perhaps) marry her in a sort of melancholic romantic ending without love.

Not only is the background of these films clearly neorealist,[18] but the characters' only hope is to help each other overcome their miserable lives in a way that can be hardly found in other comedies of the same period. A theme typical of Monicelli's mature comedies can already be seen in his early movies: The establishment appears indifferent and even hostile to the protagonists' vicissitudes. For example, when in *Guardie e ladri,* Totò's wife sadly admits that they never had a chance to get married in Church, this does not appear as an expression of religious concern, but an implicit confession that her family never received any help or comfort even from the Church. This makes Monicelli's films similar to neorealist ones (De Sica's *Umberto D,* for example) in saying that after the war the old social network has disappeared, leaving the individuals alone, and is still waiting to be replaced by a new one. The future reconstruction (represented by the rapidly growing Roman suburbs) appears already to be at best only material.

Totò appeared in other similar films such as *Destination Piovarolo* (*Destinazione Piovarolo,* 1955) and *The Band of Honest Men* (*La banda degli onesti,* 1956). Despite their light tone, all these comedies show the same concern about the risk of the dissolution of traditional small-town and old urban neighborhood bonds in the face of the country's growing urbanization and modernization. Consequently, the family is represented as the only value left, the last chance to survive in the material and moral confusion that characterizes the new urban environment. This also illustrates two important differences between this type of comedy and the future Italian-style comedy. The protagonists, played by Totò, but also by other well-known comedians such as Fabrizi, are not the product of reconstruction, but are poor men who still believe in old-fashioned values and honesty.[19] Even in the most satirical achievements of, for example, a Monicelli film, they avoided provoking the audience by directly attacking the family. Just as in the rosy neorealism or the *Don Camillo* series, the family is represented as the last remaining Italian social value, the ultimate harbor. On the contrary, as I will show, one of the major features of *commedia all'italiana* is precisely a sharp critique of family ties. Unlike the comedies of rosy neorealism—but also *Big Deal on Madonna Street*—this genre is characterized by a complete absence of romantic elements in the plot, whereas romance and married life are causes of (male) frustration. Despite the fact that a good deal of social critique is present in the abovementioned films and other similar "social comedies" of the 1950s, the real satire of family values must be found elsewhere.

Roberto Rossellini and Federico Fellini: A Society in Crisis

As we have seen, the relationship between neorealism and the future sarcastic *commedia all'italiana* does not seem to pass through rosy neorealism. Regarding the issue of family values, the first examples of over-arching social satire akin to the future *commedia all'italiana* can be found in some unusual comedies directed by Roberto Rossellini and Federico Fellini. These films show a society in which human relationships are reduced to mere exploitation, thus displaying, perhaps for the first time in the form of comedy, the risk of social and moral dissolution denounced by neorealism. Needless to say, due to their social pessimism these films were difficult to classify, and were generally commercial failures. Just as with neorealism, the public rejected the absence of any trace of social cohesion.[20]

Rossellini's films are also interesting because his name is usually associated with dramas. However, as I have already said, not only are several comic elements present in *Open City* and other neorealist dramas directed by Rossellini (co-written by Fellini), but from many points of view Rossellini's *General Della Rovere* can be considered one of the first examples of mature *commedia all'italiana* (although the similarities noted by Bondanella between this late commercial exploit and the first examples of *commedia all'italiana* are often overlooked by the critics). Furthermore, long before *General Della Rovere*, Rossellini's bizarre comedies *Machine to Kill Bad People* (*La macchina ammazzacattivi*, 1948–52) and *Where is Freedom* (*Dov'è la libertà*, 1952–54) have many points in common with the future genre. They show a small-town community deeply divided at all levels in a way that we can hardly find in other satirical comedies of the same period.

Most importantly, in *Machine to Kill Bad People*—a surreal parable, based on an idea of playwright Eduardo De Filippo, directed in 1948, but released only in 1952—the dissolution of the social bonds is no longer caused by the traumas of war, but by the material greed that comes with reconstruction. As Bondanella writes, in this film, "true to the best traditions of the *commedia dell'arte*, Rossellini's characters are dominated by selfishness, greed, and self-interest" (1993: 94). Rossellini does not concentrate greed and selfishness in a few villains, but shows it spreading throughout the whole community like an epidemic disease. Beginning with the initial scene showing the procession for the patron saint's day—an event that usually symbolizes a community's unity—*all* the characters are represented as totally self-interested individuals who are resentful of one another. If we consider this community a synecdoche of Italy of that time, we can easily see its difference from a totally distinct image, that is, the aforementioned happy ending in *Bread, Love and Dreams*, in which the final fireworks celebrate the four protagonists' future weddings and the harmony of the small town community. Quite the opposite, here, the naïve photographer of Rossellini's film, who is given a camera that is able to kill people, is horrified to realize that the only way to stop the "evil disease" in town would entail the elimination of virtually everyone.

Likewise, *Where is Freedom*—a Totò star vehicle in which producers tried to improve his reputation among the critics by using Rossellini, and vice versa, give some of Totò's commercial appeal to Rossellini's career—is particularly interesting in the way the director takes over the model of the earlier film *Guardie e ladri*. Rossellini transformed Monicelli's social critique into a even bleaker parable of an outsider who is incapable of adapting to the new society and ultimately unwilling to do so. When the barber Salvatore Lojacono is released from jail after 20 years (he had murdered his wife's lover), he must demonstrate that he is able to find—as a policeman tells him—his "reinstatement into the social fabric." Since his wife died years earlier, he finds himself alone in a postwar Rome he cannot recognize, and soon realizes that the so-called legitimate society of "good" citizens, starting with his own family, is full of hypocrisy and selfishness. The ingenuous Salvatore is so shocked and discouraged to see that all social relationships are phony and based on material interest, that he eventually decides to return to prison.

This caustic description of a community prey to greed and incapable of genuine relationships shares many similarities with the future Italian-style comedy. As I have shown, the *commedia all'italiana* is, in fact, defined by Grande as a film genre that

> presents a society that is deaf, unthinking, cynical, indifferent, blind, arrogant, aggressive, amoral, derisive, fickle, greedy for success and ready to pay any price for it, without historical depth or national sentiment, lacking a sense of the future and of collective planning (1985, 52). [This is the representation of] a deceptive artificial landscape, where no one trusts anyone and where everyone is involved in the national spectacle of widespread fraud (2003, 56).[21]

On the contrary, we would hardly find in the rosy neorealist and other successful comedies of the 1950s signs of a disintegrated "social fabric," of a world in which greed has become the only motivation behind an individual's actions. In *Where is Freedom,* even the Jewish character played by actor Leopoldo Trieste (who will become one of Fellini's favorite actors), and whose family disappeared in the concentration camps, seems more interested in regaining his property than in seeking revenge and justice from the people who denounced them to the Nazis.

The question of Rossellini's authorship of these films (particularly the second one) is not within the scope of this study. But we certainly cannot underestimate the importance of the screenwriters, since they will become some of the most important authors of the *commedia all'italiana.*[22] In particular, *Where is Freedom* was written also by Ennio Flaiano, who was Federico Fellini's closest collaborator.

Unsurprisingly, Flaiano co-wrote Fellini's first films *The White Sheik* (1952) and *I vitelloni* (1953) (in both of which the young comedian Alberto Sordi performed) whose social satire is quite similar to Rossellini's. A major difference from the latter, however, is that the male protagonists of Rossellini's films are poor men who still belong to the neorealist world, whereas Fellini decided to move away from this model and to focus instead on the middle class. Fellini's first films as a director are satires of *petit-bourgeoisie* small-town family values and their claim to be the backbone of the new nation. With *The White Sheik* and *I vitelloni*, he established the pattern of a new comedy which departs from the postwar comedy by focusing for the first time on the empty values and hypocrisy of the rising urban petit-bourgeoisie.[23]

In *The White Sheik*, Fellini mercilessly portrays a middle-class husband in all his prissiness, whose only concern during his honeymoon in Rome is not his wife's happiness, but ingratiating himself with his influential uncle who has arranged a meeting with the Pope. As Bondanella writes, "the husband is a typical petit-bourgeois product of the Italian province, characterized by his mechanical obsession with time and order, physical fastidiousness, and a complete subservience to conventional morality" (1992: 82). He is so concerned with appearance (the Italian *bella figura*) and the tight schedule that his Roman uncle has prepared for him that he pays no attention to his wife. He does not realize that she, albeit more naïve and innocent than he is, is already prey to the myths produced by mass culture portrayed in the love-story magazines (*fotoromanzi*) she reads. Fellini suggests that even *his* integrity is not so solid as it appears, and he easily vacillates once he is confronted with the lures of the big city (the real consequence of his encounter at night with the two prostitutes remains significantly ambiguous). Fellini's satire is remarkable if we think that even the 1950s films of Monicelli—whose contribution to the evolution of the *commedia all'italiana* is impossible to underestimate—do not go directly against the values represented by the family and the solidarity among the destitute. We should not be surprised that the movie was a commercial disaster.

After *The White Sheik*'s failure at the box office, in his next film Fellini did not directly attack traditional middle-class values, but tried a slightly more indirect approach, by focusing on one of the

by-products of the new society. He concentrated on characters similar to the one embodied by Sordi in the previous film: *I vitelloni.* "*Vitelloni*" are men in their late 20s who are stuck in a condition of perennial and aimless immaturity within a society that is losing its old
values without replacing them with new ones. Therefore the childish
vitellone does not really belong (or claim to belong) to the traditional
Italy like the newly wed husband in *The White Sheik.* He is unwilling
to follow the old customs, but at the same time is unable to cope with
change. In this way, Fellini not only established the main character of
the *commedia all'italiana,* but also its narrative pattern. We are dealing here with what Grande called "*the epoch of loss,* no longer seen as a
mechanism which leads to adult life and 'trains' for entry into society
[as in the typical classical comedy which focuses on marriage], but as
a permanent condition of life, without center or periphery" (2003:
87). In the surreal style which will become more and more evident in
films over the years, Fellini describes a social milieu without "center
or periphery." This is a withered society in which understanding and
compassion no longer exist and where the only pure characters—as
in Rossellini's films—are destined to succumb.

Likewise, after *La strada* (1954), Fellini's following films set in
Rome, *The Swindle and the Swindlers* (*Il bidone,* 1955), and *Nights of
Cabiria* (*Le notti di Cabiria,* 1957), are two bitter satires somewhere
between comedy and drama. In particular, they include a growing
social phenomenon produced by economic growth, that is, a new,
amoral lifestyle based on the cult of prosperity and consumerism.
The characters appear completely disconnected from their environment, and lost in a space that lacks any socio-cultural coordinates.
This space is represented by Rome, portrayed as a symbol of the new
homogenization produced by mass culture (this will become the
main theme in Fellini's 1960 film *La dolce vita*). Without a doubt,
we are dealing here with the same background and narrative patterns
as the *commedia all'italiana,* as a film genre aimed at

> grasping the rapidly-changing features of a new mass culture
> and of new ideological attitudes and customs, whose basic
> characteristic is provided by the rapid and steady reshaping of
> the environment and forms with which its intended adherence

For the guests of the New Year's Eve party in *The Swindle and the Swindlers* (1955) the sweet life has just arrived in Rome.

(conscious or otherwise) to the ongoing transformations of society triggered by the "industrial civilization" and its demands … The basic feature of this *homogenization*, obviously, consisting of the "cession" of a well-defined cultural identity, which is replaced by an underlying capriciousness, by a constant fluctuation of values and opinions (Grande 2003, 93).[24]

The Roman swindlers of *The Swindle and the Swindlers* are another group of *vitelloni* (one of them is played by the same actor, Franco Fabrizi), a little older than in the previous movie. But their immaturity and consequent difficulties in integrating cause even more problems because, although they are more experienced and cynical than the younger fellows in *I vitelloni*, urban society is changing too quickly for them. Quite significantly, the victims of their scams do not belong to the affluent classes, but are poor people from the country or from the slums around Rome.

These swindlers, like many male protagonists of the future *commedia all'italiana*, are caught between two worlds: the "rural" world of the old Italy (more wholesome, but also backwards and unappealing) and the new "urban" world (modern, but essentially unforgiving). On the one hand they no longer want to live according to the old "neorealist" values of the naïve postwar society to which the victims of their scams belong. But, on the other hand, they are unable to "grow," to take responsibility, because they are unable to go with the flow and keep up with the changes of the new urban society. Thus, unlike some of the younger characters, the aged and tired protagonist

Augusto succumbs because he is unable (and perhaps unwilling) to adapt to the unforgiving rules of the new society.

Some moments in the film could perfectly well belong to the *commedia all'italiana*, particularly the New Year's Eve party scene, in which the moral and social confusion of Rome's new affluent classes anticipates *La dolce vita*. But the second, more sentimental half, with the protagonist's final death, and the choice of the American dramatic actor Broderick Crawford for the role of the protagonist, makes *The Swindle and the Swindlers* a rather unresolved film, at times closer to the poetry of *La strada* rather than the satire of *I vitelloni*. Even in *The Swindle and the Swindlers*, Richard Basehart and Giulietta Masina play two characters who are not dissimilar to the ones they played in *La strada*. Indeed, if we could only replace Crawford with an Italian actor such as Gassman, for example, we would have a film close to the future milestone of comedy Italian style *Il sorpasso* (a.k.a. *Easy Life*, 1962). Unsurprisingly, after *The Swindle and the Swindlers*, the swindler (especially from Rome) will become a stock character in the *commedia all'italiana* (Gassman will play a famous one in Dino Risi's comedy *Love and Larceny* (*Il mattatore*, 1959).

Despite the unquestionably poetic side of Fellini's films, the pessimistic undertone of his satire is far removed from the social optimism and romanticism of rosy neorealism or from neorealism. As Renzo Renzi writes, in Fellini's comedies the humanitarian utopia is replaced by the description of an impossible harmony between the individual and the community around him:

> Neorealism was always about gaining awareness not so much of a reality but of a harsh reality. But at that time, one thought one could fight against it. In fact the film intended to criticize the characteristics of an historically given reality. Now, hope is lost and the film is a tale of defeat before an alienating reality, since it is confusing and may be metaphysical ... in the films of which we speak [*the 1957 films of Fellini, Antonioni and Visconti*], the basic theme is the conflict, by now tragic, between the individual and the collectivity, unified in the search for a solution that can no longer be seen (1986: 60).[25]

In the context of the collective narration represented by Italian postwar filmmaking, the transformation of neorealism into *commedia all'italiana* is not only a matter of increasing the comic element. Following the example of Rossellini and Fellini's early comedies, the *commedia all'italiana* turns out to be a perfect *satire of alienation*, displaying what Grande called "*the dissonant chord* between history and comedy, between the disintegration of the national fabric and the "nomadic" individuality of the new social subjects ... the dissatisfaction of the individual, disconnected from history and from a world of values by now devoid of worth" (2003: 221). This is why, as Bruno di Marino points out, the action often takes place—as in many films by Fellini and Antonioni—in the new social environment represented by the newer "modern" city districts:

> Therefore, it is natural that the cinema of this period [the early 1960s] would use as its setting real glimpses of a city as it restores itself and which expresses the idea of growth, but also of depersonalization, alienation, loneliness, loss of community identity, removal from the ritual perspective of the village, which instead were reflected perfectly in the cinema of the '50s through the outlying neighborhoods (2001: 271) ... non-places such as the snack bar are numerous (2001: 272).[26]

At the same time, the mature *commedia all'italiana* must be distinguished from Fellini's more abstract and "existentialist" dimension. In fact, whereas in the 1960s, Fellini (like Antonioni) moved away from the actual historical events that determined Italy's socio-cultural crisis, the *commedia all'italiana* directly addressed them. Therefore, in order to see this clash between the individual and society in the context of a more concrete social background displaying all the faces of modernization, we must analyze the films in which Alberto Sordi appeared after *I vitelloni*.

Alberto Sordi: A New Breed of Italian

Undoubtedly, it is mainly with Alberto Sordi (1920–2004) that the comedy film became a caustic satire of modern Italians' way of life and myths, including the two pivotal films he made with Fellini.

Sordi (left) plays Sasà, an Italian parasite searching for nourishment and protection within the Roman establishment, in *The Art of Getting By* (1954).

Unlike Totò and the other popular comedians (Fabrizi, Macario, Rascel, De Filippo, Taranto), Sordi is, from the beginning, quite different from the fixed masks of traditional vaudeville (influenced by the old *commedia dell'arte*). He embodies a more flexible figure, one that could easily be turned into a realistic character, to the extent that we cannot imagine him outside the social environment in which we all live. Sordi is extremely important for the evolution and definition of this genre because, as Masolino d'Amico writes:

> With him, we pass from the comedy-sketch to the satire of manners. After Sordi, puppets—little men with Macario's curl, Rascel's Piccoletto—appear anachronistic, or in any case rather limited … Sordi is the only one who arouses laughter through simple exasperation with an otherwise "normal" situation (2008: 92).[27]

Moreover, Sordi is one of the first examples of a comic character who is totally negative. His humor does not come from a stubborn or goofy inability—typical of older comedians like Totò, Chaplin, or the Marx Brothers—to conform to the rules of society, but, on the contrary, it comes from his exaggerated drive to succeed and to be accepted by mainstream society.

This "quantum leap" from the hardships of the working class to the ultimate hypocrisy and self-indulgence of the petty bourgeoisie represented by Sordi is essential to understanding the nature of *commedia all'italiana* and its difference from both rosy neorealism

and the popular comedies of that time featuring more traditional comedians like Totò. Sordi's anti-hero is not an outsider, but, following
the example of Fellini's *vitelloni*, he is the negative champion of the
new urban *piccola borghesia* who have experienced the first prosperity
of postwar Italy. Sordi took to the extreme the character he played
for Fellini and mercilessly portrayed him as an eternal adolescent reflecting "the behavior of the middle-class Italian in the exhausting
search for a new moral identity" (Brunetta 1991: 324). Throughout
the movies he made in the 1950s, Sordi gave voice and body to the
postwar middle-class Italian male: childish, conformist, cowardly, ir-
responsible, and sly, although usually so inept in his short-sighted
furbizia that he was frustrated in his attempts to get what he wanted.
In other words, as Graziella Livi writes, Sordi's appearance on the
Italian screen represented for comedy

> the birth of the middle-class character, comic and credible. He
> was the savage, clear identification of a type, the negative model
> produced by Italian society between the 1950s and 1960s ... a
> person, confused because the rapid passage from dictatorship
> to democracy, just at his coming of age, prevented him from
> becoming a man in a mature coherent way (2005: 108-9).[28]

It is important to recall that Sordi's characters live in a society in
which modernity means that the old religious, political, and moral
virtues, regardless of their value, have lost any significance, without
being replaced by others.

Needless to say, Sordi's path to success was long and full of difficulties, as the public was bewildered by his first unabashed attempts to
represent the monstrosity of supposedly "normal" Italians. His success in *vaudeville* was limited, and his first feature films as a protagonist, *Mamma mia che impressione!* (1951; no English title available;
produced by De Sica who co-directed it with Antonio Savarese) and
Fellini's *The White Sheik*, were commercial failures. For many years,
audiences seemed to accept him either as a secondary character (as in
I vitelloni) or with the most controversial and unsympathetic sides of
his character strongly attenuated—as in the quite farcical *An American
in Rome* (*Un americano a Roma*, Steno, 1954). Still, especially after

the great success of this film, Sordi tried to impose his more realistic and negative characters on the public, as in *The Art of Getting By* (*L'arte di arrangiarsi,* 1954)—which also represented the final collaboration between director Zampa and writer Brancati (who died prematurely in the same year).

The Art of Getting By is the story of the life of Sasà, a new kind of Italian parasite who manages to succeed from the pre-Fascist era to the post-Fascist one, from Sicily to Rome. Despite the fact that the film begins before the Fascist era, Sordi's character is the prototype of the quintessential ultra-negative middle-class male, embodying the dissolution of values and social bonds in postwar Italy. As Maria Pia Fusco writes:

> In *L'arte di arrangiarsi,* for Alberto Sordi, family and [social] relationships exist purely to be exploited. He needs his uncle, the mayor, in order to embark on his dishonorable ascent to power, but he is ready to betray him, just as he will betray all the political parties that he joins according to the advantage they provide him, along with the women he uses unscrupulously only in order to climb one step higher (1986: 133).[29]

Therefore, for this inability to establish social relationships that are not merely exploitative, *The Art of Getting By* might be considered the archetype of the comedy Italian style. Andrea Pergolari's comments about director Luciano Salce's comedies of the 1960s also apply to this film:

> The authors of these films single out the monstrosity of modern life among the bourgeoisie. These are middle-class men, without virtue, who have attained a comfortable standard of living, but with the downside of trampling on moral values, provoking a sense of dissatisfaction which undermines any possibility of tranquility in their lives. The portraits of these protagonists have a chronological span (from Fascism to the modern era) and a social one (between public and private) which allows them to be excellent examples of their stories (2002: 114).[30]

Whereas the themes of first half of the film, set in Sicily, are strongly influenced by the Sicilian screenwriter Vitaliano Brancati, the second half in Rome displays the same urban and capitalist environment in which the *commedia all'italiana* will take place. Rome is depicted not as a fixed community, but as a dynamic space, a sort of "open city" in which, instead of the ideal community based on the respect and tolerance portrayed in Rossellini's masterpiece, new more materialistic forms of social relationships are emerging. Rome becomes here "the perfect essence, both good and evil, of all possible places and types. It is the place where everything happens, the privileged space where phenomena of conservation and transformation coexist" (Brunetta 2001: 590), and the mercurial nature of Sordi's acting reveals a desperate attempt to adapt in an environment of constant change and without fixed values.

Zampa's film was fairly successful (although not exceptionally so), and the producers realized that Sordi's persona could not be entirely imposed on the public. Although he acted in a large number of films in the 1950s, he was rarely the only protagonist. Sometimes he accepted roles that were different from his most disturbing middle-class characters (*Il conte Max,* 1957, *Venezia, la luna e tu,* 1958). Still, Sordi was able to carry out his personal discourse on the meanness of the Italian middle class in some pivotal films, especially in *The Bachelor* (*Lo scapolo,* Pietrangeli, 1955), and *Il marito* (Puccini/Loy, 1958; no English title available), which, perhaps for the first time, display all the elements of the *commedia all'italiana*: negative characters who fall prey to the lifestyle myths of modernity and consumerism in the background of the expanding cities, a fundamental inability to achieve what they want, and the consequent lack of a happy ending.

One important element makes these two comedies the final steps toward the genre's definitive maturation, namely the (male) protagonist's attachment to the myth of an (economically, socially) independent life which must be reached at any cost. This attachment, which clearly reveals his unconscious fears about his own immaturity, is perfectly exemplified in *Il marito* by his refusal to work as a mere employee.[31] Brunetta points out:

> *Il marito*, one of Gianni Puccini [and Nanni Loy's] least remembered films of the period, seems to me to show clearly an

individual's sense of anxiety at the end of the 1950s, with the radical changes in values and the flight from the infernal space of the home where mother, mother-in-law and sister-in-law prevail. ... The shackling of the ex-*vitellone*, who never managed to reach a stage of maturity, within the walls of his household, ... also shows, by extension, the critical state of the entire social and anthropological model of the Italian family at the beginning of a cycle of profound transformation (2001: 599).[32]

Thus *Il marito* is the perfect satire of a man torn between the myth of the American self-made man and the traditional family-centered lifestyle. If Sordi fails as an entrepreneur and fails to escape the constraints of the traditional Italian family, this is due mainly to his incurable conformity and self-indulgence, rather than to external factors such as the many suffocating female figures of the film.

Mario Monicelli: The Comedy Italian Style Takes Over

Although Sordi's status improved during the 1950s, he had his first great popular success only with the slightly positive characters he played in the successful "trilogy of war" we mentioned at the beginning: *The Great War* (Monicelli, 1959), *Everybody go Home* (*Tutti a casa*, Comencini, 1960) and *A Difficult Life* (Risi, 1961). If we compare the two films that are usually considered the first comedies Italian style, as well as the first great commercial successes (*Big Deal on Madonna Street* and *The Great War*), it is not difficult to see the difference between them and Sordi's abovementioned characters. Director Monicelli and his screenwriters introduced a stronger dramatic element, showing death for the first time in a comedy (especially in *The Great War* with the final execution of the two protagonists). However, we must say that in *Big Deal on Madonna Street* and *The Great War*, Monicelli followed the old pattern that he had started with *Guardie e ladri*. Although the protagonists of these films are anti-heroes, they are also good-hearted proletarians, not dissimilar to the neorealist ones insofar as they are victims of a society which is much stronger than they are.

Big Deal on Madonna Street privileges the people who live in the suburbs and slums of Rome, who despite (or because of) their

The group of outcasts breaks into a dream of impossible social integration only for a brief moment at the end of *Big Deal on Madonna Street* (1958).

shabbiness, appear as communities resisting the social decay produced by rapid urbanization (although clearly not for long). Thus the film's petty thieves, who are unable to carry out an effective robbery, are not really representative of the new amoral society. They are a group of outsiders who are trying to survive and become legitimate members of society, but are unable to conform to the rapid process of modernization. Needless to say, their attempt proves unsuccessful, and they have to be satisfied with a dish of pasta and beans found in the refrigerator (a domestic symbol of social improvement that they are almost surprised to find in the apartment). These characters are not thieves because, like Sordi's, they aspire to the consumer goods of the new lifestyle, their status as "outlaws" being a sign (or a result) of their inability to adapt to a world that is evolving too quickly for them. At the same time, they do not belong to the generation of the two older comedians, Totò and Memmo Carotenuto, who represent an old-fashioned comic style destined to disappear (in the movie, Carotenuto dies and Totò decides to leave the city).[33] Of course, the younger characters are on the path of a drastic transformation which will make them—Gassman in particular—akin to Sordi's champions of the new petit-bourgeois society.

In fact, not all of them will share this destiny. Quite significantly, in the movie, the character played by Renato Salvatori, who represents the now out-of-date rosy neorealism (he was one of the male protagonists in the *Poveri ma belli* series), eventually realizes that this is not the job for him and leaves. At the end, the gang disbands, and we see the main protagonist (played by the former dramatic actor

Vittorio Gassman) going to work on a building site. We may be un-
sure of his ability to adapt in order to achieve social betterment, but
we are afraid that if he was not content with that simple dish of pasta
and beans, he will also become one of the "normal monsters" who
will populate the *commedia all'italiana* of the 1960s. As we know, his
career as a film actor will confirm this impression since he becomes
one of the genre's most important actors. His swindler in *Love and
Larceny* is already a completely different kind of thief. He has learned
all the tricks of the trade from his mentor Peppino De Filippo (another traditional comedian), but he is a much more "modern" thief.
He is a sort of genetic evolution, in the context of the newborn social well-being of the young swindlers already seen in Fellini's *The
Swindle and the Swindlers*. Thus his character can be easily compared
to Sordi's, due to his constant adaptation in order to succeed in the
shifting environment represented by the new Italian society.

   To conclude, we can say that Ferreri's assertion that the *commedia
all'italiana* was a sort of smart adaptation of neorealism in order to
achieve popular success is not correct. Many critics and filmmakers
too easily establish a relationship between this film genre and the
most popular comedies of the 1950s. The second reason is that most
of what, in my opinion, we should consider the genre's real forerunners were not great commercial successes. Ferreri's assertion is certainly
true for the rosy neorealism, but becomes misleading once we think of
the satirical comedies of the 1950s, which included some of the most
important features of the *commedia all'italiana*. Aside from Rossellini's and Fellini's initial attempts, Sordi's films are, in my opinion, the
genre's real forerunners in their depiction of a childish and inept male

Petit-bourgeois fam-
ily life is not enough
for the boom-generated
ambitions of the male
protagonist (Vittorio
Gassman) in *Love and
Larceny* (1959).

striving to succeed in a society whose moral and cultural coordinates are dissolving. But even his movies took an entire decade to achieve success and create their audience.

All of these comedies' scant or very limited success demonstrates that they pushed the social satire too far for their time. Italian society in the first decade after the war was too traditional to accept the first acerbic critiques of family values described, for example, in Fellini's *The White Sheik*. Moreover, since the late 1950s was a period of great optimism regarding the effects of the economic boom on Italian society, the majority of the audience could not understand the bleak cynicism of these films or Sordi's negative characters. In effect, the *commedia all'italiana* did not only have to find its audience in the new Italian middle class which was rapidly evolving at that time, but also shaped it through a sort of mutual interaction.[34] Being the ideal space where Italians could meet and see themselves portrayed (albeit in a negative way), the *commedia all'italiana* showed and amplified the process of social affirmation and cultural homogenization of the urban middle class. Accordingly, Paolo D'Agostini writes:

> And thus the Italy of mass communication, the "cultural industry" that, with the cinematic comedy of the 1950s and 1960s makes, perhaps for the first time, its appearance on a grand scale in the fabric of Italian society, which is rather archaic—or in any case, torn by already extremely strong imbalances, not homogeneous—also determines the first model of the "cultural mode," whose effects rise from popularity among the masses up to the intellectual class (D'Agostini 1991: 38).[35]

Unlike rosy neorealism, the "real" *commedia all'italiana* evolved as a film genre destined for the urban middle classes. This evolution parallels the evolution of this class toward a "critical mass" which will take over Italian society and film audiences in the 1960s and 1970s. In other words, the *commedia all'italiana* was successful precisely because of the contemporary evolution of a modern urban middle class which represented both its main subject and its audience. Accordingly, Paolo D'Agostini observed:

The "average" is precisely the soul, the solid base of the "*com-media all'italiana*." A double-sided average: a source of extraor-dinary vivacity and of real contact with the climate and with the general feelings of the society ... Average is the person "fab-ricated" by the authors of the comedy, "average" (in the sense of least), for many years, is the commercial benchmark, "aver-age" is the position, the setting that for more than 20 years this type of cinema occupies in the Italian movie industry, which only then begins to assume less imprecise contours. Between the mid-1950s and the mid-1970s, comedy becomes its true backbone. No wonder then, that the average becomes its ideol-ogy (1991: 37).[36]

Therefore, the ambiguity that many critics find in the *commedia all'italiana* is due to the fact that its commercial triumph correspond-ed and was connected to the success of the social class it was supposed to criticize.[37]

NOTES

1   We might ask if we can really speak of *genres* of Italian cinema, or rather of short-lived "strands" that flourished for a brief period in the wake of a successful movie. According to Luciana Della Fornace, "the cinemato-graphic trend as an inferior manifestation of the industry is presented as a socio-economic phenomenon with distinct and special character-istics only in Italy at the time when, in the wake of a film of perhaps notable artistic value, or at least commercial success, a series of movies was produced that were of lesser quality, because they were always less filled with ideas" (1983: 120). Likewise, Claver Salizzato and Vito Za-garrio write: "But can we define it (the comedy) as that which, in the absence of a *studio system* and a popular tradition of "genres," is the only identifiable trend in our (film) industry, which has allowed it to acquire codes, perhaps a "school," and certainly the possibility of exchanges (of technical and artistic frameworks) impossible for the rest of national cinema? Certainly the *commedia all'italiana* is the only contact with the genre structure of American cinema" (1985: 200). We can hardly call the directors of the Italian comedies *auteurs*, that is, directors with a recognizable signature. Comedy *in general* requires a quite unobtrusive

visual style, as opposed to a typical *auteur* one which is usually based on the *mise-en-scène* or on some peculiar camera positions and movements. The seemingly invisible style of direction is probably more fitting for the comedy genre, as opposed to other genres such as drama, the thriller and even the slapstick comic film. The *film comico*, for example, is based on a single scene, so that it can be a succession of individual *gags* which can be enjoyed independently, whereas the *commedia* requires knowledge of the story and the development of the plot as a whole: "*Commedia all'italiana* works never reveal their truest meaning in a single well-made sequence, as often occurs in the so-called 'auteur cinema,' or in a particularly amusing one as can be seen in so many comic films of the preceding decade … but always need to be discovered in the 'whole,' only during which the various points of view are determined, become concrete and are justified" (Viganò 2001: 239). Comedy films require, perhaps more than any other genre, a sort of democratic collaboration between director, screenwriters, and actors.

2   The years 1959–60 were not crucial only for the *commedia all'italiana* but for Italian cinema as a whole. The definitive consecration in the international arena came in 1960 with the critical-commercial success of Fellini's *La Dolce Vita*. Italian filmmakers—directors, screenwriters, and actors—achieved a freedom (from censorship, for example) previously unimaginable, and also a new awareness of their artistic opportunities.

3   "*La commistione di comicità e dramma, la predilezione per il tratteggio di eroi tutto sommato negativi, una viva attenzione al presente se non addirittura all'attualità, e l'intreccio spesso ambiguo di satira, denuncia morale e irridente caricatura priva di autentico spessore etico*" (the translations are all mine).

4   It is not crucial to decide whether the neorealist's "filming reality"—shooting in real locations without embellishment—is truth or a myth (the interiors of neorealist films, like those in *Sciuscià*, are often arranged sets). The most important characteristic of neorealism is not raw realism as such, but rather its new moral stance. Miccichè points out that neorealism was not an esthetic but an "ethic of esthetic": "'Neorealism' was, above all the name of a battle, of a front, of a clash: One which the advocates of the 'ethic of the esthetic' waged against the advocates of an 'esthetic (apparently) without ethic', that is, of an artistic practice which, pretending to be independent of worldly things, works toward their preservation since it is the 'spectacle' that 'distracts' from the suffering that they produce" (1975: 27).

5   "*Il cinema del dopoguerra, in misura del tutto inedita rispetto al passato, racconta le dinamiche e le trasformazioni nella vita degli italiani nei comportamenti e nella mentalità in una sorta di "diario pubblico" in cui si sovrappongono e condensano, senza soluzioni di continuità, eventi reali e*

immaginazione di mondi possibili, si succedono diverse ondate ideologiche e si dispongono, in ordine sparso, più modi di percezione e rappresentazione della varietà del Paese ... un diario scritto da un io collettivo, un registro e un libro di conti dove vengono annotati profitti e perdite, inutili dissipazioni di energie e difficoltà e durezze degli ostacoli da superare, dolore e rassegnazione insieme alla volontà di ripresa."

According to Marcus, "from the first feature work, *La presa di Roma* (1905), whose *Risorgimento* subject matter coupled the inception of the film industry with the birth of a nation, through neorealism, which made film the agent for the postwar rebirth of a nation, Italian cinema has proclaimed its status as national signifier, as *chronicler of the life of the body politic from infancy to advanced middle age*" (2002: 285, my italics). It must be said that this is not just a matter of content but the product of the way the movie theater was experienced, particularly by the postwar generations. Mariagrazia Fanchi observes that the movie theater became "[a] place for meeting and socialization ... a defiant and rule-breaking experience (going to the movies and viewing certain films is the easiest way to call attention to one's own individuality with respect to the preceding generation and to one's own distance from the traditional culture), and a means of laying reality bare (films, as opposed to television programs, are designed as circumstantial texts which oblige the viewer to reflect and to search for another meaning, implicit and profound), in those years cinema is a basic means for cohesion and construction of a generational sense of identity, the *collective* experience of *belonging to a collectivity*" (2001: 355). Accordingly, Paolo d'Agostini describes postwar Italian cinema as "the plan for a new drama, an expression of national community, which after the destruction and the reconstruction (Fascism, Second World War), needs to be able to identify and recognize itself by means of its own history throughout the twentieth century. (It is a matter of a) political program that is not aligned with (if not actually antagonistic to) that of the Conservative-Democratic-Christian restoration, which has its privileged channels among the most strictly government-controlled organs of communication (foremost of all, television), but not even one radical carrier of alternative values, a supporter of disagreement and social tensions, that is, of real and appropriate opposition" (1991: 74).

6   Not only is there a clear relationship between Fellini's production in the 1950s and the *commedia all'italiana*, but the latter has been also influenced by the dramas directed by Antonioni. However, throughout the years these two *auteur* directors engaged in a more personal discourse that became less and less connected with the Italian socio-economic situation. Still, one should not think that this mutual influence stops or is one-way, from *auteur* to popular genres only. A good example is

the little ghost-child playing with a ball in Fellini's short episode *Toby Dammit* (1967), which comes directly from Mario Bavas' horror film *Kill Baby, Kill* (*Operazione Paura*, 1966).

7   "*l'impossibilità per l'uomo comune di aderire alla «grottesca parata sociale dei valori ideologici e delle norme» che l'Italia del boom economico dispiega davanti agli italiani, per traghettarli dall'"italietta" vergognosa del fascismo alla nuova Repubblica dello sviluppo e della modernizzazione.*"

8   The huge success of Matarazzo's films demonstrates that the failure of neorealism was not due to its dramatic ending (at least not solely), but mainly to thematic novelties. Matarazzo's portrayal of the hardships of ordinary people is derived from neorealist experience, but the popularity of his sob story movies (particularly among the female audience) can be found in their reassuring conservative ideology. As they make the woman the protagonist of their story, these movies acknowledge her suffering in the postwar society. But, by making her a Christ-like bearer of all the burdens of a society in crisis, they eventually re-establish the centrality of the family and her traditional role in it.

9   "*sulle ceneri del neorealismo si sviluppò poco per volta la commedia di costume: tenendone peraltro ben presenti certi insegnamenti: l'attenzione quasi morbosa alla realtà, l'uso del dialetto, l'estrema disinvoltura nell'alternare e fondere comico e tragico, la capacità di sintetizzare in una battuta o in una macchietta un'intera situazione sociale. La commedia all'italiana non rappresenterà un tradimento, ma un'evoluzione spettacolare del neorealismo; d'altronde, se si voleva educare il grande pubblico, bisognava educarlo coi film che andava a vedere, non quelli che non andava a vedere (quanti videro La terra trema o Umberto D.?) Ha ragione Marco Ferreri [director of grotesque and excessive comedies Italian style] quando afferma che «la commedia è il neorealismo riveduto e corretto per mandare la gente al cinema».*"

During the Fascist era between 1930 and 1943, comedy was already the most important film genre. Film comedies were "the real driving force of cinematographic production between 1930 and 1944" (Rossi: 194), representing almost 50 percent of production. The notorious *telefoni bianchi* romantic titles—a kind of Italian "sophisticated" comedy—but particularly the comedies directed by Mario Camerini starring Vittorio de Sica were among the most successful. Camerini's films, as well as the first comedy directed by De Sica, contained some elements of satire of manners, such as Camerini's *Gli uomini, che mascalzoni* (1932). But the satire was strictly limited by Fascist censorship, and focused on little aspects of everyday life, a slight critique of high society and the consequent apology for lower middle-class values, as in Camerini's *Signor Max* (1937).

10   "*Il neorealismo cercava di restituire il volto drammatico ed autentico*

dell'Italia di quegli anni, mentre la «commedia all'italiana», con intenti opposti, soltanto evasivi, ha cercato di fabbricare un quadro italiano conciliante, paesano, doncamillesco, di «pane» e «amore». È cominciata così, in modo abbastanza falso, la «commedia all'italiana». A poco a poco, però, è cresciuta, ha preso a seguire sempre più da vicino e più criticamente il cammino della società. Ne ha registrato i cambiamenti, le illusioni, le realtà, dal «boom» al «crack»; ha contribuito a intaccare qualcuno di quei tabù di cui l'Italia cattolica è vittima: tabù della famiglia, del sesso, delle istituzioni."

11 *"Con il neorealismo come padre e la farsa popolare come madre, la commedia di costume è riuscita ad entrare nelle case del popolo quando, nel dopoguerra, proletariato e piccola borghesia erano alle prese con il pane. La commedia di costume è nata come risvolto comico-satirico del neorealismo."*

12 *"Non si trattava né di dar vita a un cinema di regime né di liquidar tout court l'eredità della scuola che aveva dato prestigio al film italiano in tutto il mondo: ma solo di lasciar lavorare in pace chi stava ricostruendo l'Italia, non mischiarsi nelle beghe politiche che avvelenavano la vita pubblica e assicurare all'industria cinematografica dei prodotti dignitosi e seducenti, capaci di assicurare solidi incassi senza rinunciare al decoro formale. Va da sé che ciò significava rifarsi all'unica tradizione nazionale positivamente accertabile, a livello del film di buona confezione spettacolare: la commedia brillante d'anteguerra."*

13 *"Obiettivo della garbata critica erano le consuetudini, le usanze, le tradizioni del costume piccolo borghese e popolare italiano ... L'ironia, la satira erano comprensive e cordiali: non miravano a investire gli istituti fondamentali, i cardini dell'etica e della vita civile: a conclusione del racconto, i protagonisti dovevano entrare a pieno diritto nell'ordine costituito, che mai li aveva rifiutati, così come essi mai avevano pensato seriamente di porlo in discussione."*

14 *"Il neorealismo si eclissa con l'eclissarsi di quella società caratterizzata—ancora nei primi anni del dopoguerra—dalla prevalenza della problematica contadina e di tutti i suoi addentellati: cioè le vicende delle masse immigrate nelle grandi città in conseguenza della guerra e del dopoguerra, dei profughi venuti nelle metropoli non per il miracolo industriale ancora da venire, ma per trovare alloggio o lavori terziari, o per esercitare il mercato nero [...] l'elemento fondamentale rimane la campagna, dove la città è vista ancora come sradicamento, o congegno distruttivo, agglomerato confuso di esseri umani allontanati dalla natura."*

According to Marcia Landy, "Neorealism was a symptom of the ongoing economic, social, and cultural transformations that were set in motion by the rapid modernization and capitalization of Italy" (2008: 352).

15 *"Il personaggio Allasio era destituito di intenzioni polemiche e anzi integrato perfettamente nel suo ambiente sociale, la famiglia, il piccolo mondo di*

> *quartiere, che le promettevano un futuro ricco di elettrodomestici, mobili componibili e una bella seicento, anzi una millecento nuova fiammante."*

16 Among them: Federico Fellini, Steno, Cesare Zavattini, Vittorio Metz, Ettore Scola, Age e Scarpelli. The relationship between the *commedia all'italiana* and these magazines (*Marc'Aurelio* in particular) is extremely interesting and requires a separate study.

17 "*Una volta epurati motivi e personaggi considerati pericolosi, messi in isolamento a tempo indeterminato temi legati alla Resistenza e alla lotta di liberazione, il disco verde viene concesso o a chi pedina un'Italia di funzionari tardo-giolittiani integri moralmente, ma condannati all'estinzione, o a chi canta con tono agro-dolce l'Italietta post-fascista, presa a prestito dalle scenette e caricature del «Marc'Aurelio»: priva di ideali, opportunista, qualunquista, che vive a rimorchio dello sviluppo, inventa mestieri truffaldini ... e si muove con diffidenza, incapace di guardare al di là del proprio «particulare», verso i nuovi orizzonti politici prospettati dal governo.*"

As we know, this comedy could not exist without the contribution of many authors and scriptwriters who came from the satirical magazines—such as *Il Marc'Aurelio* and *Bertoldo* (both founded by future screenwriter Vittorio Metz in 1931 and 1937)—which were the only voices of dissent during Fascism. After the war they found a new and much more effective way to express their sarcastic talents. Italian comedy absorbed the authors of the old satirical magazines and their readership, which was composed mainly of the urban bourgeoisie.

18 The actor who plays the American in *Guardie e ladri* comes from *Paisà* (he is the American priest in the monastery episode). Rossellini used him again in *Machine to Kill Bad People* (1948), and *Europa '51* (1952).

19 This is what distinguishes the Sordi or Gassman characters from those embodied by the old comedians like Totò and Fabrizi. For instance, in *Totò vs. the Four (Totò contro i 4,* 1963), made during the golden years of the *commedia all'italiana*, there are allusions to the "right" to make easy money at any cost that are typical of this genre. Totò, who plays a police commissioner, is not Alberto Sordi. In order to arrest the corrupt customs officer Mastrillo, he only pretends to make a deal with him, being tired of his meager salary:

Commissario: Mastrí, I'm sick of being a government employee at 150,000 lire a month. I'm fed up. I can't take it any more. I want to break away.

Mastrillo: I understand very well, you're right, but you realized it too late, dear commissioner.

Commissario: Eh, what do you want to do?

Mastrillo: Not me, I realized it four years ago.

Commissario: Better late than never, right? So, will you tell me how this system of swiping from the customs office goes?

(Commissario: Mastrí [Mastrillo], io mi sono stufato di fare l'impiegato stat-ale a 150.000 lire al mese. Sono stufo non ne posso più voglio evadere!
Mastrillo: capisco benissimo, ci ha ragione; però se n'è accorto troppo tardi caro commissario
Commissario: ehh che vuoi fa'?
Mastrillo: io no, io me ne sono accorto 4 anni fa
Commissario: meglio tardi che mai, vabbe'? Dunque me lo vuoi dire com'e' questo sistema di fregare i soldi alla dogana?')
As the officer reveals his (illegal) trick, the commissioner reveals his own:
Commissario: Mastrí, what did you think, that I'd become your partner? I'm an honest upright commissioner; 150,000 lire a month, but I'm a commissioner!
(Commissario: Mastrí, cosa ti credevi, che diventavo socio tuo? Io sono commissario onesto ed integerrimo;150.000 lire al mese ma sono un commissario!)
Likewise, when Totò plays a thief (as in *Big Deal on Madonna Street* or *Totòtruffa*), he is never part of the (illegal) system but always an outsider, a poor guy who tries to live from day to day. *The Overtaxed* (*I tartassati*, 1959) and *Totò, Fabrizi e i giovani d'oggi* (1960; no English title available), in which Totò plays a well-off shopkeeper, are an exception clearly influenced by the changes in Italian society. But a main reason is that when Totò and Fabrizi work together, they tend to repeat the pattern of *Guardie e ladri*, in which it is Fabrizi who plays the honest and scrupulous public officer. Totò's "immorality" has nothing to do with Sordi's selfishness, and in the end, the values of the family and friendship always prevail.

20 Spinazzola observes that, in keeping with neorealist "optimism of the will," *Umberto D*, stills contain "the positive energy of an act of faith in the resources of the conscience of the individual" (1974: 46).

21 "*Mette in scena una società sorda, distratta, cinica, indifferente, cieca, spavalda, aggressiva, amorale, beffarda, camaleontica, avida di successo e pronta a pagarlo ad ogni prezzo, senza spessore storico o sentimento nazionale, priva del senso del futuro e di progettualità collettiva. (1986: 52) [Questa è la rappresentazione di] un paesaggio sociale artefatto, ingannevole, dove nessuno si fida di nessuno e dove tutti armeggiano nello spettacolo nazionale della truffa generalizzata.*"

22 Among them, *Machine to Kill Bad People* was written by Franco Brusati and Sergio Amidei; *Where is Freedom* by Vincenzo Talarico, Vitaliano Brancati, Antonio Pietrangeli, and Ennio Flaiano.

23 After the commercial disaster of his neorealist feature film *The Earth Trembles* (*La terra trema,* 1948), Luchino Visconti directed his only comedy-drama about the frustrated ambitions of a mother who is willing

to do anything for the success for her young daughter in the cinema: *Bellissima* (1951). This film can be regarded as another precursor of the *commedia all'italiana* having much in common with Fellini's early comedies, and particularly with *The White Sheik*'s satire of mass culture and the star system. A major difference is that the protagonist, Anna Magnani, is still a neorealist character, although facing a different ordeal. She is a proletarian—actually a copy of the character of Pina she played in *Roma città aperta*—not a middle-class woman. Unsurprisingly, the "neorealist" ending is a celebration of proletarian family values as opposed to the lures of the new middle-class culture. The proletarian environment, represented by her apartment's courtyard and its inhabitants, is still sound.

24   "*Cogliere i tratti rapidi e mutevoli di una nuova cultura di massa e di nuovi atteggiamenti ideologici e di costume, la cui caratteristica di fondo è data dal tratteggio veloce e sicuro di ambienti e tipi con cui si propone l'adesione (consapevole o meno) alle trasformazioni continue della società innescate dalla 'civiltà industriale' e dalle sue esigenze ... Il tratto di fondo di questa omogeneizzazione, ovviamente, costituito dalla 'cessione' di una identità culturale ben definita, che viene sostituita da un camaleontismo latente, da una oscillazione costante di valori e prospettive.*"

25   "*Il neorealismo fu sempre la presa di coscienza non tanto di una realtà quanto di una dura realtà. Ma allora si pensava di poterla combattere: infatti il film intendeva denunciare i tratti di una realtà storicamente data. Ora si è persa la speranza e il film è il racconto di una sconfitta di fronte ad una realtà alienante, perchè confusa, può darsi metafisica ... nei film di cui si parla [i film del 1957 di Fellini, Antonioni e Visconti], il tema di fondo è il conflitto, per ora tragico, tra individualità e collettività, unito nella ricerca di una soluzione, che non si può più vedere.*"

26   "*È perciò naturale che il cinema di questo periodo [primi anni 1960] utilizzi come scenografie gli scorci reali di una metropoli che si rinnova e che esprime un'idea di crescita ma anche di spersonalizzazione, alienazione, solitudine, perdita di una identità comunitaria, allontanamento dalla dimensione rituale del villaggio, che invece era perfettamente riflessa nel cinema degli anni 1950 attraverso gli esterni nei quartieri popolari (2001: 271) ... numerosi sono i non-luoghi, come l'autogrill.*"

Spinazzola correctly sees an element of social alienation in Sordi that makes his Fellinian *vitellone* (and therefore all the male characters of the future genre) analogous to Antonioni's characters: "Therefore, he introduces into the satirical sphere the dramatic representation of a totally alienated humanity, not unlike that which, with such different stylistic methods and narrative register, was brought to the screen by Michelangelo Antonioni during the same years" (1965: 222). A major difference is that Antonioni focused on female characters, whereas the protagonist of the *commedia all'italiana*—with important exceptions—is definitively male.

27   "*dal comico-macchietta con lui si passa alla satira di costume. Dopo Sordi le marionette—l'omino col ricciolo di Macario, il piccoletto di Rascel—appaiono anacronistiche, o comunque, assai limitate ... Sordi è l'unico in questo suscitare la comicità con la semplice esasperazione di una situazione altrimenti «normale».*"

28   "*La nascita del personaggio medio, comico e veridico. Era la feroce, chiara identificazione di un tipo: il modello negativo prodotto dalla società italiana fra il '50 e il '60 ... un personaggio confuso, perchè il passaggio repentino dalla dittatura alla democrazia, proprio nell'età della formazione, gli ha impedito di farsi uomo in maniera matura, coerente.*"

29   "*In L'arte di arrangiarsi per Alberto Sordi famiglia e rapporti [sociali] sono puramente strumentali, ha bisogno dello zio sindaco per cominciare la sua disgraziata ascesa al potere, ma è pronto a tradirlo, come tradirà tutti i partiti politici a cui aderisce secondo convenienza, insieme alle donne che usa senza scrupoli soltanto per salire un gradino in più.*"

30   "*Gli autori di questi film individuano le mostruosità della vita moderna nella classe borghese. Gli uomini senza qualità sono uomini borghesi, che nella vita hanno raggiunto un livello sociale benestante, a scapito però del calpestamento dei valori morali, provocando un senso di insoddisfazione che mina la possibile tranquillità della loro vita. I ritratti di questi protagonisti hanno un'estensione cronologica (dal fascismo all'epoca contemporanea) e sociale (tra pubblico e privato) che consente di attribuire loro un alto grado di esemplarità alle loro storie.*"

31   We can say that the *commedia all'italiana* officially begins when in *I vitelloni* Sordi shouts "*lavoratori!*" and blows a raspberry to the rail workers.

32   "*Il marito di Gianni Puccini [e Nanni Loy], uno dei film del periodo meno ricordati, mi sembra segnare in maniera netta, il senso di crisi di un personaggio alla fine degli anni cinquanta, con il capovolgimento dei valori e la fuga dallo spazio infernale della casa dove trionfano moglie, suocera e cognata ... L'incatenamento dell'ex vitellone, mai entrato del tutto nella fase della sua maturità, entro le mura familiari ... segnala, per estensione, anche la crisi di un intero modello, all'inizio di un ciclo di trasformazione profonda, sociale ed antropologica, della famiglia italiana.*"

33   Once seen retrospectively, the story and the casting of *Big Deal on Madonna Street* are enlightening in understanding the future of the new *commedia all'italiana*. The old and experienced "artist" Totò is hired to teach the basic skills to a new generation of "performers" who are willing to take over. Monicelli underlines the difference between the old school represented by the former, and the new one represented by the latter as the first line of Totò's character is a drastic comment: "As a movie it is horrible."

34   Spinazzola notices that Sordi's films in the 1950s were successful only

in the biggest cities: "The Sordi phenomenon finds a proportionally much greater approval among inhabitants of the large cities than in the smaller towns: More than half of the proceeds realized by *Scapolo* in the 16 regional cities, and precisely 51 percent is due to audiences in Rome, Milan, Turin" (Spinazzola 1965: 218).

35 "*E così l'Italia delle comunicazioni di massa, l'«industria culturale» che con la commedia cinematografica degli anni Cinquanta e Sessanta fa forse per la prima volta la sua comparsa su vastissima scala nel tessuto abbastanza arcaico – o comunque dilaniato da ancora fortissimi scompensi, non omogeneo – della società italiana, determina anche il primo modello di «moda culturale»; i cui effetti dal gradimento di massa risalgono fino alla classe intellettuale.*"

36 "*la «medietà» è proprio l'anima, lo zoccolo duro della «commedia all'italiana». Una medietà a doppia faccia: fonte di una straordinaria vivacità e di un contatto vero con la temperie, con il comune sentire della società ... Medio è il personaggio «fabbricato» dagli autori della commedia, «medio» (come minimo) è per molti anni il riscontro commerciale, «media» è la posizione, la collocazione che per oltre un ventennio questo cinema occupa nell'industria italiana dello spettacolo che solo ora comincia ad assumere contorni meno approssimativi. La commedia ne diventa, tra la metá degli anni Cinquanta e la metá degli anni Settanta, la vera spina dorsale. Per forza che media, allora, sia anche la sua ideologia.*" Likewise, Franco Fortini writes: "The unsurmountable difficulty of Italian films and novels is precisely the representation of the middle-class culture, because it is a mystery, within it hides the reality least able to be simplified, least easily described a priori by formulas" (*Cinema Nuovo* 1963: 363).

37 Fernaldo di Gianmatteo is right to observe that "if there is a case in which the concept of reflection or the nebulous Lukasian category of the typical can still count for something, it is the *commedia all'italiana*, a primary manifestation of an attitude of mistrust and rejection, of gratification and of the fear that the new emerging social classes are acquiring as the country springs out of poverty and incredulously faces a world glimpsed only in its wildest dreams" (1991: 278). A major problem is, according to De Vincenti, that "the *commedia all'italiana* offers ... a critical model ... but does not offer alternative models, it does not present *other* ways of living and behaving to the public, other ways of feeling. its strength and its limitation, its unpleasantness enjoyed by the public, its subtle and deep tie with the grotesque, with the strange abnormality that makes one laugh, but does not amuse" (1991: 278).

5

TARANTULA MYTHS AND MUSIC*

Popular Culture and Ancient Rituals in Italian Cinema[1]

Flavia Laviosa

Introduction

Southern Italian tarantism, a fascinating topical subject with its mythical-symbolic and magic-religious ritualistic components, has generated great interest and curiosity for centuries. Since the early 1990s, tarantism, as a complex archaic form of music and dance therapy, along with similarly undeniable phenomena of musical healings practiced in diverse cultural contexts (Gouk 2000; Horden 2000),[2] has been the object of renewed international academic interest in anthropology, ethnology, musicology, medicine, history, sociology, psychology, and psychiatry (Bartholomew 1994; Lanternari 1995; Lüdtke 2000, 2009; Agamennone and Di Mitri 2003; Del Giudice 2003; Biagi 2004; Del Giudice and van Deusen 2005). To that effect, the purpose of this chapter is first to provide a documented historical, medical-anthropological, and ethno-musical overview of the practice of tarantism in Italy.

While the phenomenon has been widely researched and discussed in other fields of study, surprisingly it is still an unexplored area in film and media studies. There is, in fact, a lack of scholarly work

*Dedicated to Wilga Rivers

on Italian and foreign documentaries and films representing ancient rituals connected with tarantism (La Penna 2005). In order to stimulate a critical debate and fill in the academic void in cinematographic productions on the subject, this study examines Italian documentaries and films directed since the 1960s from an aesthetic as well as critical cultural perspective.

Although tarantism is extinct today, the Salento region[3] re-interprets the myth of the spider. Such unexpected, and at the same time constructed, enthusiasm has transformed music and dance in the region into products of commercialization promoted through concerts and local festivals. This phenomenon is determined by the fact that tarantism, as a ritual and a practice, is no longer observable, so, while it survives in the memory of older people, it also lives on in the space of cinematographic representation, theater performances, and music recordings. Therefore, this essay tries to define the cultural and artistic phenomenon, the so called *new*-tarantism (Nacci 2001; 2004) "by inquiring whether this current popularity and commercialization is connected with the historical ritual of tarantism, or if [such phenomenon] is only a source of rhetorical legitimization" (Lüdtke 2008[4]), or if it is linked with a re-appropriation of the role of southern Italian cultures.

Historical and Medical-Anthropological Overview of Tarantism

The tarantula spider is said to take its name from the Apulian sea harbor of Taranto, situated on the Ionian Sea where the Apulia and Calabria regions meet. According to local traditions, people bitten by the tarantula were called *tarantati* or *attarantati*. Tarantism, dance disease or dance of the *tarantati*, is a therapeutic and cathartic ritual, as well as a multifaceted anthropological and artistic phenomenon. According to the myth, in the hot summers, a spider bites people (mostly women) working in corn fields and tobacco plantations, causing a complex syndrome characterized by diarrhea, tremors, convulsions, and delirium, or neuro-pathologic symptoms like depression, paranoia, hysteria, epilepsy, and even schizophrenia. The spider types associated with the tradition of tarantism, and the ones most commonly referred to in the literature are the poisonous *Latrodectus Tredicem Guttatus* (or Black Widow) and the *Lycosa Tarentula*.

Ethno-musicologist Giorgio Di Lecce reports that the presence of venomous spiders was documented by ancient Greek and Roman historians. For example, in 250 B.C., Solino documented cases of death caused by the *Latrodectus* in Crete (Di Lecce 2001).

The spider hides in the crack, in the tobacco leaves, in the faggots, in the cracks of the parched ground, in the dry stonewalls of rural houses, but predominantly in the labyrinth of the mind. It bites at midday, like a meridian demon, arousing senses and unleashing unavowed desires. However, while the South American counterparts and the *Latrodectus* are large and lethal, the Italian *Lycosa* tarantula is a small, harmless spider. Therefore, what is interesting is that in most cases, no actual spider bite occurred.

The phenomenon of possession of tarantism originated in the Middle Ages as a pagan ritual where music and dance acquired the therapeutic function to heal from the tarantula bite, and exorcise the inhibited Eros and forbidden expression of sexual desire (Di Lecce 2001). The origins, however, of the complex mythical ritual of tarantism trace back to the mysterious and ancient cults of possession, as well as the mythological pagan rites and orgiastic ceremonies of Magna Greece. In this realm, it was believed that a greater force or spirit, divinity or mythical ancestor, entered a person's soul and forced him to dance. The most immediate reference can be found in the Dionysian rituals during which the Bacchants, in the elation of the dance and euphoria of the wine received in their souls, temporarily emptied of folly. The connection with tarantism is tenuous, but consistent and persistent—as in the eighteenth century the *tarantati* danced in the woods near springs or fountains, with wine leaves wound around their bodies, like country Maenads. Today the forest element is limited to the decoration of plants, while a bowl filled with water is reminiscent of the purifying spring.

Furthermore, the folk tradition of music therapy for tarantism seems to inherit anthropological-cultural practices, which trace back to both biblical texts and Greek mythology. Uncountable are the extraordinary events connected with the healing power of music and dance—from the myth of Orpheus, who calmed wild animals with music, to the Odyssey, where Ulysses' wounds were cured with the sound of a chant. The therapeutic role of music, which derived from the Pythagorean tradition that those suffering of mental and spiritual disease could be brought back into society with music and dance, was preserved in Apulia, a region of Magna Greece, for centuries.

Di Lecce reports that in the tenth century, a spider called *Tarantola* (*Lycosa Tarentula*) was already known in Italy. Much more dangerous was the *Latrodectus*, whose poison could cause death. Both spiders lived in Italy along the Mediterranean coasts. As documented in the 1362 *Sertum papale de venenis* written by Guglielmo di Marra, from Padua, episodes of ominous bites were cured with music and dance, thus widely spreading the practice in southern Italian regions. Later, the ritual became a Catholic rite and the Church demanded that people adapt their popular traditions to Christianity, established that the Christian calendar coincided with the days of local celebrations, decided to build churches next to pagan temples, and ordered the substitution of ancient deities with saints. In spite of the rigorous control exercised by the clergy, such pagan rituals continued throughout the Middle Ages and outside the official religious functions, thus preserving the traditional popular dances still performed today during local feasts. Similar phenomena, called the *"Ballo"* (dance) of St. Vitus, St. John, and St. Donatus,[4] occurred in villages 'infected by dancers' in the summer. The wildest dancers engaged in indecorous behavior, which was not accepted and strictly forbidden by the Christian Church.

Furthermore, the Christianized form of tarantism was strongly connected with the worship of St. Paul, the patron saint of Galatina, where a chapel was erected in his honor. St. Paul became the protector of those bitten by snakes and poisonous insects, according to legend, for his miracles against scorpions, spiders and other venomous animals.[5] Official medicine disapproved, while Church authorities discouraged the popular belief about the healing power of music and the miraculous qualities of the water in the well of St. Paul's chapel[6] in Galatina against the effects of the tarantula bite. Doctors claimed that only medical treatments cured the symptoms, whereas the clergy preached that religious faith was the real remedy for the disease. However, people in the southern regions continued to believe in and practice their traditional dance, song, and music to fight the symptoms of the poisonous bite.

Tarantism has been considered a healing ritual for those affected by the hypothetical or real tarantula bite since the fourteenth century, and thus widely studied and documented since 1300. The German doctor Justus F. K. Hecker, in his 1838 publication,[6] explained that from the Middle Ages to the seventeenth century, southern Italian villages were hit 16 times by the plague and epidemics. He wrote that toward the fifteenth century, "people bitten by poisonous spiders, or so it was believed, went every year where the lively tarantella was played and danced. Crowds of curious women went to these gatherings, contracted the disease, not of the bite, but of the moral poison, which they absorbed with their eyes, and the healing of the *tarantati* gradually became a real folk festival that everyone waited for with great anticipation"[8] (2001: 14). Around the seventeenth century, these dances and music, originated in the Taranto area, were called *tarantella*. These therapeutic dances were performed during popular feasts where musicians and participants came from neighboring villages. Gradually they became common methods for the cure of the *tarantati*.

These dances, observed and described since the Middle Ages, were marked by slow and lively rhythms and melodies. Examples documented in popular literature, between the fifteenth and twentieth centuries define a vast variety of dances of *tarantati* decorated with different objects and accessories such as swords, colored handkerchiefs and ribbons, mirrors, fans, and shells. Historian L.G. De Simone, in 1876, made a clear distinction in his descriptions between the *taranta*, the *pizzica-pizzica*, and the *tarantella*. He described the *taranta* as the healing dance, of which 12 different melodies (*muedi*) are known; the *pizzica-pizzica*, deriving from the *taranta*, was different for only a few choreographic details and later became the typical Salentine dance. The *tarantella*,[9] instead, named after the tarantula spider, was accompanied in a minor 6/8 time, and was danced in other regions such as Campania (De Simone 1996: 50). The *pizzica* (from *pizzicare*, to bite, pinch or sting), and its healing systematic practice survived until the mid-twentieth century in Salento. Tightly connected with the therapeutic ritual of tarantism, the *pizzica-pizzica* was first identified as a choreographic term in sources only at the end of the eighteenth century. The name *pizzica-pizzica* (D.E.U.M.M.

1983: 656)[10] was used to describe a lively dance for young couples, often confused with the *tarantella* dance.[11]

For centuries, the cult of tarantism was the sole source of relief for those (supposedly) "bitten" or "possessed" by the tarantula, and the only means to free people from alienation caused by poverty, social marginalization, or personal problems. The long and exhausting expiatory ritual, connected with the choreography of dance and music therapy,[12] usually took place in private homes. A blanket spread on the floor marking the sacred enclosure, musicians invited as archaic priests of an ancestral ritual, colorful ribbons (*nzacareddhe*)[13] placed around the room, green plants, and a large bowl filled with water were the symbols used to evoke curing energies. The victims danced for days to the *pizzica* rhythm played by traditional musicians.

Only through music, it was said, could the spider's poison be expelled and relief assured. Therefore, when a person manifested symptoms of panic, madness, or feelings of suffocation, his or her relatives called for the band. Violin, accordion, and tambourine[14] players performed for days the hypnotic, repetitive rhythms, and sang healing love songs. The haunting and incessant music went into the sick person's head, caused convulsive shakings and rhythmical movements, leading the person into a trance-state. The musicians played a kind of music, later called *tarantata* or *pizzica-tarantata*,[15] which consisted in a series of beats that would awake the *taranta* (spider) in the bitten person. The tempo of the music *scazzicava* (from the Salentine dialect *scazzicare* in Italian *eccitare*—to provoke or excite from within the person) the *taranta*, thus forcing the possessed to dance incessantly. At the end, the dance purified the body from the poison, freed the person from disease and spell, allegedly caused by the tarantula bite, and from neurosis.

The dance usually comprised several stages: In the first phase, the person would personify the spider, thus, he/she would lie on the floor and crawl, imitating the movements of the spider. In the next stages of the choreographic cycle, the person would get up, and his/her movements would simulate the search for the spider, the running after the insect, the attempt to crush it underfoot, and finally the liberating act of expelling—getting rid of it. The healing came only when the sick person fell on the floor exhausted, then he/she was revived by friends and family members. When the effect of the tarantula bite was finally defeated, the healing was welcomed with collective outbursts of joy.

As part of the curing process, every year at the time of harvest, people went on a pilgrimage to the chapel of St. Paul in Galatina[16] on June 27, 28, and 29, the saint's feast day. The chapel was a regular destination for the victims of the *rimorso*, intended both literally as repeated spider bites and psychologically as recurrent torment. In the chapel, the *tarantati* screamed, lamented, cried and prayed, thus causing a collective outburst of hysterics, expressed through wild dance, while imploring redemption, and hoping to heal permanently from the poison of the tarantula. Sometimes the possessed ran frenetically into the streets of the town, then gathered in the yard outside the church, and started to dance, jumping for hours, sometimes for days. Outside the church, the collective healing ritual was staged to the sounds and rhythms of tambourines, violins, and accordions playing as villagers sang. In this way, people, mostly women farm workers, who felt repressed, oppressed, ignored or exploited in their lives, could, once a year, be the protagonists of a community ritual, allowing them to manifest their mysterious and silenced pain, while musicians played and sang for them. Moreover, their relatives and friends assisted them in their suffering, and at the end rejoiced for their healing.

There were fewer real spider bites than people stricken with tarantism, as documented in Ernesto De Martino's research. It is therefore evident that conditions of psychological submission, social status and economic poverty, harsh working conditions in the fields, along with personal dramas connected with love, family, and sexuality that characterized the lives of these people, were the real causes of their alienation. The historical malaise and its pathology were the results of peasants' difficult lives in the countryside and the strict moral rules of a rural society, yet the culture itself elaborated pragmatic and effective ways to resolve such mental conditions through collectivized rituals entailing the inclusion and socialization of the sick, thus avoiding the stigmatization of madness. The music therapy, however, provided only temporary relief, as symptoms frequently resurfaced, as a result of persisting primary causes of psychological affliction. As Karen Lüdtke explains, "the tarantula's music and dance provided a safety net not only to endure severe life circumstances, but also a safety net to guarantee that the status quo of these causes was secured" (2005: 41).

In archaic societies, the village community accepted insanity as a means of escape into the irrational, dealt with manifestations of folly as permissible forms of rebellion, and provided caring assistance and emotional support through traditional music and dance. Therefore, the ritual of tarantism can be described as societal treatment for depression, which validated madness, did not marginalize the sick, and was recognized as a way of accepting mental illness within the community rather than excluding or banishing it. Consequently, the tarantula bite, whether real or supposed, acquired a strong symbolic value in so far as the animal embodied ancestral human fears and obscure temptations, while the musical rhythms, the repetitive chanting, and the *pizzica* dance represented the antidotes produced by a highly suggestive liberating ritual.

Following the Second World War, pesticides exterminated the tarantula from southern Italian regions and with it, as popular belief explains, also the tradition of tarantism. However, as Lüdtke suggests, more recent research, bringing socio-economic factors into the discussion, "has inevitably questioned this popular rationalization. Officially, but not quite in practice, tarantism became a memory, shamefully dismissed, […] [and intentionally] relegated to a distant past" (2008: 2). The archaic ritual of tarantism, a cultural solution to the precarious life of poorer social classes, was later defined as a peasant form of superstition and backwardness.

In 1959, southern Italy inspired Ernesto De Martino's[17] seminal work and anthropological inquiry *La terra del rimorso*.[18] De Martino and his team,[19] attracted by the opportunity to explore the unknown aspects of Italy during the years when southern regions were experiencing crucial socio-economic changes, studied the subordinate world of the poor, while trying to rethink and redefine the post-national unification *Questione Meridionale*.[20] Then, in the 1960s, it became common practice to celebrate "progressive folklore" and, in the spirit of this enlightened anthropological approach, De Martino's analysis of symbolic relations between religious beliefs and ritual forms, societal values and mental disorders provided "crucial reflections for overcoming the alleged inevitability of clashes between civilizations, the eclecticism of cultural relativity, and the overestimation of com-munitarian idealism" (Cupolo 2006: 183). De Martino concluded that, "Tarantism is a complex phenomenon whose many-sided as-pects cannot be resolved only in psychiatric terms"[21] (1996: 302), thus recognizing the depth and wealth of the historical, cultural and artistic substrata of this ancient practice.[22] Thus, the healing rhythms of the historical tarantism, played to tame the obscure forces hidden in people's minds and bodies, gave voice to their ancestral grief and soothed their despair. For these people, as long as the music played, the pain of life became bearable.

Visual Representations of Popular Culture and Tarantism

Tarantism has interested scientists, historians, Catholic Church au-thorities, anthropologists, ethnomusicologists, art-therapists, travel-ers, and writers on the occult for centuries. It has also inspired a large number of artists including novelists, poets, filmmakers, dancers, musicians, photographers, and filmmakers. Henrik Ibsen for example in his 1879 play *A Doll's House* introduced the theme of the *tarantella* as the dance that Nora performs on Christmas Eve; D. H. Lawrence also manifested his fascination for tarantism in his 1920 novel *The Lost Girl*,[23] and Italian poet Salvatore Quasimodo composed superb prose in his culturally perceptive and emotionally disquieting poetic commentary to Gianfranco Mingozzi's documentary *La taranta*[24] (1962). A recent novel with a modern interpretation of tarantism is *Il bacio della tarantola* (2006) by Giovanna Bandini.

Since the 1960s, the sacred and ancient ritual of tarantism has been the object of the intrusive curiosity of the mass-media, disrespectful attitudes of visitors, insensitive judgment of pseudo-researchers, and the academic interest of anthropologists and ethnographers, all pho-tographing, audio-recording, filming and documenting both private and public manifestations of the phenomenon. Subsequently, rich photographic records of tarantism include the famous and aestheti-cally impressive ethnographic reportages by Chiara Samugheo,[25] An-nabella Rossi,[26] Marialba Russo,[27] Sebastiana Papa and Lello Maz-zacane,[28] André Martin, and Franco Pinna[29] conducted in the 1950s, 1960s and 1970s. The dramatic impact of these vivid images from ar-tistically poignant photographs by these professional reporters leave an indelible memory of the powerful, yet unsettling moments of folly and helplessness of people cured through the practice of tarantism.

These visual documentations of the phenomenon are complemented by a variety of older as well as more contemporary cinematographic representations. A selected list of anthropological and ethnographic documentaries include (none of these was released in the English-speaking market so no English titles are available): *Meloterapia del tarantismo pugliese* (1959) and *La terapia coreutica-musical del tarantismo* (1960) by Diego Carpitella; *La tarantolata: la vedova bianca*, the eighth episode of the film *Le italiane e l'amore*[30] (1961) and *La taranta* (1962) by Gianfranco Mingozzi; *Il male di San Donato*[31] (1965) by Luigi Di Gianni; *Sud e Magia*[32] (1977) by Gianfranco Mingozzi; *Nel Sud di Ernesto De Martino* (1978) by Luca Pinna; *Sulla terra del rimorso*[33] (1982) by Gianfranco Mingozzi; *Morso d'amore: viaggio attraverso il tarantismo pugliese* (1985) by Annabella Miscuglio;[34] *Viaggio a Galatina* (1989) by Rina Durante;[35] *San Paolo e la Tarantola* (1989) by Edoardo Winspeare and Stefanie Krenser-Koehler; *La danza del piccolo ragno: La tarantella pugliese/Der Tanz der Kleinen Spinne: Tarantella*[36] (1992) by Raimund Köplin and Renate Stegmüller; *Tarantule Antidoti e Follie* (2004) by Marina Gambini;[37] *Un ritmo per l'anima: Tarantismo e terapie naturali* (2004) by Giuliano Capani; and *Il sibilo lungo della taranta: musiche e poesie sui percorsi del ragno del Salento* (2006) by Paolo Pisanelli.[38]

Tarantulas and tarantism have inspired also foreign directors and producers. *Tarantola* (1955) by Jack Arnold; *Tarantella*[39] (1995) by Helen DeMichiel, while the fear for the spider has been recurrent in a number of films from the horror feature *Aracnofobia* (1990) by Frank Marshall, and the more ironical *Arac Attack* (2002) by Ellory Elkayen. Even Harry Potter, in Act II, fights against voracious tarantula spiders, and Frodo is confronted with spiders in *The Lord of the Rings*.

Both the first ethnographic experimental studies directed in the 1960s, and the more contemporary proliferation of works released from the 1980s onward, are expressions of the growing interest in anthropological documentations of tarantism as a popular culture phenomenon. These artists have mobilized diverse cinematic forms of intervention, locating themselves inside a universe of unknown socio-cultural realities. They take on the responsibility as leading advocates for southern Italian people, mostly women, and purposefully use their cinematic skills to document a new form of social realism. Furthermore, their films are expressions of cultural militancy and artistic commitment for the South's collective experience of struggle. These directors' definitions reproduce and structure the discourses of realism portraying prototypical characters and figurations and magnifying the complex and unequivocal truth about the South's political, class, and gender struggles. Furthermore, their documentaries illustrate the forms of alienation manifested in women living in rural communities, paying special attention to women's expressions of escape and rebellion. These visual documents represent forms of reinterpretation of women's difficult roles in traditional societies. Organized around socio-anthropological, medical, and musical themes, these documentaries report and address the consequences of cultural conflicts in women's lives in southern regions in the past.

However, the representations of tarantism in these documentaries have been deeply questioned, arguing that anthropologists and ethnographers have exploited and ideologized the phenomenon. Although visual anthropologists filmed staged manifestations of tarantism most of the time, they inevitably filmed authentic events as well. Consequently, they intruded into people's private dramas, arguably exploited peasants' stories and, with their peeping cameras, invaded the secret rituals and moral codes of archaic cultures with the aim to support their progressive ideals and apply their innovative investigative methods. On the other hand, those documentaries on tarantism are rare texts, belonging to a precious popular culture, a patrimony kept in Italian archives and representing the sole sources of visual information on the phenomenon.

In addition to ethnographic documentaries, tarantism has been a topic of interest for Italian filmmakers. An interesting production of both fictionalized and historically inspired films on themes related to tarantism, include long features, such as *Flavia, the Heretic* (*Flavia, la monaca musulmana,* 1974) by Gianfranco Mingozzi; *La sposa di San Paolo*[40] (1990; no English title available) by Gabriella Rosaleva; *Pizzicata* (1996; no English title available) and *Life Blood* (*Sangue vivo,* 2000) by Edoardo Winspeare. These films vary in the ways that

Tarantata, followed by players, walks by the convent in *Flavia, the Heretic*
(1974)

they offer examples of fictionalized versions of tarantism, often giving
merely distorted representations, or romanticized narratives of the
ancient rituals.

Flavia, the Heretic[41] (1974) was in part inspired by the historical
siege of Otranto and genocide of the Christian population by the
Turks in 1481. Set in Otranto, at the end of the fifteenth century, the
story is about the true dramatic life of Flavia Gaetani, the daughter of
a local despot, who had been forced by her father to become a nun.
Flavia seeks emancipation, becomes a sort of feminist *ante litteram* in
her attempt to claim her rights and those of her sisters for freedom
from male tyranny. So, when a fleet of Saracens lands on the shores
of Otranto, Flavia allies with their leader Achmed, soon becomes his
lover, and leads Muslim soldiers through secret passages from the sea
to the town. Harnessed with the vestments of a priest, she administers a series of executions, slaughtering the Christian reprobates.
However, she is not able to prevent the Saracens, during an orgiastic
feast, from bringing violence and death into her own monastery. As a
result of this outbreak of violence, Flavia's desire for freedom is disap-
pointed and her love betrayed. Achmed and his soldiers sail back to
their land of origin, leaving her behind in the hands of the angered

Tarantate enter the convent in *Flavia, the Heretic.*.

Christians. Condemned to death, she is skinned alive.

This film is relevant to a discussion on cinematic representations of tarantism for a scene at the beginning of the story, portraying a group of *tarantate*. Coming from neighboring villages, these young women abruptly enter the church of the convent where Sister Flavia lives. The women scream, have hysterical attacks, suffer convulsions and fits, as they have all been bitten by the tarantula. Their wild and indecorous behavior troubles Flavia's mind and plants the seeds for her rebellious actions. The women, however, are expelled from the church before they can find spiritual peace and physical healing.

The film itself belongs to the "nun-exploitation" Italian-style genre. This is supported by a dry and essential direction and a screenplay which combines anticlerical furor and libertarian feminist apology"[42] (Attolini et. al 2007: 192). Subsequently, it was censored and accused of criminal blasphemy for its explicit sexual content, nudity, violent language, disturbing images of typical fifteenth century tortures, and its moral attack on the foundations of the Christian religion. The portrayal of the *tarantate* at the beginning of the film is an overacted, sensationalistic, gratuitous, visually offensive, and disturbing series of border-line scenes, simply adding to the film a sexually exploitative purpose. The attempt to give an historical representation of young

Cosima and Tony dance the *pizzica de core* in *Pizzicata* (1966).

tarantate is weak, distorted, and unconvincing, as it turns out to be more of a sexually enticing pretext than a real thematic objective in the narrative structure of the entire story.

La sposa di San Paolo[43] (1990), directed by Gabriella Rosaleva,[44] is a fictionalized story of a *tarantata* set in late sixteenth century. A group of traditional musicians and singers accompany Anna, a young woman bitten by the tarantula, on a pilgrimage to St. Paul's chapel in Galatina. During their journey, they experience the most adventurous and extraordinary encounters. Among the many people they meet, there is even a messenger of the pope sent to Galatina. His mission is to understand the reasons for the common and frequent violent crises that plague young and old women in the region, and the forms of collective exorcism practiced to defeat the devil, symbolized by the mythical seductive tarantula, through dances and music. The bishop wonders how it is possible to heal from the bite of the poisonous spider with dances and music, but in the end he will witness this extraordinary force and phenomenon when Anna and the musicians play the rhythms of their ancient culture. Young Anna is confronted with the obscurantism of the Christian Church, and tarantism in this film becomes a metaphor for social repression, psychological submission, and economic conflict in southern Italian society. As Francesco Faeta states, "This film belongs to a certain kind of cinema interested in the distorted representation and false celebration of tarantism."[45]

Pizzicata[46] (1996) is Edoardo Winspeare's[47] debut film, which stems from themes explored in his ethnographic documentary *San Paolo e la tarantola*[48] (1991). *Pizzicata*, the first film entirely shot in Salento,[49] is the sum of local traditional music, song and dance. The title comes from a combination of the words *pizzica* (the dance of joy, courtship and love) and *tarantata* (the dance of death). The *pizzica* dance, very suggestive, sensual and seductive, served as a loosening of values and a release of passions for the southern Italian people—everything that was not accepted by society was conveyed in the *pizzica*.

The story takes place in Salento on an evening illuminated by German anti-aircraft bursts in 1943. An American scout plane crashes with its pilot, the Italian-American Tony Marciano,[50] just outside the village. On the eve of the Allies landing, the young man finds shelter and care in the house of a farmer, Carmine Pantaleo,[51] a widower and father of three daughters and one son, who is at war. Their farm, in the middle of the countryside, allows Tony to heal from his injuries and reconnect with his own roots, since, as it turns out, he was born in a neighboring town. Tony works his way into the Pantaleo family, first by pretending to be a relative, then by falling in love with and being requited in his feelings by daughter Cosima.[52] However, she is promised to handsome and rich Pasquale. Jealousy and revenge ensue and tragedy inevitably unfolds. After a symbolic, yet emotionally charged dance-duel during a village feast, Tony is stabbed to death by Pasquale. Cosima's reaction to the tragic loss of her love culminates in excruciating pain, exploding into compulsive shaking and convulsion, typical symptoms of the *tarantate*, as she crawls on the white sheet laid for her on the floor of her house waiting for the music therapy ritual to start. Only in this way she will eventually recover from her mourning for her dead lover.

The film, rich in singing and dancing, is structured around three spiraling key moments all following the rhythm and sequence of the *pizzica* in its various expressions. First, the tempo of the story is stroked by the *pizzica de core*[53] (*pizzica* of the heart), a sensuous dance with a flirtatious and celebratory tune that allows men and women to brush against each other, not touching, but looking intensely into each other's eyes. This music and dance are performed during the village feast when Tony woos Cosima, and she returns his feelings in the gentle, yet suggestive popular dance.

Next, the *pizzica sherma, schermata*, or simply *scherma* (dance of the knives/swords)[54] (Tarantino 2001), danced only between men, is a symbolic dance that recalls the movements of a duel, with fingers mimicking knives. This rhythm is played in the film during the men's dance in the village celebrations, when Tony and Pasquale engage in a highly stylized dancing fight, evocative of a warning and ominous duel of honor, while manifesting their male rivalry and jealousy over Cosima's heart. Daniela La Penna explains that in these two scenes with the community in feast the pulse of the *pizzica* revives the film's narrative pace and she describes how the director introduces a more rapid montage by inserting "white" frames in order "to achieve a blinking effect, [...] [thus] conveying visually the convulsive rhythm of the music" (2005: 191). Finally, the *pizzica-tarantata*[55] (healing dance), both individual and collective with swooning, screaming women, performed as an exorcism for women bitten by tarantulas, serves as a dramatic introduction in the film, foreshadowing tragedy, and also concludes the movie, thus giving a concrete emotional context to the practice of tarantism, as well as an open-ended closure to the protagonist drama.

Characters' passions, stories and frustrations are expressed in the film through the highly emotional language of music and the figurative representations of dance. Winspeare defines this film as "a declaration of love"[56] (Laviosa 2005: 253) to the past and the rural society of his homeland Salento. It uses old popular songs and traditional dances, thus giving a choreographic frame and musical commentary to a rich and mysterious South. When first released, the film was viewed as a seductive manifesto for depicting an archaic Salento not yet contaminated by modernity, and was perceived more as a documentary, than a fictionalized representation of tarantism. Toriano states, "Winspeare should be credited for bringing Salentine culture to international audiences. His film, however, is only a romantic plot that seems to be a a metaphor for reality, while it is actually the depiction of a kind of unreality. The director projects a false sense of awareness of the phenomenon of tarantism. His film is empty of meaning and it seems to negate the propulsive elements of research of archaic values."[57] *Pizzicata* has been considered a film belonging to the ethnographic genre and to that effect La Penna states that Winspeare translates his commitment to Salento in "a hybrid gaze that is partly nostalgic and partly ethnographic" (2005: 189). The film is in fact a prototypical expression of an idyllic and idealized rural South, and the representation of a stylized and romanticized version of tarantism.

Life Blood[58] (2000), also directed by Edoardo Winspeare, is "an act of love towards Salento"[59] (Laviosa 2005: 250). The film portrays the places, faces, sounds and dialects of contemporary Salento. The film, inspired by the real life of the protagonist, Pino Zimba, tells "a real story about deviance and redemption with real, not realistic characters."[60] In the outskirts of Lecce, two brothers, 50-year-old Pino, a smuggler, fruit vendor and talented musician, and 30-year-old Donato, a small-time criminal, drug addict and gifted tambourine player, struggle through life. Their father's death—an accident, for which Pino feels responsible and which results in Donato's refusal to talk to his brother—represents the obscure pain tormenting their souls.

Pino lives off small jobs, smuggles cigarettes, is involved in the illegal immigration business and trafficking of Albanians, and occasionally works for a local mafia boss. In this way he supports his family, old mother, his brother Donato, and a lover. His aspiration, however, is to succeed in music with his talented brother so that they can put an end to their precarious life and their connections with local criminality. Donato, though, is a weak man; he prefers to engage in petty crimes and drug dealings, and spends a dull life in the town square in the company of unreliable friends. The advice of his mother and his girlfriend, Teresa, and encouragement that he should step out of such a self-destructive life style lead nowhere. Even his sister Maria who manages to interest a producer in launching Pino's music, is unable to change Donato's mind.

While Pino performs with his group at a local feast, Donato falls again into the trap of his heroine addiction and gets involved in a burglary with one of his friends, Giovanni, a young and unscrupulous criminal. The robbery fails, thus provoking the fury and revenge of the local mafia. Killers are on the hunt for Donato and Giovanni, while Pino, warned about the imminent tragedy, tries to reach his brother, asks for information from one of Donato's friends, but the young man, scared, shoots Pino. Giovanni, found by the mafia gunmen, is killed. Though severely injured, Pino keeps driving in search of Donato. When he finally finds him, he asks his brother to play the tambourine for him for the last time. Only Pino's brotherly gesture of love eventually shakes Donato's repressed feelings of deep anger and guilt, violent resentment and regret. Captured by such a rage of passions, he plays a *pizzica-tarantata* leading to a cathartic release of his hurt feelings, and ultimately to moral redemption.

The homonymous film sound track, *Life Blood*, includes songs and instrumental pieces of the traditional repertory played by the *Officina Zoè*.[61] The plot follows the crescendo rhythm of the *pizzica, pizzica-pizzica,* and *pizzica-tarantata*, as the music poetically comments on the story, underscoring the dramaturgy of its heroes' lives. Lamberto Probo's and Pino Zimba's vital beats of tambourine playing, Cinzia Marzo's and Raffaella Aprile's piercing vocal talents, accompanied by organs, violins, flutes, guitars and castanets, explode in a flow of forceful, unrestrained energy, wild and suggestive at the same time. The pulsing music scores, along with the intensely paced editing of images, as parallel narrative channels, blend, merge and harmonize, as the tragic story unfolds.

In the most powerful scenes[62] the music progressively reaches a climax, matching the tension and pathos of the drama; then it softens, releasing emotions in a liberating end. At times, the rhythm starts slowly with a melody played by the violin, guitar, organ or accordion, and gradually acquires the energizing beat of the percussion instruments.[63] Other times, the music begins with rapid, close and repetitive beats, until it reaches a high peak of tension, immediately followed by a feeling of exhaustion and relief. The intense, tight, fast pace of the *pizzica* bursts into fraught expression, and inevitably induces a natural state of trance, the utmost form of symbiosis between the mind and the spirit. The emotional and frantic music seems to come from within the body, and to flow through the blood, whereas the obsessive beats irresistibly inspire the dance, while the songs tell stories of pain, poverty, and love passions in the same way as in the past when these rhythms and lyrics were vehicles and sources of healing.

The director's stylistic editing choices of shots and counter-shots frenetically juxtaposed, along with the quickly paced extreme close-ups, establish a tense emotional and cinematic tempo. In the scene when Pino interprets the traditional song *Sale*,[64] an expressive close-up of the actor singing on the stage arranged in the town square, lit and crowded for the celebrations of the local patron saint, is inter-cut with the shot of a rural landscape, dark, and desolate where Donato and his friends Zaccheria and Giovanni have met. The striking disparity between the socialization and entertainment of the community in feast and the psychological estrangement and social separation of a group of restless young men in the countryside at night is marked by the pressing and tight beats of the music that form the diegetic in the town in feast, and become extra-diegetic and oneiric in the scene of Donato's fix. From Pino's opening notes, the scene follows Teresa, whose powerful singing becomes screaming, a pained cry against the background of a crowd cheerfully dancing, while immersed in her rhythmic dance, she enters into a state of performative trance. The repeated sequences of Teresa singing and dancing on stage, are inter-cut with disturbing shots of Donato lying in the back seat of the his friend's car, under a different state of trance: the narcotic effect of his heroine injection.

The incessant succession of these combined scenes sets the tone for a dramatic transition from the town's joyful, socializing and collectivized *ballo* (dance), to the isolated countryside setting, expressing the alienated and solitary *sballo*[65] (drug effect), thus drawing attention to and pausing on the narcotic effect of the "fix" as both a parallel to and a contrast with the exalting and enthusiastic atmosphere of the local feast. The shooting of different cinematographic times, one of the action and one of sound is dramaturgically effective. The time of the long shot, edited in slow motion, of Donato's distorted perceptions for his altered state of consciousness and the slowed movements of his intoxicated body, are in a symbiotic emotional fusion as well as in dissociation with the pressing tempo of Teresa's staged singing, to signify the strident coexistence of the cathartic euphoria of music and the trance of the dance, with the temporary ecstasy, trance state and oblivion of the heroin. Will Teresa's traditional therapeutic playing, singing and dancing eventually heal Donato's modern malaise?

The film's didactic tone lends itself toward the conclusion and equation that when community ties of interdependence collapse, and traditional ways of relief and discharge of alienation lose the support of societal inclusion, relationships between the individual and the collectivity inevitably fall apart. Therefore, *Life Blood* is a metaphor for modern tarantism, for the moral pain and psychological desperation of urban contemporaneousness, expressed as the drama of victims of criminal deviance, drug addiction, social marginalization, incommunicability, alienation, and, consequently, profound loss of identity.

Neo-Tarantism: From Traditional Healing Practice to Contemporary Performative Art

Between the late 1980s and early 1990s ritualized *pizzica* "resurfaced, turning into a local craze, mesmerizing masses of dance and music enthusiasts. Reinvented and revived, this music has come to attract crowds and sponsors, [film directors, and documentary producers] fabricating and marketing a unique sense of regional identity on the basis of its captivating rhythms and powerful origins" (Lüdtke 2008: 3). Consequently, Salento has become the epicenter of a cultural movement that goes beyond southern Italian regional borders and has been the initiator of the rediscovery of popular culture and in particular of the *pizzica*, after years of silence on the topic of tarantism because, as previously mentioned, it is considered a form of archaic superstition and shameful peasant backwardness. Such revival is part of a broader change in musical preferences as expressed by the Italian posse and reggae-muffin groups who use local dialects in their lyrics[66] and propose new paradigms of relationships between local cultures and international musical interests (Durante 1999).[67] As a result of this phenomenon, an enthusiastic niche of young people, eager to follow the collective fascination of the rediscovery of tarantism, has raised the *pizzica* to the status of an identity emblem, while many folk-revival players and dancers have spread the *neo-pizzica*.[68] The modern choreographic wave and "*pizzica* fever," redefine the *neo-pizzica* as a means to restore ancient rhythms and folk practices, revitalize songs in vernacular, re-elaborate traditional dance styles, and produce films in a sort of *neo*-neorealism.[69] The contemporary *pizzicomania*, defined as "*neo*-tarantism" (Nacci 2001; 2004), although improbable as a return of the original tarantism, reflects the desire of the new generation to produce, perform and enjoy music and dance as a rediscovered socio-culturally community-based healing practice from contemporary forms of alienation.[70]

Among the numerous festivals where these new artistic expressions are performed, it is necessary to mention the internationally recognized annual concert The Night of the Tarantula (*La Notte della Taranta*). Founded in 1998, this is a cultural project[71] with the goal to organize, within the Hellophone (ancient Greek speaking) area, concerts in which local rhythms hybridize with other musical traditions, thus revitalizing Salentine melodies and producing a new synthesis of diverse ethnic sounds and songs.[72]

Toriano, however, in sharing the philogical position of anthropologists, ethnographers and musicologists, argues:

> The *new-pizzica* and the subsequent concept of *salentinità*[73] are only the products of cultural mystification. Tarantism, as an anthropological phenomenon is connected with the archaic rural culture, is the expression of psychological discontinuity, breakdown of the individual, refusal of and rebellion against societal order; it is not a form of political antagonism. The varied forms of *pizzica* revivals are empty rhetorical manifestations of popular culture, very much like pizza and mandolin for Naples, while *La Notte della Taranta*, the symbol of such rhetoric, is merely an exploitative commercial device.[74]

Lüdtke adds to the debate by writing, "Tarantism has become touristic. To many it is no more than a myth of the past framed in glossy tourist brochures. According to widespread views, the recovery of well-being is of no issue in this context, in which academic, political and commercial motives are seen to predominate" (2005: 44).

Nonetheless, this movement of Salentine artists and sponsors stems from a synthesis of post-modernity and tradition, leading to the institutionalization of rhythms and dances from Salento as central elements of *neo*-traditionalism and *neo*-meridionalism. This awareness rejects the idea of a unified and "single thought," and aspires to embrace the manifestation and valorization of a "meridian thought," as expressed by sociologist Franco Cassano, "of a South thinking for itself"[75] (1996: 5), in other words, of a South that regains its ancient

Dance performance of the *Arakne Mediterranea* August 10, 2003.

dignity of "subject of thought," rather than accepting the subordinate position of being the "object of thought." Cassano further explains that "the meridian thought is also intended as a way of treating with regard and having respect for (*avere riguardo*), as well as in the sense of revisiting (*riguardare*), as rediscovering the South."[76] The contemporary revival enthusiasm is arguably an exploitative way to captivate audiences or spread new commercialized artistic products and pseudo-traditional performances, but it is fundamentally a form to reclaim emancipation from what has been denied for centuries to the South as a result of a politically deliberate process of de-historicism of a culture. Such resurgence speaks for a new sense of self-respect, indicates a time of rediscovery of a denied past and erased history, and manifests the urge to reacquire control of its own future. Therefore, the contemporary Salentine movement reflects an ideological and philosophical position of a self-centered South seeking autonomy, identity, and delineating the coordinates of a political and cultural self.

A valid example of this cultured revival is Di Lecce's[77] group *Arakne Mediterranea*, named after the Greek myth of Arachne,[78] which comprises musicians, singers, and dancers, the expressions of the "*coreutico*" (choreographic) element.[79] Di Lecce's rigorous philological research elaborates a unique performative choreography of traditional music and dances. *Arakne Mediterranea's* dancers use masks reminiscent of the *Commedia dell'Arte* of the seventeenth century, as well as of ancient Greek theater, and wear traditional costumes, as those shown in old prints from the 1600s and 1700s.[80] Di Lecce discusses the performers of the seventeenth century tarantella, the most ancient and authentic version of contemporary *pizzica*, "These are modern young Salentine women who adapt and represent their ancestors' popular and rural dances. Their performance can be defined as both 'being' and 'presenting,' as they interpret themselves and at the same time the history of their people from Salento."[81]

Another relevant expression of artistic and historical revival of a vast musical patrimony is the unique research done by the *Ensemble Terra d'Otranto*. Founded by Doriano Longo and established in 1991, this group of artists studies therapeutic forms of music and rituals belonging to the erudite and popular Salentine tradition composed in the seventeenth and eighteenth centuries. Further, the *Ensemble* performs Salentine Baroque composers[82] using original or faithful copies of antique instruments and adopting the style and techniques of the time. In addition to taking the regional classical music to a wider international public, these musicians promote traditional singing and dancing by organizing seminars, courses and festivals.

The new generations' interest in the re-appropriation of songs in Salentine Greek dialects,[83] and attention for the ethno-choreographic inquiry, are signs of critical reflection on the popular dance traditions from the rural context to the theater performance, as well as of motivation to recuperate reclaimed traditions as roots, archetypes and expressions of a local *habitus*. The post-modern definition and fruition of popular culture lies in the need for re-enchantment and the search for a different form of socialization defined as collective hedonism of a "freed time," whether it is the artistic trance, or more simply the community in feast (Apolito 2000). Through this complex transformation, Salento has reacquired its role of anthropological laboratory at the intersection between post-industrial identity needs, multimedia globalization trends, and cultural inter-ethnic syncretism.

In conclusion, this essay has examined a variety of topics and addressed several ideological and artistic issues pertaining to the southern

Italian practice of tarantism. First, an historical, anthropological, and ethno-musicological overview of the rituals connected with tarantism has provided a sense of the medical, psychological, cultural and musical complexity of this ancient phenomenon. Second, an exploration of the stylistic and thematic choices and the different objectives of anthropological documentaries testifying the rituals of tarantism has led to assess the validity and effectiveness of these recordings as social and cultural documents, and to address questions of representation in examining whether tarantism has been respectfully portrayed, or exploited and ideologized in these documentaries. The distinctive purpose of this analysis has also been to open an academic debate on tarantism in film and media studies, and to start an intellectual inquiry on the varied authentic, distorted or romanticized representations of tarantism in film productions. Furthermore, this essay has examined how and why the *pizzica* has exploded in the Salento region in the past 20 years, thus generating consequences on a national and international level, and fostering the cultural and artistic phenomenon of the so called *new*-tarantism. Finally, the discussion has focused on whether this current popularity and commercialization are only forms of emblematic justification, or if instead they are more deeply connected with a new appreciation and re-appropriation of the role of southern Italian popular cultures and values in contemporary Italy.

NOTES

1   This essay was made possible thanks to professional contributions from the following people to whom I wish to express my gratitude: the late Giorgio Di Lecce (1953–2003), ethnomusicologist, musician, choreographer and dancer, professor of History of Dance at the University of Lecce and founder of and performer in the group *Arakne Mediterranea*; Franco Cassano, sociologist and philosopher and professor at the University of Bari; Giacomo Toriano, professor of Film/Documentary Direction at the Academy of Fine Arts in Lecce, musician, composer and co-founder of the group *La Mela d'Oro*; director Edoardo Winspeare; Francesco Faeta, visual anthropologist and professor at the University of

Messina; and Lia De Martino (Ernesto De Martino's daughter) founder of *Annoluce*, a cultural association interested in theoretical and applied research on popular traditions in Matera, for their interviews. I also wish to thank Sue Clayton, British feature film writer and director, program director of the MA Screen Writing for TV and Film in the Department of Media Arts at Royal Holloway, University of London; Dorothy Louise Zinn, anthropologist and professor at the University of Matera; Karen Lüdke, medical anthropologist and independent researcher in Lecce; Doriano Longo, musician and professor of Baroque Violin and Music at the Conservatory Tito Schipa in Lecce, artistic director, violin and tammorra player for and founder of the *Ensemble Terra d'Otranto*; Immacolata Giannuzzi, artistic director, singer and dancer, with her brother Luigi Giannuzzi, manager and player for the group *Arakne Mediterranea* in Martignano, for their suggestions on bibliographic references, film, documentary and photographic sources; and my brother Osvaldo Laviosa, musician and musicologist in Bari, violin and acoustic guitar player in the group *Arakne Mediterranea*, for helping me find rare documentaries and films as well as old publications on tarantism. I also wish to thank Stefania Massai, director of the Museo Nazionale delle Arti e Tradizioni Popolari (MNATP) in Rome for granting special permission to access their photographic and film archives. Special recognition and gratitude goes to Dr. Marisa Iori, officer of the audio-visual collection at MNATP, for her dedicated assistance in facilitating the consultation of their rare ethnographic photos and films, and for explaining the historical, aesthetic, and anthropological aspects of their resources. All these people's generous collaboration marked the inception of my research, academic writing, publication and divulgation of the representations of popular traditions in southern Italy. Interviews were video- recorded and transcribed with interviewees' formal permission. All translations of Italian citations and interviews are mine.

2 For example, the phenomenon of *argismo* practiced in the Italian island of Sardinia, and similar practices of music as medicine performed in Gypsy communities, Native American cultures, Latin America, India, the Middle East, North Africa, and other African countries, is widely studied in medical anthropology and musicology.

3 Salento, the extreme end of the southern-eastern Italian region Apulia.

4 St. Donatus is the protector of those affected by epilepsy and mental diseases. People go to the chapel of the saint in Montesano every year on August 6 and 7 to be healed.

5 In addition to this, the legend says that St. Paul, on his way to Damascus, was hit by the divine spur, causing a violent ecstatic crisis.

6 According to the legend, St. Paul became the patron saint of Galatina because he rewarded the man who had offered him hospitality

in Galatina, by giving therapeutic power to the water of his well, so whenever the sick drank the miraculous water and invoked the saint in the chapel, they would be healed from the bites of poisonous animals and insects.

7   Justus Friedrich Karl Hecker, born in Erfurt on January 5, 1795, studied Medicine at the University of Berlin where he taught History of Medicine from 1834 to 1850, when he died. His vast research on the history of epidemics produced his monograph *Die Tanzwuth, eine Volkskrankheit im Mittelalter* (1832). This book was translated into English and published in London in 1833; then into French and published in Paris in 1834; and finally into Italian and published with the title *La Danzimania-Malattia popolare del Medioevo*, by Ricordi e Compagno in Florence in 1838.

8   (*Chiunque fossse stato morsicato dal ragno velenoso, ovvero da uno scorpione, o credesse di essere stato morsicato, presentavasi ogni anno ovunque risonava l'allegra Tarantella. Quivi accorrevano in folla le donne curiose e contraevano la malattia non già del morso del ragno, ma del veleno morale, che esse evidentemente, succhiavano con gli occhi, e la cura dei tarantati divenne, a poco a poco, una vera Festa Popolare, che aspettavasi con la più viva impazienza.*) Primary source, Hecker, 1838: 60.

9   The *tarantella tarantina*, from Taranto is less famous than the *tarantella napoletana*, from Naples (De Simone 2001: 50).

10 Diego Carpitella's definition of *pizzica-pizzica* explains this kind of dance and music: "Apulian tarantella is a dance where the woman dances successively with two men (and vice versa) at the sound of a song played with a guitar, accordion, cupa-cupa, and tambourine. It is performed during local country feasts or for the music therapy of tarantism" (*Dizionario Enciclopedico della Musica e dei Musicisti*, Torino: UTET, 1983: 656). The areas where such dances are still prominent and preserved are Salento, the Taranto and Bari provinces, the Matera province and the Jonian area in the Basilicata region. Today the practice of the dances in their original version is almost completely extinct, as the repertoires recuperated through the testimony of the older generations are minimal and incomplete.

11 In the past, the dance involved invitation by using a handkerchief. Through the study of ethnographic video documentation of re-enactments of traditional dances, it was established that the *pizzica-pizzica* belongs to the large Apulia-Basilicata subgroup of the southern tarantella. The dance is performed in couples in the middle of a circle of spectators, players and dancers, consists of frontal, circular, round dancing with brief confidential approaches and tight turns.

12 According to German naturalist W. Katner, who took part in De Martino's expedition to the South in the 1960s, tarantella first appeared in

Taranto in the seventeenth century. Chopin, Liszt, Weber, and other composers used the rhythm of the dance in the form of a *perpetuum mobile*. The tarantella by Mendelssohn is the last movement of the symphony called "Italian."

13 The therapy also included the use of symbolic colors; in fact, sick people often gripped red ribbons or handkerchiefs in their hands and waved them. As Giorgio Di Lecce explains, "In the past, such ribbons, called *nzacareddhe* and representing the colors of the spiders, were used to adorn the icons and statues of saints during the local feasts and were blessed in churches. People tied them to their arms or around their foreheads for protection" (Interview with G. Di Lecce. Lecce, October 13, 2002).

14 Sometimes also a guitar player would join the band of musicians.

15 Giorgio Di Lecce explains that the music played to *scazzicare* (provoke or excite the tarantula) was called *pizzica-tarantata* by Luigi Stifani (Inchingolo 2003). Di Lecce also documents that one of the last testimony of *pizzica-tarantata* took place on June 29, 1993 with the final dancing of a woman who had performed such ritual for 20 years (1994: 181-186).

16 Galatina is at about 20 kilometers southeast of Lecce in Salento.

17 Ernesto De Martino, who was born in Naples in 1908 and died in Rome in 1965, was an anthropologist, ethnographer, musicologist, ethnomusicologist, philosopher, and engaged intellectual. He studied with Benedetto Croce and Adolfo Omodeo. He wrote about magic, shamanism, ethno-psychiatry, and southern Italian societies. He taught History of Religions at the University of Cagliari from 1959 until his death. De Martino went to Salento in 1959 with a team of psychiatrists, psychoanalysts, ethnomusicologists and anthropologists. *La Terra del Rimorso* was the result of their large survey work. The philosopher Benedetto Croce was De Martino's *mêtre à penser*, while Antonio Gramsci's notes on folklore were fundamental to the development of his thought. *La terra del rimorso*, a classic for university courses in anthropology in Italy, was reprinted in 1994, 1996, and 2002. Dorothy Louise Zinn translated and annotated De Martino's book *The Land of Remorse* (2005).

18 *La terra del rimorso*, Milano: Il Saggiatore, 1961, is considered a cult book.

19 De Martino's team comprised psychiatrists Giovanni Jervis and Letizia Comba, anthropologist Amalia Signorelli, ethnomusicologist Diego Carpitella, photographer Franco Pinna, social assistant Vittoria De Palma, and journalist Annabella Rossi, author of *Lettere da una tarantata* (1970) on the experiences of women affected by tarantism. De Martino's was the first research that conducted audio-photographic recording of tarantism. The result of this research was the production of the documentaries *Meloterapia*

del tarantismo, by Diego Carpitella, and *La Taranta,* by Gianfranco Mingozzi, shot in summer 1960, under De Martino's supervision.

20 The expression *Questione meridionale,* first used in 1873 in the Italian Parliament, after the 1861 national unification, refers to the discussion on the problems pertaining the socio-economic gap between southern regions (formerly under the Bourbon kingdom of two Sicilies) and the North, and includes the analysis of the political decisions made by the new ruling Savoy kingdom to overcome such differences. The topic has always been highly controversial, thus inspiring two schools of thought: one of *Risorgimento* matrix stating that differences in development between the North and the South were the result of pre-existing socio-economic conditions of inferiority of the South in comparison with the North; and the second of southerner matrix ascribing the responsibility of decline of the South to national unification and to the new Tuscan-Padanian governing classes' politics of exploitation and colonization of the South. In recent years, violent discussions have raged within the academic debate on the topic from representatives of both schools.

21 (*Il tarantismo è un fenomeno complesso i cui molteplici aspetti non si possono risolvere solo in termini psichiatrici.*)

22 De Martino's statement confirms that he was, as his daughter Lia describes him, "an extraordinary scholar. He tried to understand the needs and problems of the South not only as an anthropologist, but also as a human being in search of answers to the tragic living conditions of the people he met and interviewed. For these reasons, the historical and scientific value of his research and findings is still very current for his profound humanistic approach to the cultural phenomena that he investigated" (Interview with Lia De Martino. Matera June 19, 2006).

23 Published in 1920, Lawrence's novel *The Lost Girl* (written in 1912–1913) won the *James Tait Black Memorial Prize,* the only official literary honor he ever received. The novel tells the story of Alvina Houghton, a young woman suppressed by her conventional upper-class life in a mining town in the Midlands. When a group of Italian-theater artists come to her town, she meets a flamboyant Neapolitan musician, Ciccio, and rebels against the repressive life of a proper bourgeois woman. Alvina and Ciccio fall passionately in love, marry and flee to his native village in southern Italy. A few months later, with the start of First World War, Ciccio leaves to fight for his country against Austria, and Alvina is left alone. Sue Clayton writes, "Lawrence, who lived for many years in Italy, was probably aware of the symbolic significance of the southern Italian dances and music, as he makes frequent reference in the novel to the Orpheus myth—the woman being seduced out of a dark underworld by music, an energizing and life-giving force. An analysis of Lawrence's text would be relevant to assess whether the *pizzica/ tarantella* metaphor

could be used to explain how Alvina undergoes cathartic change, and becomes connected with the norms of the culture in this southern Italian mountain village." Clayton also points out that "Hélène Cixous' notion of women's 'writing from the body' corresponds to Lawrence's—and the dances'—sense of the female body as a site of meaning and catalyst for change." Further, Clayton makes the character Alvina use a quotation by Cixous that reads, "[she] alone desires and wishes to know from within, where she, the outcast, has never ceased to hear the resonance of fore-language" (e-mail correspondence with Sue Clayton, January 24, 2006).

24 This short film was an Academy Award nominee in 1963.
25 Photos in the Chapel of Sts. Peter and Paul on 28 June, 1954 in Galatina.
26 Photos on 29 June 1960 in Galatina, in June 1960 in Nardò and in Galatina, in 1976 Galatina, and in March and April 1963 in Ruffano.
27 Photos during the celebrations of the Sts. Peter and Paul on June 29, 1973, in Galatina.
28 Photos during the celebrations of Sts. Peter and Paul on June 29, 1970, in Galatina; Lello Mazzacane during the celebrations of Sts. Peter and Paul on June 29, 1971, in Galatina.
29 Complete collections of their extensive works are available at the MNATP in Rome.
30 An Italian-French production. Episodes are directed by Marco Ferreri, Piero Nelli, Nello Risi, Gianfranco Mingozzi, Giulio Macchi, Carlo Musso, Florestano Vancini, Giulio Questi, Gian Vittorio Baldi, Francesco Maselli, and Lorenza Mazzetti. Based on Gabriella Parca's book *Le italiane si confessano*, and supervised by Cesare Zavattini, this is a documentary, with non professional actors, inquiring about women's roles in a variety of love relationships.
31 Shot in Montesano in Salento during a popular feast, the documentary presents magic-religious rituals in part similar to those practiced for tarantism. During these rituals miraculous healings take place.
32 This RAI2 production comprises four episodes shot between 1976 and 1977 in the regions Campania, Basilicata, and Apulia.
33 Films shot in 1961–1962.
34 Co-directors: Maria Grazia Belmonti and Rony Daopoulo.
35 Screenplay written by Rina Durante, and soundtrack composed by Giacomo Toriano.
36 Giorgio Di Lecce co-authored the screenplay and acted as the protagonist of the documentary. Produced by ED. Bayerisch Rudfunk, München, for the German Television and broadcast in January 1993.
37 The documentary *Tarantule Antidoti e Follie* (2004) by Marina Gambini, is part of the TV program *Sulla via di Damasco*, Sfide del Terzo Millennio,

presented by Don Giovanni D'Ercole, and directed by Leandro Lucchetti. The videotape and homonymous CD were generously donated by Doriano Longo.

38 The following list of documentaries was kindly suggested by Karen Lüdtke: *La scherma di San Rocco* (1985) by Gigi Spedicato; *Viaggio a Galatina* (1993) by L. Santoro and R. Durante; *Stretti nello spazio senza tempo: viaggio nel tarantismo salentino* (1995) by F. Bevilacqua; *Me pizzica lu core* (2001) by M. Daudy; *La notte della taranta e dintorni* (2002–2003), *Ritorno a Kurumuny* (2003), *Ritratti di Salento* (2005) by P. Canizzaro; *I video 2002–2003* (2003) by Alla Bua; *Santu Roccu: la pizzica scherma* (2005) by M. Ferini; *Craj-Domani* (2005) by D. Marengo; and *Amateve!* (2006) by A. Gallone.

39 The film, written by Helen De Michiel and Richard Hoblock and starring Mira Sorvino, was shown at film festivals and on public broadcasting stations in the United States. Produced by Independent Television Service.

40 This film is a remake of Rina Durante's *Viaggio a Galatina*.

41 Screenplay by Sergio Tau, Raniero Di Giovanbattista, Francesco Vietri, and Gianfranco Mingozzi. Music by Nicola Piovani. Florinda Bolkan played the role of protagonist. Shot in Trani (Bari), in the space in front of the Cathedral and in the monastery Colonna, and in parts of the countryside of Ostuni (Brindisi).

42 (*Nun-exploitation all'italiana. E questo grazie soprattutto ad una regia quanto mai asciutta ed essenziale e ad una sceneggiatura capace di coniugare furore anticlericale e apologia filofemminista e libertaria.*)

43 Screenplay by Gabriella Rosaleva, Rina Durante, and Antonella Grassi. Shot in Bari, Manfredonia (Foggia), Carovigno (Brindisi), and Melendugno (Lecce). According to Giacomo Toriano, this film is a remake of *Viaggio a Galatina* (1993) by L. Santoro and R. Durante (Interview with Giacomo Toriano. Lecce August 9, 2006).

44 Rosaleva also directed two films on witchcraft and the Inquisition: *Il Processo di Caterina Ross* (1982), and *Sonata a Kreuzer* (1986).

45 (*Questo film fa parte di un certo cinema interessato a dare una rappresentazione distorta e una falsa celebrazione del tarantismo.*) E-mail correspondence with Francesco Faeta, February 4, 2006; and in conversations with Faeta at the *How to study the Souths? An International Workshop*, Camigliatello (Cosenza), June 25-30, 2006.

46 The film was recognized as a Wertwoll film by the German Ministry of Culture. It was awarded prizes for Best of the Fest at the Festival of Cinema in Edinburgh; Special Mention at the Festival of San Sebastian; Best First Film at the Festival of Annecy; Best Film at NICE in New York; The Youth Prize at the Festival Latinà in Paris; the Public Prize for Best Actor and Special Mention to the director at the Sulmona

Cinema Festival; and for Best Film at the Independent Cinema Festival in Arezzo.

47 Edoardo Winspeare (1965) was born in Klagenfurt, Austria. Of Anglo-Saxon aristocratic origin on his father's side, who is also of Spanish, French, Neapolitan and Sicilian origins, and a mother with Middle-European origins, partly Hungarian, Polish, Austrian and Belgian, he grew up and lives in Depressa, a town in Salento (Interview with Winspeare, Taranto, June 24, 2002). He studied Modern Literature in Florence and Cinema at the Munich Film School, which was founded by Wim Wenders. There, he worked as assistant to the director, cameraman, sound editor and technician. Between the late 1980s and the early 1990s, he traveled around the world working as a photographer and directing several documentaries: *I Tedeschi del Volga* (1989), *Il ghetto di Venezia* (1989), *L'ultimo Gattopardo* (1991), *San Paolo e la tarantola* (1991) co-directed with Stefanie Kremer-Koehler, and *I grandi direttori della fotografia: Luciano Tovoli* (1992). He also directed the short *A toilette's short story* (1989). For several years, he was active in the revival of Salento folk culture, researching local music and dance and organizing gatherings for young and old *pizzica* musicians. This experience led him to his debut, the long feature *Pizzicata* (1996), followed by *Sangue vivo* (2000), *Miracolo* (2003), and *La guerra privata del tenente Guillet* (2006) (Attolini et al. 2006: 124-128).

48 Directed and produced by Edoardo Winspeare for the Munich Film School where he studied.

49 Screenplay by E. Winspeare. Shot in Tricase, Presicce, Botrugno, Depressa, Galatina, the countryside of Salve, on the Otranto coast, and at Punta della Palascia. Soundtrack by *Officina Zoè*. Dialogues are in the Salentine dialect, subtitled in Italian.

50 Fabio Frascaro.

51 Cosimo Cinieri is the only professional actor in the film.

52 Chiara Torelli.

53 *Pizzica de core*, an expression coined by ethnomusicologist Giorgio di Lecce, refers to the *pizzica di corteggiamento*, courtship, which is usually danced in popular feasts, at weddings, baptisms, family reunions, and anniversaries. It is a fast-paced jumping dance between a man and a woman. It is danced by young and old people, as it is the expression of feelings of joy and love. This dance of enjoyment, sometimes with erotic allusions, is also called *pizzica-pizzica* or tarantella.

54 Practiced in the Lecce, Brindisi and Taranto provinces, this is a duel version of the *pizzica* and is performed on the nights of August 15-16, during St. Rocco's feast, at Torrepaduli, near Ruffano (Lecce). There are different ways of fencing and the fencers are often connected with the prison communities or the resident Gipsy Rom societies, wrote Antonio

Gramsci in his *Lettere dal carcere.* They mime the knife with the fingers, gestures are dictated by fencers' codes, and traditional symbolism is often difficult to interpret. This is an antagonistic dance between two men. In the past, duelers held knives, and their dance and challenging performances were accompanied by tambourine players and lasted all night long. Today the knives are replaced with the forefinger and the middle finger that hit the chest of the enemy, the performance is executed with agile and elegant dancing movements.

55 *Pizzica-tarantata* holds its origins in the ancient healing ritual of the *tarantati* performed in their homes and during their religious pilgrimage to the chapel of St. Paul in Galatina, on June 28-29.

56 (*Dichiarazione d'amore*). Interview with Edoardo Winspeare. Taranto, June 24, 2002.

57 (*A Winspeare bisogna riconoscere il merito di aver proposto la cultura salentina ad un pubblico internazionale. Tuttavia, il suo film è solo un'operazione romantica, e il racconto sembra essere la metafora della realtà, ma invece è un film di irrealtà. Il regista è proiezione di una falsa coscienza del fenomeno del tarantismo, il suo film è svuotato di contenuti ed è la negazione della componente propulsiva di una ricerca dei suoi valori arcaici.*) Interview with Giacomo Toriano. Lecce August 9, 2006.

58 Screenplay by E. Winspeare and Giorgia Di Cecere. Shot in Tricase, Alessano, Lecce and on the Salentine coast. The sound track was composed and played by the *Officina Zoè.* The film was considered of national and cultural interest. Dialogues are in Salentine dialect, subtitled in Italian. Appreciated by national and international critics, the film gives voice to the Salentine dialect and to the regional music. The film participated at the Sundance Film Festival, was awarded the New Directors Prize in Donostia-San Sebastian at the International Film Festival in Spain; the Antigone d'Or prize at the Festival International Cinema Mediterraneen Montpellier in France; and three prizes from Grolla d'Oro for Best Film, Best Music and Best Producer at the St. Vincent Festival in 2000 for Italian Cinema.

59 (*Un atto d'amore verso il Salento.*) Interview with Winspeare, 2002.

60 (*Una storia vera sulla devianza e sulla redenzione con personaggi veri, non realistici.*) "Pino Zimba has been a smuggler, a fruit vendor in his life, and the children in the film are his own. So I have written a story around him." (*Pino Zimba è stato un contrabbandiere, un fruttivendolo, e i bambini nel film sono i suoi figli. Così ho scritto una storia su di lui.*) Interview with Winspeare, 2002.

61 The players of *Officina Zoè* are also the protagonists of the film *Life Blood.*

62 The cigarettes smuggling, the illicit landing of the Albanian girl, the concert scenes, and the dramatic closing of the film.

63 Tambourines, tammorre, and drums.

64 *Sale* (traditional song and music by Cinzia Marzo, Donatello Pisanello and Ambrogio De Nicola). Salentine dialect: "Sale, vulia mangiare cent'anni sale / pè na donna ca me disse su dissapitu." English translation: "I would like to eat salt for a hundred years for a woman who said that I am insipid."

65 The jargon expression *sballo* interestingly refers to both the exhilarating effect of drugs and to the exalting atmosphere of a feast or party.

66 Examples of these groups are: the *Mau Mau* from Turin, the *Pitura Freska* from Venice, the *99 Posse* and the *Almamegretta* from Naples, and the *Agricantus* from Sicily. They represent new forms in the international market of the world-music, as their artistic expressions are characterized by the presence of non-western, mainstream musical elements.

67 The current situation started with older musicians, such as Luigi Stifani and the group *Gli Ucci* representatives of the first folk-revival in the 1980s. It is precisely the fusion of these musicians and new performers, like *Canzoniere di Terra d'Otranto*, that gave rise to a second Salentine artistic revival, thus generating a unique *musicscape* resulting from the cross-fertilization between the traditional musical experience of the 1970s, and the younger cultural needs of the 1990s. Another important factor has been the birth of the reggae-muffin group the *Sud Sound System*, whose music shows hybrid elements derived from metropolitan culture and rural traditions. This group sings in Salentine dialect and is the expression of the new youth culture. It is a new local version of the posse and hip hop that developed in Italy in the 1990s, starting from social centers, especially in Bologna, Naples and Rome and in universities occupied by students of the *Pantera* movement. ("*Pantera*" is the journalistic expression used to refer to the protest movement started by Italian university students in 1990. This name was chosen in reference to a panther that escaped from a private home at the beginning of 1990 and wandered in the Roman countryside). Major groups, claiming cultural re-appropriation, include: *Officina Zoè, Canzoniere Grecanico Salentino, Arakne Mediterranea, Banda Ionica, Nidi D'Arac, Aramirè,* and *Mascarimiri.* Therefore, hybridization became the modality to reclaim and restore a traditional patrimony, and to adapt it to new forms of cultural consumption.

68 The *neo-pizzica* is different in style and structure from the traditional version.

69 With non-professional actors and in the local dialects. For these reasons, Winsperare's films have been tentatively defined as expressions of the so called *neo*-neorealism cinematographic movement. However, his cinema is more interested in stories about contemporary society and culture, than in being *neorealist* or documentaristic.

70 Drug addiction, depression, stress, eating disorders, loneliness.
71 Promoted by the Union of Municipalities of the Grecia Salentina (for more details see note 68) and the Institute Diego Carpitella.
72 The celebrated series of concerts, unified under *La Notte della Taranta*, is held annually in mid-August in the nine towns of the Grecìa Selentina, as well as in Alessano and Cutrofiano, and culminate in the final mega-concert in Melpignano, with about 100,000 spectators every year. The main artistic contribution is provided by the *Orchestra Popolare Notte della Taranta* , conducted by Maestro, Mauro Pagani, who, since 2007 has substituted Maestro Ambrogio Sparagna. Singers and authors of international reputations such as Massimo Ranieri and Giuliano Sangiorgi (2007), Lucio Dalla and Carmen Consoli (2006), Francesco De Gregori and Piero Pelù (2005), Giovanni Lindo Ferretti, Franco Battiato, and Gianna Nannini (2004) have participated as guests to the final concert over the years. In 2003, Stewart Copeland, former percussionist of the group *Police*, was guest of honor and his spectacular performance was recorded on DVD.
73 Salentinità, refers to the spiritual, cultural and traditional characteristics of the region Salento and her people.
74 (*La neo-pizzica e il derivato concetto di salentinità sono solo prodotti di un fenomeno mistificatorio. Il tarantismo, come fenomeno antropologico, è collegato alla civiltà contadina arcaica, è l'espressione di una discontinuità psicologica, del rifiuto di un ordine e della ribellione verso l'ordine sociale; non è una forma di antagonismo politico. Queste varie forme di revivals della pizzica sono vuote e retoriche manifestazioni della cultura popolare, proprio come la pizza e il mandolino per Napoli, mentre La Notte della Taranta, simbolo di questa retorica, è semplicemente un espediente commerciale.*) Interview with Toriano, 2006.
75 (*Un sud che pensa il sud.*)
76 (*Il pensiero meridiano va inteso sia nel senso di avere un riguardo verso il Sud, sia nel senso di riguardare, cioè tornare a guardare il Sud.*) Interview with Franco Cassano. Bari June 19, 2003.
77 Interview with Di Lecce, 2002.
78 The fable of Arachne (also Arachné) is a late addition to Greek mythology, recorded in Ovid, Metamorphoses, Book 6: 5-54, 129-145; and mentioned in Virgil, Georgics: iv, 246. Arachne's name means spider (áñá÷íç). She was a fine weaver in Lydia (Asia Minor) who claimed that her skill was greater than Athena's, the goddess of weaving. Athena was angered by Arachne's pride, but gave the young woman a chance to redeem herself. Assuming the form of an old woman, she warned Arachne not to offend the gods. Arachne wished for a weaving contest, so she could prove her skill. Athena dropped her disguise and the contest began. Athena wove the scene of her victory over Poseidon that inspired

the people of Athens to name their city after her. Arachne's tapestry instead featured Zeus being unfaithful with Leda, Europa, and Danae. Even Athena admitted that Arachne's work was flawless, but was outraged at her disrespectful choice of subjects. Finally losing her temper, Athena destroyed her tapestry and loom, and struck Arachne on the head. Arachne realized her folly and was crushed with shame, so she ran off and hanged herself. Athena took pity on Arachne, sprinkling her with the juices of aconite that loosened the rope, which became a cobweb, while Arachne herself was changed into a spider.

79 "The *coreutico* element, from the Greek *orkesis* (orchestra comprising the choir and actors in the Greek tragedy) and *orò* (choreography), unifies music, singing and dance. *Arakne Mediterranea* represents the fusion of these three artistic elements" (Interview with Di Lecce, 2002).

80 "These were plain, white, and long clothes, on top of which peasant women put small decorative details, such as a colorful apron, or an embroidered blouse, for festive occasions, such as weddings and village feasts. Our dancers decorate their white costumes with red, green, and yellow ribbons, the colors of the tarantula spider" (Interview with Di Lecce, 2002).

81 (*Queste moderne ragazze salentine adattano e rappresentano le danze popolari dei loro antenati che si ballavano in campagna. Rappresentare è insieme 'essere' e 'presentare,' cioè queste artiste, nel momento in cui salgono sul palcoscenico, interpretano se stesse e anche la storia del Salento.*) Interview with Di Lecce, 2002.

82 Such as Pasquale Pericoli, Pietro Migali and Leonardo Leo.

83 Grìko or Grecanico, comprises a cluster of Greek dialects spoken in the Grecìa Salentina, Salentine Greece. The nine villages where such dialects are spoken are: Calimera, Corigliano d'Otranto, Castrignano dei Greci, Martano, Melpignano, Martignano, Soleto, Sternatia, and Zollino. This linguistic community is officially recognized and legally protected by the European Union as an ethnic group.

6

POPULAR CINEMA
AND VIOLENCE

The Western Genre

Flavia Brizio-Skov

The western, like gangster films, is the most endemic of American genres, because, as Cawelty argues, out of all the genres it is the only one that expresses the uniqueness of the American experience.[1] The conquest of the West was a determining factor in the creation of the American national identity. The Far West, which existed historically for a relatively brief period, was transformed into an archetype first by the travel diaries of explorers, dime novels, biographies, and autobiographies, then by novelists, photographers, artists, newspaper editors, politicians, popular legends, folklore, *chansons de geste* of storytellers, and, finally, the cinema.[2] The genre's popularity is demonstrated by the fact that between 1940 and the mid-1960s, westerns made up 30 percent of all American film production; in the mid-1970s, they began a phase of decline but, despite everything, remain the most important filmic genre of the twentieth century.[3]

The conquest of the West, or the pioneers' triumph over every kind of adversity, involves the battle between "civilization" and "savages," and in this conflict, the Indian is always destined to disappear. Just as violence is intrinsic and indispensable for the civilization of the frontier, so it is for the western; no cowboy film exists without a gunfight. The fundamental role of violence in the western has motivated us to want to analyze this essential component of the genre in order to emphasize how the history of scenic representation of violence goes hand in hand on one side with the history of the American censorship code and on the other with the historical, ideological and cultural changes of American society.

The western, like all popular culture genres, offers a "formula" that characterizes it, and this apparently restricted content made it an ideal vehicle for expressing the dominant ideology: the "regeneration through violence," which is the basis of the frontier as theorized by Turner in 1893, became a constant of a genre that, through different stories, reproduces itself *ad infinitum.*[4] Of course, great differences exist in the representation of violence within the genre, or between the classic western, the western *all'italiana*, and the post-western.[5] Therefore, our task is to analyze in detail and chronologically the changes that occurred within this cinematographic genre.

In 1903 the first western in the history of cinema, Edwin S. Porter's *The Great Train Robbery*, the story of an attack on a train by some bandits and their pursuit by law enforcers, the so-called posse, made its debut. The film ends with the surrounding of the bandits, the gunfight between the two groups, and the head bandit shooting toward the target (therefore, toward the viewers), something that caused a sensation in the public of the time. Already in its "infancy" the western genre exhibits, therefore, those characteristics that are intrinsic to the genre: action and violence. From 1903 until 1926, year in which *The Iron Horse*, John Ford's last silent film, appeared, the copious films of the horse opera dominated the screens with their simple formula of good vs. evil and damsel in distress,[6] a cinematographic world in which Tom Mix and others captured the viewer by mythologizing the past in a storyline of adventures and triumphs of justice. The western's fortunes, however, ceased with the economic crisis of the 1920s, but in 1930, with Raoul Walsh's *The Big Trail*, King Vidor's *Billy the Kid*, Wesley Ruggles' *Cimarron* (1931), Cecil B. DeMille's *The Plainsman* (1936), and, finally, John Ford's *Stagecoach* (1939), the western entered its "adult phase." If, as Kezich says, the stylistic and narrative simplicity of the horse opera films of the first 20 years of the 1900s was due to the fact that the language of cinema had not yet found its decisive elaboration, this elaboration

happened in the 1930s with the arrival of sound.[7] After the productive standstill due to the economic Great Depression of 1929,
the Hollywood industry recovered its rhythm, but the western had
changed. It presented motives that were more complex than those
of the horse opera; it concerned itself with the individual's relation
with the community, and class, race, and justice problems emerged.[8]
This western of the mature phase, which later became the critics'
classic western, dates from *Stagecoach* (1939) to Sam Peckinpah's
The Wild Bunch (1969).[9] The classic western maintained its violent
charge, elaborating in the filmic imaginary the problem of justice in a
still-lawless society, a naturally white society where redskins, outlaws,
corrupt sheriffs, dishonest bankers, railway owners, and overbearing
cattle barons alternate in the role of the "bad guys." At this point, let
us look at why violence is so intrinsic to the western genre.

Turner recognizes in the American frontier not only the coil of
the country's economic growth implicit in the wealth of uncontami-
nated resources, but also the moral regeneration of the settlers; the
famous phrase—"Go West, young man!"—exemplifies in a nutshell
the significance of the frontier, a land where not only the dreams of
personal success (the self-made man) can be realized, but also where
a better society can be born.[10] Therefore, the West is an incredible gift
that God gave to man as a second chance for a new life. Of course,
the fact that the untamed land is inhabited by men of another race
and culture does not factor into the equation. Even in the cinematographic West the Turnerian perspective lingers; with the exceptions
concerning the arrival of the post-western or the revisionist western,
the hero of the western always expresses the vision of the white man
of Anglo-Saxon origin. For him, the wilderness is a continent to conquer, to subdue—to civilize—in order to give rise to a new society
where everyone can live in peace and prosperity, and by "everyone,"
of course, one means only whites. And this is how the violence returns as an indispensible component: to conquest the virgin land one
must kill the Indians.[11] The "cowboy vs. Indian" dichotomy becomes
an axiom. That which on one hand appears as the story of the great
American epic, the glorious conquest of the West, on the other hand
appears as the story of Indian genocide. It follows that the frontier
myth is based at its origins on a concept of regeneration through

violence that later carries over to the cinematographic archetype. At an ideological level, the principle of regeneration through violence entails the justification of violence in the western. Since the western is offered as the incarnation of the myth of America's origins, it suggests that violence is a necessary phase of that process through which the American society was created and the democratic values were defended and asserted.[12] In fact, all the cinematography of the classic western, for almost 40 years, bases itself on the necessity and justification of violence.

It is not possible to evaluate all the filmic production of the classic period, but one can roughly identify the general dynamic that underlies the violence of the classic western or isolate a model from it. The western film is a type of collective dream of an ideal space in which justice triumphs at any price. The four terms that characterized the myth of the frontier—battle, success, progress, and democracy—are also the ideological components of the filmic production. The model of the classic western is always based on three entities: the hero, the community, and the "savages"/"bad guys."[13] Of course, the combinations vary and not all the components appear in every film. The hero with whom the viewer identifies is usually the protagonist who, confronted with a series of extreme situations, must make a decision. He must defend the caravan from the Indians, vindicate a wrong, fight a duel, etc., and he must use violence as the solution to the problem because the situation is such that he could not do otherwise. From this point-of-view, violence is justifiable; in a primitive world still without laws, the law of the "good man's" gun must prevail so that "tomorrow" civilization can prosper. The viewer, in fact, is almost never shocked by the violence in the classic western because the hero always kills for justifiable reasons, to save others or for the survival of the majority; only the "bad" kill for personal or utilitarian reasons, and, as a consequence, they deserve to be punished. In this filmic world, Indians do not kill for utilitarian reasons, but their presence itself threatens society because their existence hinders the "progress" of the white man. The fact that many classic westerns end with a final duel validates the moral integrity of the hero who postpones violence as long as possible. Indians, who, unlike the "bad men" can be killed at any moment, are the exception to this rule; they appear in the action scenes and not necessarily in the "crescendo" of the finale.[14] The two films that exemplarily embody the moral rectitude, the hero's ability of self-control in difficult situations, and the use of violence for the good of the community are *Shane* (1953) by George Stevens and Fred Zinnerman's 1952 film, *High Noon.*

Of course, a popular genre like the western defines itself through fixed formulas within which, however, the story, characters and setting can be manipulated in different ways. In order for a popular genre to remain vital, it must encourage artistic transformations that allow for a continuous evolution of the patterns. This depends on the artistic ability of the directors and all those involved in film production, or, more precisely, all those who shape the development and growth of the genre, but it also depends on cultural and ideological factors that influence the choices of the producers and the script decisions, and, ultimately, on the "taste" of the public.[15] From the 1940s until the 1960s, the western genre undergoes various evolutions, especially following the end of the Second World War, and often shows a hero who is about to become an anachronism with respect to his time. The hero, with his principles and his violence justified by the service to the community, is unable to integrate himself in it; his ability to kill relegates him to a marginal position, to a role of exclusion, his values do not have a place in the new society that he has helped create. This refers, for example, to Ford's *The Searchers* (1956) and *The Man Who Shot Liberty Valance* (1962), and Sam Peckinpah's *Ride the High Country* (1962), but there are many other films in which the hero, after having settled everything and having killed the "bad guys," leaves by horse and disappears in the prairie. The hero asserts his identity in the action, but the qualities that allow him to perpetrate violence seem to have become incompatible with the society in which he operates and for which he has operated. This is a sort of "twilight" thread that penetrates many postwar films. In these stories, on one hand one grieves the end of the heroes, but on the other hand, one justifies their "departure" precisely because the qualities of courage, extreme individualism, tenacity, use of violence—the qualities that the heroes share with the bad guys (with the difference that the former have a moral integrity that the latter lack)—cannot subsist in a society headed toward modernity. Therefore, the future of

American society is clearly that of James Stewart in the role of the lawyer Ransom Stoddard, promoter of civil values of law and order, and not that of John Wayne in the role of the cowboy/gunman Tom Doniphon.[16]

The fact that almost all the great directors tried their hand at the classic western genre, some setting new standards—thinking of John Ford, Anthony Mann, Delmer Daves, Budd Boetticher, Robert Aldrich, Henry Hathaway, Howard Hawks, William Wellman, Andrew V. MacLaglen, John Sturges, Henry King, John Huston, Raoul Walsh, and Sam Peckinpah—contributed to its popularity from the postwar until the 1960s. It is important, however, to keep in mind that other factors also contributed to the western's success.[17]

The way of representing violence goes hand in hand with the creation of the formal language of cinema, because the violence manifests itself with regard to filmic style. The fact that violence can be vividly represented on the screen and give the filmmaker the opportunity to manipulate the cinematic form to represent battles, massacres, and fights, saw to it that violence, from the beginning, would be an essential component of the seventh art. Of course, from the 1920s on there was a preoccupation with creating within the same film an equilibrium between violence and crimes, characters and situations represented in a way that the "good" counterbalanced the so-called "immoral actions." In this regard, the film industry, worried by the activity of various censor committees that were crusading against the "immorality" of cinema, created the Motion Picture Production Code in 1927. The Hays Code, as it was popularly known, went into effect in 1934 and ruled until 1968.[18] The history of American cinema is, in reality, also the history of this censorship code that the Hollywood industry imposed upon itself.[19]

For 34 years, the representation of filmic violence remained within the code's orders, but the directors, as remedy to these restrictions, devised a series of film techniques that are now part of the cinematic syntax worldwide.[20] According to the Code, the cinema had to offer an edifying and moral example of human life, avoiding violence, unbridled passions, sex, nudity, profanities, etc., and, in the event that crimes or abuses of power were represented, it was imperative to ensure that the "bad guys" were punished, or the film would be cut. From this the famous happy ending—and the consequent death of the bad men—of American cinema and of the western genre was born. And if it is undeniable that the western genre is the film genre that has suffered the least from the Code's cuts, unlike the criminal-gangster, horror, and science-fiction genres, its relative liberty is due to the fact that, despite representing many scenes of violence, such as fistfights, gunfights, killings with knives, arrows, whips, lynchings, hangings, etc., the story within which this violence is expressed is almost always morally irreproachable. One commits violence to defend oneself from Indians, to free hostages, to kill bandits, in sum, to defend oneself from the bad guys or to punish them. Even in regard to war films, the Code turned a blind eye, even in cases of brutality and torture, because the more the soldier's conditions appear horrible on the screen, the greater the value of he who heroically sacrifices his own life to defend his country seems. One sees this in the films on the Second World War against the Nazis and the Japanese, in which the filmic violence becomes an indirect form of propaganda. The same thing happens with the western. The hero's violence is the violence of the "just." The hero has his own moral integrity; he must defend the community, the caravan, vindicate an offence, a crime, his is the biblical law of "an eye for an eye, a tooth for a tooth." He, too, like the soldier, performs a painful, but necessary, duty.

Among the Code's restrictions there was also a ban on showing the effects of violence on the human being; these could be suggested through a particular cinematic syntax that could leave room for the reader's imagination, but they could never be directly shown. As a result, in all the western films of the period, after a tremendous fistfight that has completely destroyed a saloon, no one seems to have even a bruise and the characters hit by bullets graciously fold into themselves and, without a groan, fall out of the frame. The Code operates the "sanitation" of violence and, by showing it without consequences, pain, spasms, or cries, trivializes it and makes it acceptable to the audience that is never shocked, but can risk leaving with the belief that violence is not such a grave thing for those who receive it.

The other factor that contributed to the success of the classic western is of an ideological nature. As Slotkin argues, interest in the violence that characterized the western and the frontier myth made it so that this genre became the ideal vehicle through which the ideological concerns with the Cold War and growing postwar American imperialism could be played out on an imaginary level.[21] According to the critic, in the 1950s and 1960s, with the Korean War, the Vietnam War and the growing American involvement in the so-called Third World countries, the importance of the frontier myth gained new life, and, as a consequence, also the western. The "Indian wars," seen as a fight between white civilization and non-white primitive barbarians, become the metaphor for various military endeavors. America, champion of civilization, brings progress to people of other races who refuse to accept it, and, as a consequence, must be carried with violence on the path of progress; in short, the idea of "must kill them in order to save them," an idea that, translated into the filmic mythology of the western, translates into the story of the hero, champion of justice, who saves a recalcitrant community from the risk of falling into the hands of the token bad guy. The flexibility of the genre allows many ideologies to come into play, but the idea of the necessity of violence to bring order and progress in the world, a predominant concern of the American political program of the time, acquires prominence also on screen. Consider the possible parallelism between a film like *The Magnificent Seven* (1960) and the Korean War (1950-53), or between the Vietnam War (1959-75) and the multitude of westerns that tell of the endeavors of a *gringo* or a group of *gringos* "south of the Rio Grande," or in Mexico at the time of the Revolution.[22]

In 1967, Sergio Leone's *A Fistful of Dollars* (*Per un pugno di dollari,* 1964) appeared on the American screens; the film had an enormous public success, was made with a cost of 120 million lire, and earned $3.5 million in the American market. With this film and the following two of Leone's trilogy, *For a Few Dollars More* (*Per qualche dollaro in più,* 1965) and *The Good, the Bad and the Ugly* (*Il buono, il brutto e il cattivo,* 1966), the spaghetti western phenomenon began.[23] This "made in Italy" western, filmed in Spain, in the former Yugoslavia or in Ciociaria, revolutionized the classic genre. Despite the fact that Anglo-Saxon critics, with the exception of Christopher Frayling, did not concern themselves with the phenomenon for quite a while, spaghetti westerns make up a fundamental moment in the history of the genre and, indirectly, are also a cause of its decline, as we will see.[24] As previously discussed, in order for a cinematographic genre to remain vital, it must continuously reinvent its patterns within the formula that sustains it; the "spaghettis" fully accomplish this task because they regenerate the classic western.

If, in the collective dream of the classic western, justice always triumphs at any price, in the films from across the ocean, this does not happen. The four terms that characterized the frontier myth and the filmic production of the western—battle, success, progress, democracy—reduce to two, battle and success. Regeneration through violence does not occur; only violence that has as its goal the acquisition of money for personal reasons occurs. Violence is no longer used as a means to achieve justice and, therefore, a more just society and, in the end, the prosperity of the community. These new "heroes" move within a hostile world in which justice does not exist and the law of the strongest reigns. The protagonists destroy the "bad guys" in order to take possession of the loot or because they cannot stand bullies and so, by eliminating them, they incidentally perform a good service for the community. In this filmic jungle in which the rule is "to bully in order to not be bullied," the new "heroes" do not seem to concern themselves too much with justice; every means is licit to obtain what one wants. Violence is amplified and reaches points of brutality, and there are scenes of torture, the killing of children and women by the "bad men," and memorable bust-ups. The "hero" usually comes out crushed and almost at death's door, to then recover, helped by some Good Samaritan and, once recuperated, carry out his tremendous vendetta by killing all the present bad guys, who are always quite numerous. The resurgence of violence in terms that exceed the Hays Code is the obvious consequence of the fact that this production, not being American, was not concerned with the Code, and it is also due to the fact that the Code itself by the 1960s was often ignored in Hollywood too. The Code, in fact, would be replaced in 1968 with a more flexible system.[25]

Despite what has been stated above, the universe of the spaghetti western is not an amoral world, but rather the product of a different culture that sees reality with a loss of innocence as a result of various ideological and historical factors. In the 1960s, Italy goes from a backward and agricultural country to an industrialized country; it becomes a "modern" nation and culturally begins to free itself from a long-gone and heavy legacy. Therefore, this is a period of passage and great change in which the beginning of the crisis of ideologies that will bring terrorism in the following decade occurs. The western *all'italiana*, understood by the public and misunderstood by the critics, with its charge of iconoclastic violence is a typical product borne from the confusion and ideological turmoil of the 1960s, a filmic product that in its best outcome points out the ideological and moral confusion of a country that was passing from backward cultural, political and social values to the "modern" ones of an industrialized country. The spaghetti western is an emblematic parable of the ambiguity of the modern world, where justice does not always triumph, where money counts a lot, and where the "heroes" have weaknesses and virtues like common mortals.

After Auschwitz, Hiroshima, the Cold War, political assassinations, the various third-world revolutions and counter-revolutions, after the big and small imperialist and colonial wars, the dictatorships, after the difficult years of the postwar and reconstruction, it was no longer possible for Italian society, as it had in 1945, to believe in the "American dream" of the classic western. The accusation of cynicism and amorality from many critics toward the spaghetti western is false, the filmic stories of our anti-heroes reveal to the attentive observer that violence and injustice exist, that things don't always go as they should, that there is corruption in power, and that between Good and Evil there is not always a precise and clear differentiation. The shocking violence of the gunman, if compared with the violence of the historical events against which he sometimes clashes (the American Civil War, the arrival of the train system, the Mexican Revolution, etc.), becomes a trifle, its dishonesty a venial sin; deep down, what's wrong with stealing from those who steal, and killing the bad guys is not so bad when the actors of history, the people in power, commit continual massacres in the name of country, law, progress, and civilization. The Italian western deconstructs the genre, undermining the foundations on both an ideological and stylistic level.[26]

The classical model based on three entities—hero, community, savages/bad guys—is reduced to two: hero and bad guy. There is not even a shadow of "savages" in the spaghetti western (in this it was revisionist before its time). Of course, the consequences of the disappearance of the Indians are considerable; with them also the frontier myth of Turnerian memory disappears and, as a consequence, also the possibility of the "regeneration through violence." The Indians have always had in the classic western the function of "cementing" the community, which, in the face of danger, must unite in order to face the enemy. During the attack of the savages, the white people, in order to survive, must put aside all tensions, conflicts, and disagreements that exist in the community. The Indian attack functions as a catalyst; thanks to it—for example, in the case of *Stagecoach*—all the stagecoach travelers forget their social differences and their political divergences, and help each other in the extreme situation. The violence of the Indians "regenerates" the community, as all the characters, that is, all those who survive such violence, become better by discovering the noblest part of their "American identity" through the danger they experience.

With the disappearance of the Indians in the western *all'italiana*, in the role of the bad guys remain the white men who, in exchange, become more sadistic than the bad guys of the classic western. Even the "new heroes" change; they are bounty hunters, gunmen without a name, outlaws who dress strangely and live on the edge of society. The deconstruction of the genre is not limited to the stylistic level, or to the protagonist, who from the "immaculate" classic one becomes scruffy, but corrodes also the space in which these characters move. In this new western the deterritorialization of the Far West takes place. The landscape, a fundamental element of western cinematography, such as John Ford's Monument Valley, for example, becomes an arid, wild, inhospitable desert; the communities, when they appear, resemble ghost towns, and one is not surprised that the anti-hero wants to escape as soon as possible from such a corrupt and dangerous environment. In the case of the spaghetti westerns, therefore, one must speak of the "myth of the myth," since the genre thrives above all on the history of cinema, but the myth has lost its historical-ideological foundation on which the classic genre depended. The consequences of this removal are many and profound; as such, they end up bearing on the lifeblood of the American genre. It is exactly the liberation from the censor code restrictions and from the Turnerian myth that gives Leone and his followers the freedom to achieve new formal solutions and styles; I am referring above all to the representation of film violence. The Italian western inserts a different collective dream into the filmic space, deconstructs a myth, and substitutes it with an ironic, cunning, easy-going, and ultra-violent image of contemporary "reality."

The incredible public and box office success of many of these films in the American market show that also the audience was ready to receive them, that these films met with the taste of the overseas public. It becomes clear that even the American viewers did not have difficulty identifying with the "new heroes." At this point, one must infer that the flexibility of the western "formula" allows for a plurality of messages that in some way satisfy all the categories of both Italian and foreign audiences. The filmic text of the Italian western opens itself, in fact, to a hegemonic interpretation as celebration of the capitalistic individualism, to a revolutionary one, with the use of violence to strike against an unjust society, to a quasi-feminist one, with the refusal of the patriarchy, and finally to an escapist one, flight from the ordinary into a fantastic and more exciting world. It becomes evident that the moral reference of the Italian western is the real world of the time that, in a society like the one of the 1960s, both Italian and American viewers were the product of modernity. Beyond the music and the iconography, the ultra-violence of the gunman mirrors that of the contemporary world, and, therefore, paradoxically, the Italian western that thrives on the "myth of the myth" becomes, on a symbolic level, more "real" than the classic western that had claims of verisimilitude, in the sense that the filmic stories, in some way, could have "occurred" in the nation's past, a claim that the Italian western does not have. The Italian western has as a reference the contemporary society and its faults, represented with no pretenses of verisimilitude within the filmic space, while the classic western has as a reference the American history of the frontier in its epic form.[27]

The Italian western produced 462 films in a decade (1964–1974), and then disappeared from the screens, but its enormous popularity influenced greatly the American western production

With slow motion and intercutting, *The Wild Bunch* (1969) shows the
massacre of innocent people and outlaws perpetrated by the "law" at the
beginning of the movie.

of the following years. Leone's five westerns and the films of his
followers became a model. In 1969, in fact, Sam Peckinpah with
The Wild Bunch produced a western that revolutionized the history
of the American genre. Mindful of the spaghetti westerns' lessons,
Peckinpah built a film in which the equation battle/success/progress/
democracy is reduced to only one element, battle. His anti-heroes are
outlaws who move among diverse and disparate communities north
and south of the Rio Grande. The "wild bunch" ends up being the
best group of individuals among all the "groups" of the filmic story
because the law enforcers are a gang of renegades sponsored by the
railroad owners who, tired of the train robberies, do not seek justice,
but want the elimination of the outlaws at any cost, even at the cost
of killing innocent victims. In Mexico, where our anti-heroes are hiding, there are the counter-revolutionaries of General Mapache who
take advantage of and rob the country indiscriminately. So, in the
end, our bandits decide to resort to violence, the only art in which
they excel, and to die in a general massacre that ratifies not only their
end, but also the end of all the counter-revolutionary sadists. Their
death, incidentally, benefits also Mexican society by liberating the
campesinos from the general's counter-revolution and banditry. The
film opens with a carnage of civilians, started by law enforcement,
and concludes with a massacre in which blood flows in streams.

Peckinpah used a special editing technique to render what he himself calls the "stylization of violence," which, far from having to do

In the massacre at the end of *The Wild Bunch*, the bunch kills the entire army of Mapache's Federales and gets killed in the process.

with any form of "realism," had the function of "stylizing" violence and transforming it into a work of art, the art of filmic representation of violence. Peckinpah's idea was that television, with its savage images of war (Vietnam), massacres, civil violence, etc., had trivialized violence, inserting it among advertisements and serving it in such high doses that the public was becoming used to it as a "consumeristic show." Television had, according to Peckinpah, domesticated violence, had desensitized the public, by now immune to the effects of a reality saturated with killings. Raising the bar of violence through stylistic artifices, Peckinpah broke, or at least believed he did, the cycle of violence as a "consumeristic good." Breaking all the conventions and rules of the Hays Code, the director proposes to tear the public away from the addiction to violence, not only televised, but also that of the big screen, where for decades the "sterilization" of violence happened due to the Hays Code, which forced filmmakers to show killings without pain and without blood. Whether the American director succeeded in his intent is a problem that transcends the confines of our analysis; nevertheless, the representation of violence in the genre, after the Italian western and the big screen release of Peckinpah's 1969 film, changes face.

Starting with the lesson of the Japanese master Akira Kurosawa, Peckinpah films the action with more cameras, then includes slowed-down sequences between normal sequences in the film editing and alters the causal sequence and chronology of the framing of certain lines of action, displacing them in the montage. The result of this "aesthetic of violence" is the transformation of violence into show. The blood and deaths in this particular style shock the viewers, but at the same time, rivets them. So, paradoxically, the intention of making the spectator more conscious of the "violence" causes the opposite effect; the public becomes avid consumers of the impressive images of death created by this "aesthetic of violence."[28]

At this point one is inclined to ascertain that the future of the western genre is at a turning point. The American westerns produced after 1969 tend to differentiate themselves a lot from the classic western.[29] Once the frontier myth has been deconstructed through the alteration of the conditions on which it was based—battle, success, progress, democracy—and once the classic formula of the genre—hero, community, bad guys/savages—has changed, only two possibilities become available: Begin to revise history and what really happened in the conquest of the West, or start with the modifications to the formula used in the western *all'italiana* and by Peckinpah, and go beyond.

In the pro-Indian westerns of the 1950s, such as Delmer Daves's *Broken Arrow* (1950), Robert Aldrich's *Apache* (1954), Arnold Laven's *Geronimo* (1962), John Ford's *Cheyenne Autumn* (1964), and others, a re-evaluation of the Indians was attempted. However, it was done dividing them into good and bad or into those who were friends and those who were enemies of the white men. Also the white men were divided according to the same logic: those who were good and in favor of the Indians and those who were bad and against them. In so doing, the underlying historical-political problem was trivialized, reducing it to imponderable and inscrutable reasons (Good vs. Evil) over which man had little or no control, such as "there have always been good and bad, rich and poor, fortunate and unfortunate, etc.; therefore, there is nothing to do but submit to destiny." In addition, one notes that the Indians who were good helpers of the hero were almost always those who were in favor of integration and assimilation to the white man's society.[30]

In 1954 the U.S. Supreme Court, in the famous Brown vs. the Board of Education of Topeka, Kansas, case, decreed the end of segregation in public schools. In 1971, with the release of *Bury My Heart at Wounded Knee* and its extraordinary success, assisted by Marlon

Brando's refusal of the Oscar in 1973 in support of the rights of Native Americans, the thaw begins. The awareness of Indian genocide begins to gain ground in the American national conscience, the counter culture, the campaigns for civil rights of the various minority groups, and the protests against the Vietnam War contribute to creating the impression in many Americans that the Vietnam War was the replica of the old war against the Indians, with the difference that, this time, the Indians were winning. The revised western of the 1970s is, therefore, a film in which the figure of the "savage," the Indian, is no longer the "bad guy" to kill, but a victim of white men who hunt him because they want his land. The Indian becomes the "different one," the one marginalized by white society who often finds himself forced to use violence as a last resort against extinction.

In the revised westerns like *Tell Them Willy Boy is Here* (Abraham Polonsky, 1969), *Little Big Man* (Arthur Penn, 1970), *Soldier Blue* (Ralph Nelson, 1970), *Jeremiah Johnson* (Sidney Pollack, 1972), *A Man Called Horse* (Elliot Silverstein, 1970), *Dances with Wolves* (Kevin Costner, 1990), and *Geronimo* (Walter Hill, 1993), to name the most notable examples, the formula of the classic western is turned upside-down. The hero—sometimes, the heroine—always exists, but the four components of the frontier myth change, reducing to three: battle, success and/or failure.[31] The communities linger, but there are Indian communities that face the white ones. One sees this in the case of *Soldier Blue*, where two communities alternate, that of the soldiers and that of the Indians, with the cavalry in the role of the bad guys who exterminate the defenseless redskins. The violence of the Indians, if compared with that of the "law" or the establishment, is reduced to a desperate fight for survival. The impersonal violence typical of the classic western, with the assault on the stagecoach by the "savages," filmed in the distance, in the revised western becomes personal violence. The transformation is evident not only via the hand to hand combat between the Indians and the cavalry, but also because the Indians of the filmic story appear as a community with its laws, its leaders, its "heroes," and, therefore, as a different society than the white one, yet always equal to it. And even if it is undeniable that the abovementioned films, with the exception of *Geronimo*, have a white man as protagonist, it is also true that for a re-evaluation of

Jeremiah John-
son attacks and
kills single-handed
the war-party of
Crow Indians who
killed his family
(*Jeremiah Johnson*
(1972).

the Indian world implemented by whites, there needed to be a white hero who, for various reasons, "Indianized" himself and understood well the culture of the "different," so that, by being a part of both worlds, he could show how the white society was the source of many evils, among which the marked tendency toward racism and geno-cide of different races.

Along the same lines of *Soldier Blue,* one can include *Little Big Man* and *Dances with Wolves,* films that make up the fulcrum of a sub-genre that re-examines on screen for a change the history of the losing side (and not the history of the winners as in the classic west-ern) with a certain poetic license. Of course, in this view the famous "regeneration through violence" does not occur; violence remains an end in itself and always sanctions the "end" of the Indians. In this vein, a film like *Jeremiah Johnson* must position itself by straddling between the philo-Indian revision and the post-western (or the west-ern that brings forth the modifications of the formula started by the spaghetti westerns and *The Wild Bunch*). Here the re-evaluation of the "savage world" happens on diverse and unusual bases. Jeremiah Johnson (Robert Redford), the hero of the filmic story, battles for a long time against the Crow Indians in vindictive man to man battles, since they killed his Indian wife and adopted white son. The sav-ages on the other hand killed his family because he had led a cavalry squadron across a territory (a burial ground) which was sacred and inviolable to them. It was of little importance if Jeremiah, despite knowing the inviolability of the territory, infringed on the rule in order to save a group of pioneers trapped by snow on a mountainous pass. The white hero, in order to help the "civilization" of his compatriots, commits an offensive act against the Indian community in which he lives. Jeremiah, in addition, being a hunter who until this point had lived peacefully in the wilderness with the "savages," knows the laws of the Indian world. The violence of the Indians is the response to the white men's violence for not respecting the dead. From this fact a spiral of violence is unleashed and after awhile the hunter becomes a legend; the redskins build a sort of tomb-monument to him that celebrates his courage, his warrior ability, and recognize him as one of them so much that, in the end, both the hero and the Indian chief, Red Crow, come to a silent reconciliation that allows the hero to live in the Crows' wilderness, sanctioning the conclusion of the hostility between the two parties and sealing the definitive abandonment of white civilization by the protagonist.[32]

The novelty of the film is not only in the fact that the Crow Indians seem like a society superior to the white society, due to their self-sufficiency and ability to live in peace in the wilderness, while the white men are either only concerned with the war "of the moment" or remain trapped in the wilderness (as in the case of the pioneers who must be saved), but in the fact that the film closes with the cessation of violence, which, if continued, would lead to the extermination of one or both the sides involved. The refusal of the "regeneration of violence" that is the foundation of the film and the celebration of the importance of peaceful coexistence between the human beings who make up this earth, the pacifist message of the film, though finding validation in the political-social climate of the time and in the protests against the Vietnam War, nevertheless undermines the foundations of the frontier myth.[33]

The modifications brought about by the Italian westerns, *The Wild Bunch* and the Indian-revisionist westerns, lead to a turning point. On one side they regenerated the genre, but on the other they sanctioned its decline. The classic formula remains alive and kicking, but it bases itself on a myth whose validity the audience no longer recognizes, the consumer-viewer has changed in time. The "good against

In *The Missouri Breaks* (1976) the "regulator" (a splendid Marlon Brando) practices his killing techniques with an unusual weapon.

evil" equation no longer seduces the public as before; nobody believes that, thanks to violence, justice will prevail. In addition, the bad men are reduced to only the "white men," since the Indians are re-integrated among the "good guys." What options remain for the American western genre of the 1970s? The new western or post-western is forced to overturn the classic formula.[34]

From this new perspective, the new heroes become anti-heroes; yesterday they would have been included in the group of the bad guys, but today the point of view of the film is turned upside-down. The point of view becomes that of the outlaws (*The Wild Bunch*), the mercenaries (*The Professionals*),[35] the cattle stealers (*Missouri Breaks*), and the ex-killers (*Unforgiven*). The world is viewed from the eyes of the minorities, of the marginalized groups, and, as a result, the bad guys change; now they are the Pinkerton agents, the bounty hunters hired by cattle barons, the sheriffs who exercise the violent arm of the law, in short, the establishment that resorts to the use of violence apparently in the name of the law, but, in reality, because it wants to maintain power and economic profits.

In the post-western of the 1970s and beyond, one can no longer exercise violence in order to reach progress and civilization and, as a consequence, a more just society, but violence exists for reasons that hide different interests. "Success" follows "battle," but this usually only happens on a personal or group level and almost never extends to the entire society, nor does it lead to democracy or community progress. In the post-western world also the reasons for using violence become complicated. Just as the Indian-revisionist western looks at history in a new way, the post-western looks at society with a critical eye and re-reads the clichés of the formula in reverse. In a certain sense, this reading reveals itself, as in the case of the spaghetti western, to correspond more with the contemporary reality and also, paradoxically, seems to be closer to the reality of the Far West.

The historic West was a land in which not only the genocide of Indians occurred, but also where railway owners, capitalists without scruples, bankers, and corrupt politicians quarreled over enormous interests. Where Indians and settlers were often destroyed when they found themselves getting in the way of the so-called progress that was often synonymous with war between capital and workforce, with the punctual defeat of the workforce. In the Far West, every wave of civilization destroyed that which preceded it; the Indians and the trappers were destroyed by the advancement of farmers, these by the cattlemen, the small merchants by the advancement of big industry. Every group progressed at the other's expense.[36] The crude representation of an often-unjust world, in which the ones who win not only do write history, but also make laws in their favor, materializes in the post-western.

In order to demonstrate the above, let's take a film like Arthur Penn's 1976 *Missouri Breaks* which fits the profile of the post-western prototype. A young horse thief is captured by a rich cattleman, who, tired of losing his animals, hangs him without a trial. The other horse thieves (the anti-heroes), friends of the murdered, hang the cattleman's master mason. The cattleman hires a hit man (Marlon Brando as the "regulator") to kill the thieves. The bounty killer kills a second thief; in retaliation the surviving thieves steal the cattleman's horses. The killer sadistically kills all the remaining thieves except one (Jack Nicholson), who in turn takes revenge by murdering the killer and the cattleman. It is clear that the spiral of violence begins when he who holds power administers "justice" excessively and, therefore, unjustly.[37] The "law," or the cattleman and the community, responds to the robbery with an unusual violence. They not only hang the man guilty of the robbery without a trial, but they assume also the role of judges within the community in which they live and arrive

Ned Logan (Morgan Freeman) gets brutally whipped to death in *Unforgiven* (1992) by sheriff Little Bill (Gene Hackman).

to the point of giving the bounty killer, once hired, not the job of catching the guilty, but the license to kill them.[38] At the end of the spiral of violence, the two survivors, the cattleman's daughter and the surviving thief, decide not to continue on the "warpath" of their elders and put an end to the quarrel, choosing the option of a peaceful coexistence.

At this point, one wonders what of the frontier myth exists in a prototype film such as *Missouri Breaks*. The myth of the frontier, deprived of two terms, progress and democracy, reduces itself to battle and success, but the deconstruction of the classic western does not stop here. Arthur Penn's filmic text is self-reflexive; that is, it exhibits references to the "story of the West" in the dialogue of the characters, or, better, it exhibits awareness of belonging to a cinematographic genre that is based on fixed clichés originally derived from the elaboration of the Turnerian frontier myth and then translated into the filmic imaginary of the classic western, which, through irony, are overturned. While the classic genre based itself on the famous phrase, "Go West, young man," many characters of the film (the cattleman's daughter, a farmer, the protagonist/"hero" [Jack Nicholson]) do nothing but discuss how to get away from the Far West, how to go as far east as possible so to board a ship and never again see "these damned mountains."[39] Therefore, the self-reflectivity of the filmic text, combined with the condemnation of the "regeneration through violence" and the deconstruction, through irony, of the myth of the frontier make *Missouri Breaks* an exemplary post-western.

Clint Eastwood's *Unforgiven* (1992) holds another prominent position. The film is a sort of "encyclopedia" of the western genre because it questions two fundamental themes of the classic western: the use of violence and the concept of justice. The film does not limit itself to the "deconstruction" of the classic formula, but subverts it. First of all, the characters are an almost complete gallery of classic western types: the sheriff, the bounty hunter, the young aspiring gunman, the ex-outlaws, the friend of the hero, the saloon owner, the prostitutes, the cowboys, and the writer of dime novels. Nevertheless, a closer look reveals that the sheriff, Little Bill (Gene Hackman), is a sadist who administers "justice" with a whip; the bounty hunter, English Bob (Richard Harris), is a corrupt assassin who kills the Chinese for the railway owners; the main hero, William Munny (Clint Eastwood), is a reformed ex-outlaw who returns to become a ruthless killer; hero number two, Ned Logan (Morgan Freeman), is a reformed outlaw who is tortured and killed for a crime he did not commit; hero number three, Schofield Kid (Jaimz Woolvett), aspiring, near-sighted, and a bit of a braggart (boasting of shootings he never committed), is a "gunman" who, horrified by the violence, abandons the pistol forever; the saloon owner, Skinny (Anthony James), is an oppressive "capitalist" who boasts his ownership rights of prostitutes as if they were horses; the prostitutes are an exploited and badly treated minority; and the cowboys are a chauvinist bunch who react to any pressure with violence. The gallery of classic characters becomes problematic, since the only positive and innocent character in the story, the number two hero, Ned, is the only one punished and killed. This leaves the viewer with the impossibility of having the good guys to oppose the bad guys; in the film in fact there are only bad guys.[40]

Unforgiven should be considered a study of the western genre violence, since the entire filmic text consists of and progresses on through violence. The violence of the classic genre was born from the necessity to maintain "law and order," from the necessity to defend oneself from the bad guys, and from the necessity to take revenge on a crime suffered. In the western *all'italiana* another motive is added: violence for personal gain. In Eastwood's film, all the above types of violence appear. At the beginning of the film, violence is born from the fact that the prostitute Delilah laughs at the tininess of cowboy Quick Mike's masculine attributes. As a consequence, the man with the help of another cowboy, repeatedly slashes the young woman's face with a knife. But since cowboys, according to the sheriff, are outside of the "vagabond/outlaw/bad guy" category, but are just "local boys," working people who have simply committed a "foolish act," they are punished with a fine to pay in horses to the saloon owner, because the "damaged goods" belong to him. The act of violence is simply reduced to a loss of capital, since the slashed prostitute can no longer "produce." The second reason for violence comes from the fact that the prostitutes, offended by the umpteenth offense, decide to allocate $1,000 as bounty for whoever kills the two cowboys guilty of the violence (in reality only one is guilty, the other is an accessory to the offense). The three heroes, Ned, William Munny, and Schofield Kid, and English Bob, the professional gunman, arrive in Big Whiskey to kill the cowboys and obtain the bounty, but the sheriff, applying his version of "justice," tries to discourage the four bounty hunters by first beating up English Bob and then William Munny. It is clear that the four bounty hunters—the three heroes and English Bob—are led to violence for personal reasons: They want the thousand dollars of the bounty. The prostitutes on the other hand want the cowboys' death out of revenge, and the sheriff beats and kills because he takes joy from administering power in a personal and sadistic manner and also because he wants to maintain the status quo, or a city in which nobody, except him and his henchmen, can bear firearms. The violence acquires here, as in *Missouri Breaks*, a spiral character; from the slashing of Delilah (first scene of the film) comes the bounty on the head of the cowboys, then the beating of English Bob and Munny, and finally the killing (by Munny and Schofield Kid) of the two cowboys. This last event causes Ned's death and unleashes the final vendetta of Munny, who, in order to vindicate his friend's death, kills in cold blood five of the sheriff's deputies, the bordello owner, and Little Bill, in a crescendo of unusual violence; he finishes off two wounded deputies and Little Bill before exiting the saloon.

It could also be argued that Ned's unjust death is the occasion that allows Munny the opportunity to return to being the ruthless killer he once was. As Leighton Grist states, Munny, thanks to a triggering event (the killing of Ned), channels his repressed sexual energy (rejection of sex since the death of his wife) and his decade-old "abstinence" from violence and whiskey (due to the regenerating influence of his wife) into action, with all the possible psychological implications of the case. In the end, violence for our "hero" becomes a liberating act. Violence regenerates Munny, but, ironically, his regeneration does not bring about the progress of the community, but the degeneration of the hero who reverts to being the ruthless criminal he used to be. The success of the anti-hero does not imply at all the progress of the community, since he earns something from the violence only for himself. With the money from the bounty he moves to San Francisco and opens a profitable business. One could assume that with the disappearance of the sheriff, his henchmen and of the bordello owner, this community would be "liberated" from the exploitation/oppression in which it had fallen. However, the survivors of Munny's massacre (a few deputies) do not seem to be principled citizens and one can predict that things, unfortunately, will return as they were; another corrupt sheriff and another saloon owner will have the best. The violence in Eastwood's film does not have the "anarchic-revolutionary" charge of the Italian western, as in, for example, *A Fistful of Dollars* or *For a Few Dollars More*. In Leone's films, violence is a way to strike an unjust society. Here violence seems to be cyclical: in a cruel and unjust world, violence continues to reproduce itself because change is not possible; everything remains the same.[41]

Furthermore, all the groups of characters in *Unforgiven* react ruthlessly. In this filmic world there is no justice; in fact, the only one not guilty is killed. The title of the film is emblematic of a world, the Far West, where violence is the only solution to all problems, but where violence does not bring "justice" as in the classic western, because it is only destructive, and the "regeneration through violence" brings little-desired results, as in the case of Munny who returns to be a killer as before. Every social group in Big Whiskey justifies the use of violence by saying: "They had it coming," revealing a retribution logic in which the punishment exponentially exceeds the crime committed and revealing a logic according to which every group justifies its own (violent) actions by transferring the moral responsibility to the others, automatically liberating itself from any responsibility. This

Far West is a totally unbalanced world. One cannot even say that the violence in this filmic world is a prerogative of those who administer power nor is it a masculine prerogative as in the classic western. Here also the women (the prostitutes) pour into the vendetta all the resentment accumulated in the unending situation of exploitation and abuse in which they live. They end up resorting to the same methods employed by the system that oppresses them; even they operate within the same violent logic of the masculine power. Their choice is unreasonable, just as it had been unreasonable to slash the girl and to kill the cowboys; the violence amplifies the situations and does not regenerate anybody. Therefore the filmic message of *Unforgiven* has to be found in the representation of a patriarchal/dominant order that reacts violently to every little solicitation and in a group of oppressed minority, the prostitutes, for whom the sense of injustice results in seeking satisfaction using the same logic and the same methods of the masculine power. According to Grist, "Central to *Unforgiven*, then, is the implication that any consideration of America's social order must focus on the problem of violence. This has to be seen in the context of the climate of violence in contemporary America."[42]

Unforgiven is a filmic text that deconstructs violence, making it appear as it is: brutal and squalid. Delilah's slashed face, the painful death of the two cowboys, and their pleas to be spared are agonizing. The consequences of violence are felt also by those who commit it, not only by the victims. Ned is unable to shoot the cowboy and feels all the weight of the horror of killing. The Schofield boy is in shock after killing the cowboy; the irreversibility of the act committed follows him, distresses him, and for this he decides to abandon forever the gunman career. Only Munny, as a real "professional of violence," carries out his "mission" with determination and extreme efficiency.

Finally, it is important to emphasize that the film is also a text in which the frontier myth is personified in the character of Beauchamp, the dime novel writer. Beauchamp has written about English Bob's deeds in a small volume, entitled "The Duke of Death," that is often mentioned in the film. In this book, a certain duel that occurred between English Bob and another gunman, Corky Corcoran, is recounted. Little Bill, however, who happens to have been present when the event occurred seems to have a very different version of the event.[43] The sheriff makes Beauchamp and, indirectly, the viewer aware of the fact that things did not happen in the romantic and noble way proposed by the volume. Little Bill, in fact, cites the book, altering its title, and with disdain calls it "The Duck of Death," mocking English Bob and the mythology of the West at the same time. If *The Man Who Shot Liberty Valance* (1962) ended with the journalists who preferred to leave the myth intact and refused to say how things really went, opting to keep the legend alive, here one sees the process in reverse. If this revision, this critique of the frontier myth, on one side makes *Unforgiven* a post-western prototype, on the other side it carries on that process that, having begun in the 1960s with the western *all'italiana*, will lead to the decline of the genre in the 1980s.

A multitude of reasons for the end of the western have been formulated; in our opinion, the alteration of the classic formula and the various combinations of possibilities that materialize with the appearance of the Italian western on one hand enlivened the genre and on the other shortened its existence. While the classic western kept the formula intact and varied it within certain limits, the turnover carried out by the spaghetti western and by the post-western forced the formula into one-way street. The post-western, representing the community as a place in which the forces of "order" are more violent than the outlaws, reveals the ideological crisis, the distrust of the America's global omnipotence, and the loss of faith in its moral superiority. Once the western is deconstructed, the frontier myth's foundation undermined, the "regeneration through violence" negated, and the formula altered, it becomes difficult (even if it remains possible) to innocently return to presenting once again the model of the American dream/myth proposed by the classic western. After a diet of films by Leone, Peckinpah, and the other filmmakers who follow, the public's taste had changed; one could no longer represent Indians as bad guys; nobody believed anymore in the regenerating power of violence, the bad guys were often better than the good guys. The necessity for violence and its justification is negated by the post-western. At this point, working in the western genre means to act within an overturned formula that becomes constrictive; *déjà vu* is a constant threat. Of course, there are exceptions to the rule, films like Kevin Costner's *Dances with Wolves* received seven Oscars in 1991 and

Clint Eastwood's *Unforgiven* won four in 1993, but other films such as *Tombstone* (George Pan Cosmatos, 1993), *Wyatt Earp* (Lawrence Kasdan, 1994), *The Ballad of Little Jo* (Maggie Greenwald, 1993), and *Geronimo* (Walter Hill, 1994), do not attain similar success.

As Michael Coyne notes, during the climax of the classic western, between 1939 and 1941, Hollywood produced 30 major westerns (of high quality) that stand out from the 137 westerns of the whole production. American triumphantly came out of the Great Depression, and the western became the paradigm in which the victory of a nation against adversity was celebrated; the pioneers' epic could not be seen as anything, but representative of the community spirit.[44] A few years later, the analogy between "the cavalry is here" and the Anglo-Saxon victory over Nazi-Fascism at the end of the Second World War further consolidated, in the filmic imaginary and the viewers' conscience, the role of America "champion of the values of liberty and democracy" in the world. In 1946, Hollywood produced 38 westerns in only one year, and 82 million people went to the cinema every week. The western formula gave the possibility to articulate on the screen the problems that agitated American society. The western becomes a "vessel" that can contain many things: One can show a past that in reality speaks of the present, in which doubts, uncertainty, and ideals are explored, without, however, ever putting in doubt the underlying validity of these ideals. Unfortunately, the Cold War, the Vietnam War, and the events of the 1960s fuel a progressive and unstoppable ideological crisis. The western began its existence with optimism and simplicity, and in time it became more complex; it passed from a stereotyped formula to films that have nothing stereotyped. Each era has in some way soaked the filmic text with its ideology, its fears, its morality, and its vision of the world. As with all popular genres, the western changed over time in order to accommodate the demands of the public, its desires, and its concerns and, in the end, has created a filmic universe that subsists in its own world and has little or nothing in common with what actually happened in the frontier, but that succeeded in subjugating the imagination and the conscience of many generations of audience by representing on screen, not what had happened, but what could have happened or should have happened. Reduced to skin and bones, the formula on which the classic western is based is reduced to the battle between good guys and bad guys and the everlasting victory of the former; the complexity of the world is reduced to a simple dichotomy between white and black and, on a mental level, a moral exigency shared by most of humanity is satisfied. Of course, this battle between Good and Evil was overturned over time (after 1968); the viewer of the 1970s would like to believe in a world so elementary, but has by now irreparably lost his "innocence." The western created generations of outlaws, gunmen, and sheriffs, romanticizing them and transforming the "man with a gun" from an individual with moral doubts into a "hero" or an "anti-hero," transforming the violent actions into heroic actions, satisfying, in 90 minutes of filmic time, the demands of a viewer longing to see that which could/should have been, but wasn't. In the classic western, as Rita Parks maintains, the ideal substitutes the real. The fact that the events on the screen could have happened in the real world confirms in the viewer the belief that these "events" are possible, because, if theoretically these "deeds" could have happened, then it means that they could possibly happen.[45] In short, the western genre self-nourishes its own myth by itself. Nevertheless, despite its intrinsic regenerating power, the genre undergoes a strong downturn from the 1980s on.

Slotkin sees a strict correlation between the decline of the western genre and the end of the "frontier myth." According to the critic, the Vietnam War and the conflicts of the 1960s gave rise to great political and ideological crises that finished by fragmenting the political consensus on which the American society ran from 1945 on. A political and ideological crisis of such greatness involves, according to the scholar, a revision of the beliefs and, in particular, of the idea that the American political leadership and government in general might be made of trustworthy institutions, that the political discourse might give a reasonable and factual representation of events and that democracy might be a mechanism that articulates the desire of the people. When the American troops in Vietnam, instrument of a culture that sees violence as a means to achieve progress (the "regeneration through violence" of the Turnerian myth), fail, the moral regeneration does not happen; the "justification of violence" disappears and by consequence the process of demoralization that, from the military arena spills into to the political and social, is triggered. At the ideological level, the principle of regeneration through violence entails the justification of violence in the western mythology. Since the western is offered as the incarnation of the myth of the American origins, it suggests that violence is a necessary phase of that process through which American society was created and through which the democratic values were defended and made worthy. Since all the cinematography of the classic western for almost forty years is based on the necessity and justification of violence, once the myth is shattered, the ideological and cultural crisis of the nation begins.

The indestructible faith in a democracy as carrier of justice and progress which expresses the desire of the peoples through political action and the idea that every generation will do better and produce more than the preceeding one begins to waver. Doubts about the ability of the nation leadership to carry out deep analysis of problems, efficient laws and politics and even to present honest budgets are cast. The myth of the frontier succeeded in imagining a nation as a cultural community, and even if it was a myth created in exclusive terms regarding race and sex (only for whites of Anglo-Saxon origin), it nevertheless was successful; it had succeeded in building a national identity in which almost all whites could recognize themselves. If, as Slotkin maintains, the myth is "the language in which a society remembers its history," perhaps today there would be the need for a "new myth" that encompasses the new history and reflects the material changes that went through American society, its culture, and its politics, a myth that incorporates also the defeats and delusions accumulated from 1960 on. But myth is a complex phenomenon, in part linguistic, historical, and hegemonic, fruit of memories and beliefs, built by culture and conditioned by human factors, therefore, the incapacity of Hollywood to halt the decline of the western indicates the incapacity of the capitalistic system to create new myths and demonstrates that the ideological-cultural production is a phenomenon that often escapes hegemonic control.[46]

Although we agree with Slotkin in regard to the ideological crisis of the modern world, we would argue that the crisis of the western happened equally as a result of the revision of the formula used by the western *all'italiana* and the post-western. Once the myth of the frontier implicated in the cinematographic archetype is deconstructed, few roads opened for those who wished to venture into it. It became easier once the formula was stripped of its ideological and historical implications, to transfer it into the action genre. This is how, in an urban context, the battle between Good and Evil becomes the struggle between policeman/detective/hero and the criminals of the moment: drug traffickers, assassins, psychotics, terrorists etc. Violence exists in high doses, but once the concept of regeneration and progress linked to the frontier has disappeared, one witnesses a process of de-politicization and at the same time a reinforcement of the conservative concept of law and order; the war between Good and Evil no longer has any political connotation and returns to its simple and original moral structure (that of the horse opera). Often films are born which, if compared to the complexity of many major westerns, still seem to be minor, despite having great box-office success.

Considering the above, I would like to conclude by hypothesizing that, if a future for the western genre exists, this should be principally linked to the production of the post-western, that is, a film that embodies the crisis of the values of modern society, where the regeneration through violence is no longer possible because it is undermined by the ambiguity between Good and Evil and the injustice present in society. In such films, the identification with the heroes, fundamental for the filmic fruition, would not be a problem for the viewer, he, too, being a product of the same ideological crisis embodied by the protagonists.

NOTES

1   John J. Cawelty, *The Six-Gun Mystique Sequel*, Bowling Green, Bowling Green University Press, 1999: 1-56.
2   Rita Parks, *The Western Hero in Film and Television* (Ann Arbor, UMI Research Press, 1982): 22-77. As Frank Dobie maintains in regard to the myth of the West, "What happened doesn't matter. What people like to believe does" (63).
3   Gregory Desilet, *Our Faith in Evil*, Jefferson, McFarland & Company, 2006, in particular the chapter titled, "The Western as the American

Myth" (213-223). Of course, one does not want to insinuate that the western as a genre disappears; by "decline" one means that the high annual production of western films, which remains more or less constant between 1940 and 1975 (therefore, for a long period), dizzily declines from the end of the 1970s on. In 1946, Hollywood produced 32 westerns, in 1950 58, in 1961 16, in 1968 13, in 1976 26, in 1977 only six, from 1978 to1982 only four. See Michael Coyne, *The Crowded Prairie*, London, I.B.Tauris, 1997. In every chapter, proceeding chronologically from 1939 until 1976, the author offers precise dates on the production of westerns for every decade.

4   Frederick Jackson Turner, *The Frontier in American History,* New York, Holt, Reinhart and Winston, 1962.

5   By post-western we mean all the revisionist production that begins after Peckinpah's *The Wild Bunch*, 1969, that is, the philo-Indian westerns and those in which the "classic formula" is turned upside-down.

6   Tullio Kezich, *Il mito del Far West*, Roma, Bulzoni, 1975: 7-13 and 73-77. Kezich maintains that films like *The Plainsman, Cimarron,* and *Billy the Kid* already differentiate themselves from the horse operas. I agree with his opinion. These films appear on the screens at the beginning of the 1930s and, therefore, should be seen as a phase of transition of the genre, because the western is taking its first steps into sound, and the influence of silent film is still felt on the screen.

7   *Ibid.*: 76.

8   According to Rita Parks, the arrival of sound as "spoken" does not cause great modifications to the western genre, as the visual aspect, iconography, and action remain more important than the dialogue. However, what changes in the passage from silent to sound is the noise. The hoof beats of the horses, the shots, the jangle of the spurs, the crack of the whips etc., and the music of the soundtrack add a new dimension to this cinema that raises its level. Of course, in John Ford's films and in the major westerns, both the action and the characters acquire importance. In these westerns all the components are ably used in balance. In the classic western, not only the biographical-historical aspect but also the ironic, satirical, erotic and social one are developed, and the conflict between individual and community is dramatized. In the 1950s the western touches on more controversial issues, such as race and sex. The environment and the customs become more accurate, from the 1940s on, the *milieu* is reconstructed with more authenticity, but the characters, even when they are historical are translated into an amalgam that seems to have "historical authenticity," but in reality is created with the sole scope of producing an exciting story for the viewer, in order to enchant him. See the case of the multiple renditions of Jesse James. Cf. Rita Parks: 88-99.

9   There are many classifications of the western, see above all *The Six-Gun Mystique Sequel* by John J. Cawelty (Bowling Green, Bowling Green University Press, 1999), *The Crowded Prairie* by Michael Coyne (London, I.B.Tauris, 1997 and *Six-Gun and Society* by Will Wright (Berkeley, University of California Press, 1975). I consider the classic western period as being between 1939 (*Stagecoach*) and 1969 (*The Wild Bunch*), because after 1968 the influence of the spaghetti western started to be felt in the United States as Sergio Leone's *A Fistful of Dollars* appears on the American screen in 1967. The films of Sergio Leone and Peckinpah's *The Wild Bunch* by encompassing the lessons of the overseas cowboys, revolutionize the classic western so that the American genre changes and the road to the post-western gets paved.

10 The phrase is commonly attributed to Horace Greeley, famous editor of the New York Tribune (1840-70), but it appeared for the first time in another American newspaper, the Terre Haute Express, in 1815, in an article by John Soule.

11 There are exceptions to this rule. In the period of the classic western, films like Delmer Daves's *Broken Arrow* and Anthony Mann's *Devil's Doorway* in 1950, Andre De Toth's 1955 *The Indian Fighter,* Delmer Daves's 1956 *The Last Wagon*, Richard Brooks's *The Last Hunt* of the same year, Arnold Laven's 1962 *Geronimo*, and John Ford's 1964 *Cheyenne Autumn* are all pro-Indian films. Nevertheless, the perspective in general remains paternalistic: A white man seeks to make peace between the white men and the good Indians who are friends of the scout/hero in question, but they are threatened by corrupt white men and bad Indians. Exceptions seem to be the wonderful film by Anthony Mann, *Devil's Doorway* and the beautiful *The Last Wagon*, which narrates the story of a white man raised by the Comanches and completely "Indianized" who saves a few survivors of a wagon of pioneers killed by the Apaches. A complex film that dramatized racism, the necessity to make justice by oneself, the difference between the violence of the individual and the collective violence of war, a film that opens with the half-caste (Richard Widmark in grand form) who kills the men who killed his Indian wife. The pro-Indian tendency is overpowered by the majority of the classic westerns in which the Indians are always the enemies with instances, as in the case of Charles Marquis Warren's 1953 *Arrowhead,* of exacerbated "anti-Indianism."

12 Richard Slotkin, *Gunfighter Nation: The Myth of The Frontier in Twentieth-Century America*, New York, Atheneum, 1992. In this monumental volume that is the third of a series that examines the frontier myth in detail from the point of view of social history and cultural ideology, Slotkin takes into consideration the relationship between western cinema and the history of American political choices inspired by the fron-

tier myth. This is a fundamental work for understanding America and its culture. The other two volumes are *The Fatal Environment: The Myth of the Frontier in the Age of Industrialization*, 1800–1890 of 1985 and *Regeneration Through Violence: The Mythology of the American Frontier*, 1600–1860 of 1973.

13 For a definition of the formula, the characteristics of the western genre, the storylines, etc., see John Cawelti, *The Six-Gun Mystique Sequel* (Bowling Green, Bowling Green University Press, 1999): 1-64.

14 Of course, in many films, the attack of the Indians happens near the end of the film to give "our men" of the cavalry the means to arrive with trumpets and unsheathed swords. See, for example the splendid wagon attack sequence in John Ford's *Stagecoach*.

15 John G. Cawelty, *The Six-Gun Mystique Sequel* (89-112).

16 A film like John Ford's 1962 *The Man Who Shot Liberty Valence* is a complex work that, among other things, asks itself if American society rose thanks to an assassin, that is, thanks to the killing of Liberty Valence, justified by Tom Doniphon, who shoots him to save Stoddard. The discussion is complicated by the fact that at the end of the film, once it is discovered that Valence's real killer is not Stoddard but Tom, the journalists prefer to continue with the legend and brush aside the truth. There are many implications: Should we deduce that American history is all a bunch of lies, a history that refuses to tell how things really went, that prefers myth to reality, that at the foundation of a population's identity there is an unpunished homicide? At this point, the reader asks himself if Ford was indirectly speaking of the genocide of the Indians or if the assassin might be the scenic metaphor of that excessive—but necessary—violence that is at the foundation of the conquest of the West.

17 The films of the above directors who, according to the author of this essay, represent the best examples of the classic western are: Anthony Mann's *Winchester 73* (1950), *Bend of the River* (1952), *Naked Spur* (1953), *The Man From Laramie* (1955), *The Last Frontier* (1955), *Far Country* (1955), *Man of the West* (1958); Howard Hawks' *Red River* (1948), *Rio Bravo* (1959), *El Dorado* (1967); Budd Boetticher's *Seven Men from Now* (1956), *Decision at Sundown* (1957), *The Tall* (1957), *Ride Lonesome* (1959), *Comanche Station* (1960); Delmer Daves' *Broken Arrow* (1950), *Jubal* (1956), *The Last Wagon* (1956), *3:10 to Yuma* (1957); Henry King's *Jesse James* (1939), *The Gunfighter* (1950), *The Bravados* (1958); John Sturges' *Escape from Fort Bravo* (1953), *Backlash* (1956), *The Gunfight at the OK Corral* (1957), *The Law and Jake Wade* (1958), *The Magnificent Seven* (1960); Sam Peckinpah's *The Deadly Companions* (1961), *Ride the High Country* (1962), *Major Dundee* (1964). With *The Wild Bunch* (1969) Peckinpah inaugurates the post-western and therefore we will deal with this film and the following

when speaking of this period; Robert Aldrich's *Vera Cruz* (1954), *Apache* (1954), *The Last Sunset* (1961); Henry Hathaway's *North to Alaska* (1960), *The Sons of Katie Elder* (1965); William Wellman's *The Ox-Bow Incident* (1943), *Across the Wide Missouri* (1951), *Westward the Women* (1951); Andrew McLaglen's *McLintock* 1963, *Chisum* (1970), *Cahill* (1973); Allan Dwan's *Montana Belle* (1951), *Silver Lode* (1954), *The Restless Breed* (1957). There are 14 westerns by Ford, and I will not list them because they all are classics thanks to the psychological and social complexity of the filmic story, the stylistic poetics and the vastness of the themes (the cavalry, the Indians, the life in the fort, the community, the colonies, the pioneers' wagon trains etc.) make Ford the founding father of this cinematographic genre. There is also a group of baroque, wonderfully unusual, and innovative westerns such as *Duel in the Sun* by King Vidor (1948), *Rancho Notorius* by Fritz Lang (1952), and *Johnny Guitar* by Nicholas Ray (1954), in which sexual, puritan, repressive, and racist symbolism, violence, and drama masterfully mix. And, finally, there are some films like *The Westerner* by William Wyler (1940), *Destry Rides Again* by George Marshall (1939), *The Unforgiven* by John Huston (1960), *Gun Fury* (1953) and *Along the Great Divide* (1951) by Raould Walsh, *Firecreek* by Vincent McEveety (1967), *Badman's Territory* (1946) by Tim Whelan, *Hondo* by John Farrow (1953), and *The Outlaw* by Howard Hughes (1943), which deserve to be remembered.

18 In 1922, the Hollywood industry, in order to protect itself from the various boards of censors that grew like mushrooms in several American cities at the time, created the Motion Picture Producers and Distributors of America and named Will Hays its president. Hays introduced a series of rules that film-makers had to respect in order to placate the ire of the censors and the various temperance leagues, and also required Hollywood production houses (the studios) to submit summaries of the screenplays that they planned to make for assessment by the association. In 1927 Hays created a list of "taboo" arguments for cinema, which, if they were not respected, could cause cuts to the film or could even prevent the film from entering the distribution circuit. In 1934 the list became the Production Code, also called the Hays Code from the name of its author, and it remained in place for 34 years until 1968 (after 1968 the current Rating System begins). Nevertheless, starting from the mid-1960s directors tended to ignore the Hays Code, as in the case of Arthur Penn's *Bonnie and Clyde* (1967), Robert Aldrich's *The Dirty Dozen* (1967). Cf. Stephen Prince, *Classical Film Violence* (New Brunswick, Rutgers University Press, 2003): 87-251; *Screening Violence*, ed. Stephen Prince (New Brunswick, Rutgers University Press, 2000) and *Violence and American Cinema*, ed. J. David Slocum.

19 In 1968 the Production Code was replaced with the Code and Rating

Administration System (CARA), which is the system still in place today in the United States in spite of some minor modifications that occurred over the years. This system presupposes the division of the public into niches; that is, while television remains the mode of communication of the masses, films of the big screen are catalogued by G-M-R-X according to the "content": There are films appropriate for kids, those for adults, etc. In CARA, violence is catalogued by starting with the emotional relationship of the aggressor to the act represented on the screen. For example, a film in which the killer murders with pleasure will have a high rating (X), and it will be recommended for an adult-only audience; a film in which the detective is forced to kill in self-defense will have a lower rating that will allow a wider audience (teenagers, children, adults) to access the film, etc. Of course, CARA was instated because the cinematographic industry feared that the introduction of age strips for film access would be imposed in America as they were in Europe; if this had happened, many films would have been prohibited to teenagers who were among the major "consumers" of cinema in the 1960s. Cf. Stephen Prince, *Classical Film Violence* (New Brunswick, Rutgers University Press, 2003): 252-289.

20 On the history of violence in American cinema and on the existence of the Production Code, see the above-cited illuminating volume by Stephen Price on the American film censure and its consequences.

21 Richard Slotkin, *Gunfighter Nation*: 379-487.

22 I am referring, for example, to Charles Marquis Warren's 1953 *Arrowhead*, John Ford's 1956 *The Searchers*, Sam Peckinpah's 1965 *Sierra Charriba*, and Robert Aldrich's 1972 *Ulzana's Raid*, to cite only the most notable films.

23 For an exhaustive treatment of the spaghetti western phenomenon, see the chapter entitled "Dollars, Bullets, and Success: The Spaghetti Western Phenomenon."

24 By Christopher Frayling see *Something To Do With Death* (London: Faber and Faber, 2000) and *Spaghetti Westerns* (London, I.B.Tauris, 1998).

25 In 1967, Arthur Penn's *Bonnie and Clyde* was released, which, along with Robert Aldrich's *The Dirty Dozen* (1967), raised the coefficient of screen violence in open violation of the Hays Code. The enormous success of these two films and Penn's new contrived way of representing the killing of the two protagonists, Bonnie and Clyde, gave life to that "poetic of violence" that will be further taken advantage of and perfected by Sam Peckinpah in *The Wild Bunch*.

26 For the iconography of the anti-hero of the western *all'italiana*, see the chapter "Dollars, Bullets, and Success: The Spaghetti Western Phenomenon." The anti-hero is the opposite of the classic western hero; that one

was as neat and polished as this one is dirty and in bad condition, rides a donkey, and seems to have not shaven in weeks.

27 The spaghetti westerns, however, in their hyper-realism of violence, are less "real" than the classic westerns. That means that, while the violence in the latter is shown with parsimony—one witnesses the restraint from violence of the hero till the very end of the movie—in the western *all'italiana*, violence "happens" on the screen continuously. There are shootings, battles, fistfights every five minutes of scenic time. It follows that if people had been killed in the historical West as they were in the cinematographic world created by Leone and others, the Far West probably would have been depopulated within a decade. In the classic western, violence is essential; without violence, the western would not subsist because only horses, cowboys, and a panorama would exist, but the story would be missing. Nevertheless, violence is never administered in high doses as in the Italian westerns. The classic western seems to indicate that killing was something serious also in the Far West and that, even then, people, if they could, tried to be killed as little as possible. If one thinks of all the times in the classic western in which someone threatens another with a gun, but then puts it back into his sling, it becomes clear that often in these films the threat is more important than the action. This makes the classic western closer to the "real world of the West" than the spaghetti westerns. We should not forget that the Italian western, by substituting the model of the American dream with a super-violence of more modern origins, paradoxically, at the filmic metaphoric level, mirrors more realistically the modern world.

28 Cf. Stephen Prince, "The Aesthetic of Slow Motion Violence in the Films of Sam Peckinpah" (175-201) and "The Aesthetic of Ultraviolence" (79-174) in *Screening Violence*, ed. Stephen Prince (New Brunswick, Rutgers University Press, 2000).

29 There are many "classifications" of the western genre. The one of Will Wright, elaborated in *Six-Guns and Society-A structural Study of the Western* (Berkeley, University of California Press, 1975), remains fundamental still today for understanding the western, even if it differs from my classification of the classic western. Wright claims that the classic western lasts from the 1930s to the 1950s, then there was a wave of westerns based on the vendetta theme and finally in the 1960s and 1970s there came the films based on the "professionals of violence" (hired gunman, bounty killers, *desperados* etc). Although Wright's study is enlightening, I do not concur with his classification of westerns based on plot, it seems to me interesting, but reductive. Classifying all western films according to four models (classical theme, transition theme, vengeance theme, professional plot) does not seem a rational way to relate to a vast filmic production because there is the risk of forcing the categorization,

considering the infinite possible combinations of the formula. In addition, Wright does not include the Italian western and its influence on
American cinema in his equation.

30 A group of pro-Indian films, such as *Geronimo* and *Devil's Doorway,* are
exceptions because they consider the Indian society different, but equal
to the white one.

31 See the case of *Soldier Blue,* in which the heroine is a woman, but also
other films like *The Ballad of Little Jo* and the more commercial *The
Quick and the Dead.*

32 At the end of the film, Jeremiah lives in the Rocky Mountains as a "savage," in solitude, out in the open, at an altitude at which no white man,
except for another fellow mountain man who left behind civilization,
can survive. In the final scene, Jeremiah is surrounded by deep snow
and he does not know whether it is March or April. He has left white
society behind forever and his existence, like that of the Crow Indians,
is in perfect harmony with the natural world and the wilderness.

33 Of course, the classic western survives within the genre with good results, if one thinks, for example, of films like Tom Gries's *Will Penny*
(1968), Henry Hathaway's *True Grit* (1969), Howard Hawks's *Rio Lobo*
(1970), George Sherman's *Big Jake* (1971), Mark Rydell's *The Cowboys*
(1972), Andrew V. McLaglen's *Cahill* (1973), and Don Siegel's *The
Shootist* (1976). However, in these films revisionist cues appear here and
there, we encounter the introduction of an actor of color as the "right
hand" of the protagonist, or a hero who aids the badly-treated Indians
(usually from the innkeeper of the notorious saloon) or a daring and
outspoken female co-protagonist appears.

34 By post-western we mean all those westerns produced after 1969 (*The
Wild Bunch*) that do not specifically deal with Indians and that, therefore, are not Indian-revisionist, but nevertheless turn the formula upside-down, in that the bad guys of yesterday are the heroes of today.

35 Richard Brooks's *The Professionals* is a film from 1966, but it must be
considered an exception to the rule, since, although it appears two years
before *The Wild Bunch,* it anticipates the theme with its "professionals of
violence" who are hired by a rich Yankee to bring back his wife, whom
he says was kidnapped by a Mexican revolutionary. When they realize
that they have been duped, they rally on the wife's and revolutionaries'
side and renounce the bounty. It is a rebellious and subversive film like
Peckinpah's *The Wild Bunch*

36 Cf. Cawelti, *The Six-Gun Mystique Sequel,* op. cit., pp. 1-89.

37 Note that Marlon Brando in the role of the "regulator" splendidly embodies the "professional," the one who, once hired, carries out the job
(even if he is not paid) out of professional honor, who does his work
with art and creativity; in fact, he kills the robbers in a talented manner,

disguising himself, singing. In short, he kills for the love of the hunt, for
the joy of killing. This hit man is not far in his use of ultra-violence and
sadism from the psychopathic killer of many thrillers.

38 In *Jeremiah Johnson*, the spiral of violence begins because the hero, in
order to help the white men, infringes on Indian law. In *Missouri Breaks*
it is the law that starts the sequence of violence.

39 The dialogues of the film are clever in representing the Far West as a land
where only grass and nature exist, where justice is brief, and where life
is boring. Jane, the daughter of the cattleman, expresses herself always
in these terms, but also other characters share her views. For example,
see the impostor who during the trial calls himself "The Lonesome Kid"
and poses as a first-class outlaw à la Billy the Kid; see Jack Nicholson
in the role of Tom Logan, head of the robbers and anti-hero of the
film, who, hijacking a train (without using any violence, but quite in-
expertly), jokes about Jesse James and his exploits; see the farmer (who
buys stolen horses from one of the robbers) who hopes to make enough
money to allow his son to become a merchant so that the son of his son
can go to Rhode Island, that is, go as far as possible from the Far West.
In short, the Frontier myth is continually demythologized.

40 One could argue that the young aspiring gunman (Schofield Kid) in
reality redeems himself at the end of the film, abandoning the gunman career. Nevertheless, his surrender happens only after the murder
of Quick Mike, the cowboy guilty of slashing Delilah. Therefore, even
he, by punishing the cowboy with a sentence much greater than the
crime, commits an unjust act; moreover, when the murder of the cowboy happens, young Kid's motivation is only money, because the three
heroes know that the prostitute was not cut to pieces (as they errone-
ously believe at the beginning of the film when they accept the bounty
job). Without doubt, the young man's refusal of violence opens a spiral
of light for a future in which society can be more just.

41 In my opinion, the fact that Munny, after carrying out his vendetta,
leaves the saloon and threatens to return to make a massacre if the citizens of Big Whiskey do not bury Ned (exposed in a coffin outside the
saloon) and do not quit cutting prostitutes, does not seem to be a warning that encourages or contemplates a future change in the community,
but rather an act that confirms Munny's awareness. It seems that the
"hero" knows that this community is rotten and, therefore, only with
extreme threats and only for a little time he can attain some results. In
short, the logic of violence will continue to dominate.

42 See Leighton Grist's article, "Unforgiven," found in the volume *The
Book of Westerns*, edited by Ian Cameron and Douglas Pye (New York,
Continuum, 1996): 297.

43 As Leighton Grist notes in her article "Unforgiven" (see note 42), the

story of the duel between English Bob and Corky Corcoran narrated by Little Bill as proof of what "really happened" raises the problem of the relationship between violence and repression of sexual energy from which all the "true" gunmen, Little Bill, William Munny, and English Bob, suffer. See also the gun as a phallic symbol in the case of Corky Corcoran, called "Two Pistols," on account of a sexual member longer than the barrel of his Colt; see the pistol with the bent barrel given by the sheriff to English Bob before expelling him from the town; see the fact that both Little Bill and Munny do not seem to have a sex life, they are men who are fully "realized" only through violence; see the phrase of Munny who, facing Beauchamp's stupor, after the slaughter in the saloon, responds, "When it comes to killing, I have always been lucky," showing that he has an innate propensity for violence. For a treatment of Freudian symbols in the film, the pistol as a phallic symbol, etc, see Grist's article: 297-301.

44 Michael Coyne, *The Crowded Prairie: American National Identity in the Hollywood Western* (London, I.B.Tauris, 1997): 16-83.

45 *Ibid.*: 52-77.

46 Richard Slotkin, *Gunfighter Nation* (347-660).

7

WOMEN'S DRAMA, MEN'S BUSINESS*

Sexual Violence Against Women in Italian Cinema and Media[1]

Flavia Laviosa

Introduction

Sociologist Mary White Stewart explains that during the 1970s and 1980s political debate focused on the need to characterize rape as assault and as distinct from sex, so that the role of physical and psychological coercion was made evident. Rape, as feminists argued, was about power and was in fact described as an attack on a person's body, identity and soul, an assertion of power, a reenactment of oppression of an individual, coupled with a culturally approved justification for such subjugation. Furthermore, "sex was defined as rape when it was unwelcome, forced and imposed" (White Stewart 2002: 157). According to White Stewart, "to insist that rape is about power, not sex, demanded that the focus shifted from the woman's body, or a woman as seductress, or woman as doing something to ask for sexual violation, to a man's behavior. Men's behavior was clearly defined as being driven by the need to control, own, oppress, or punish rather than by sexual need or animal lust or desire" (White Stewart 2002: 158). Nonetheless, the writer argues that "although rape is not sex,

*Dedicated to Ann and Eli Germanovich

it is about sex" (White Stewart 2002: 158) because women's genitals and mouths are sexually violated by men against their will. She explains further that rape is rooted in a socioculturally defined relationship between sex, gender and power and is a specific expression of male dominance as a violation and humiliation of a woman's sexual self.

Mary Robinson, United Nations High Commissioner for Human Rights (1997–2002), reported that

> in 1992, the U.N. Committee on the Elimination of Discrimination Against Women (CEDAW) formally included gender-based violence under gender-based discrimination.[2] The process of anchoring the issue of violence against women firmly on the international agenda culminated in the adoption, without a vote, of resolution 48/104 by the General Assembly on December 20, 1993, entitled the "Declaration on the Elimination of Violence Against Women" (Robinson 2004: 162).

Two years later, at the end of the Fourth World Conference on Women held in China in 1995, the vast majority of nations adopted the Beijing Declaration and Platform of Action. This international document indisputably stated that women's rights were human rights.

In line with growing international awareness and increasingly gender-sensitive legislation, the passing of Law 66 against Sexual Violence in 1996[3] marked a major legislative victory in Italy. After 20 years of political debate[4] and feminist battles, a legal consensus was reached on a revised definition of the philosophical and ethical nature of rape. In article 519 of the previous legislation, the 1931 Rocco Penal Code, sexual violence had been described as an offense against the theoretical concept of morality and the abstract principle of public decorum; therefore, there was no human victim and the assailant could avoid imprisonment by simply paying a fine. The permissive attitude towards sexual abusers enacted by the previous legislation was overthrown by Law 66. Sexual violence was finally recognized as a crime against a person's dignity and integrity, and subsequently, the judicial system sought to enforce more severe punishments.

The purpose of this chapter is multifaceted, as it attempts to bring together several aspects—legal, political, cultural, sociological and psychological—of sexual violence against women in Italy. Secondly, it gives an overview and in-depth analysis of cinematic and theatrical representations of rape against women, and how this crime has been handled by the media, specifically in the following texts, discussed in chronological order: the two versions of the film *Two Women* (*La ciociara,* De Sica, 1960, and *La ciociara,* Dino Risi, 1989); the feature *The Most Beautiful Wife* (*La sposa più bella,* Damiani, 1970); the theater play *The Rape* (*Lo Stupro,* Rame, 1975); media coverage of Circeo Massacre (1975); the documentary *Trial for Rape* (*Processo per stupro,* Dordi, 1979); the feature *The Pack* (*Il branco,* Marco Risi, 1994); and the film *The Wedding Dress* (*Il vestito da sposa,* Infascelli, 2003). Lastly, this essay explores how Italian institutions, the legal system, and women's organizations have dealt with this sociological phenomenon and epidemic criminal behavior.

Two Women: From Novel to Fiction

Several filmmakers have explored the subject of rape and represented it in a variety of sociocultural, political, historical, geographical and gendered contexts in Italian cinema. One of the first images of gang-rape is dramatically portrayed in the film *Two Women* (1960), Vittorio De Sica's adaptation of Alberto Moravia's eponymous 1957 novel. The screenplay was penned by Cesare Zavattini. Equally compelling is Dino Risi's 1989 television remake,[5] which kept the original title *La ciociara.* It is the story of a widow, Cesira, who lives with her teenage daughter Rosetta in Rome, struggling with the fears and dangers of the Second World War. When their safety is threatened by the frequent bombings, Cesira decides to pack their belongings and flee with her daughter to the mountain retreat where she was born.

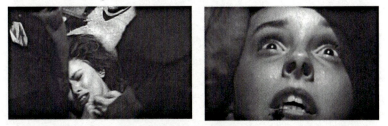

Cesira (left) and Rosetta are shown in closeups as they are raped in De Sica's *Two Women* (1960).

Rosetta lies on the ground after being raped in Dino Risi's *Two Women*.

When, in 1944, the Allies advance against a desperate German resistance, the two protagonists set off back to Rome. During their long journey, they see French African troops roaming the country roads in Jeeps. Exhausted by the long walk, the women seek shelter from the heat in the ruins of an abandoned church in a deserted village. Moroccan soldiers follow them, violently separate mother and daughter and assault them. In both De Sica's and Risi's productions, the two rape scenes mark a climatic moment of emotional intensity in the story. In both films the repeated sexual violence against the two women is symbolically set in a devastated church, against the backdrop of a demolished altar, on broken wooden pews. The rapes are represented through extreme close-ups of Cesira's and Rosetta's terrified faces, metaphorically inundated by a blinding beam of light, thus strikingly underscoring the wartime moral annihilation desecrating the destroyed place of worship.

In reference to De Sica's *Two Women*, Ellen Nerenberg explains that, "Out of a sense of cinematic decorum, the camera moves from a distance that would have shown the body entire [...] to a medium distance at body level where the rapes are certain, but not displayed on screen" (Nerenberg 2004: 88). Both directors' stylized illustrations of the scenes of sexual assault express the intensity of the drama by keeping the physical violence off screen, while focusing on the psychological aftermath of the trauma on Rosetta.

The Most Beautiful Wife: From Reality to Docu-film
Another important film discussing sexual violence against women is

Damiano Damiani's *The Most Beautiful Wife*[6] (1970), a socially committed feature denouncing the crime of rape. The film's subject is
based on the real life story of Franca Viola, a Sicilian girl who refused
her rapist's offer of marriage in order to restore her honor and avoid
his being incriminated for sexual violence. On December 26, 1965,
in Alcamo, Sicily, 17-year-old Viola was kidnapped by Filippo Melodia, a rejected suitor, with the help of 12 male friends. She was raped,
kept hidden and isolated for eight days in a countryside shack.[7] According to the moral values and cultural norms of the time, a girl
who was no longer a virgin could marry her rapist and thus restore
her and her family's honor, or remain single and be dishonored for
the rest of her life. These moral codes were justified and protected
by the Italian law. In fact, article 544 of the 1931 Rocco Penal Code
admitted the so-called *matrimonio riparatore* (shotgun marriage), because sexual violence was legally defined as an offence against morality, not against a person. According to this article, a man accused of
the crime of sexual violence, even against a minor, could redeem his
crime by marrying the victim.

Contrary to the usual custom, Franca Viola did not accept the
compromise of a shotgun marriage. Her father, approached by in-
formers during the kidnapping, pretended to agree to the marriage,
while preparing a trap in collaboration with the Alcamo police. Soon
after the event, the Viola family, which had not abided to local cultural rules, was subjected to frequent acts of intimidation. The case
immediately generated a heated national debate and became the object of numerous parliamentary debates. During the trial, the assailant Melodia's lawyer tried in vain to disgrace Viola, stating that she
had agreed to the *fuitina*—the traditional escape for love, in order
to obtain her father's approval for a shotgun marriage, a common
practice in those days. However, Melodia was sentenced to 11 years
of imprisonment[8] and heavy punishments were also inflicted upon
his accomplices. Journalist Liliana Madeo remembers, "Franca Viola
represents a milestone in the very long history of the relationship between women in Sicily and law, women and men, sex and traditions.
Her story is a light burning in deep darkness"[9] (Mancini 2006).
Subsequently, Viola[10] became a symbol of freedom and dignity in
Sicily for women who, after her, were victims of similar assaults

and who, inspired by her example, had the courage to resist a shotgun marriage. Years later, in 1981, article 544 of the Penal Code was abrogated and replaced with article 1 of Law 422,[11] which abolished the possibility of redeeming a crime of sexual violence through subsequent marriage.

Lo stupro: From Reality to Drama

The nature of gang-rape, as one form of this sexual crime, is politically denounced and graphically portrayed in the dramatic monologue and theater piece *The Rape*[12] (1975), written and performed by theater writer and actress Franca Rame. In this autobiographical text, Rame relates, from a victim's perspective, the horrific events surrounding her abduction, rape and torture at the hands of four men in the back of a van.[13] On March 9, 1973, while on her way home, Rame was kidnapped in Via Nirone in Milan. She was raped by a group of neo-fascists as punishment for her feminist and left-wing political militancy, which she shared with her husband, writer, director and theater performer Dario Fo,[14] winner of the 1997 Nobel Prize for Literature.[15] Two years after this traumatic episode, she wrote the monologue highlighting the violence inflicted on her body: cigarettes stubbed out on her breasts and face, cuts to her skin with razor blades leaving a 20 centimeter-long gash, knife slashes across her cheekbones, along with repeated insults and orders, such as "come on bitch, make me come."[16] Rame was subjected to profound repeated sexual violence perpetrated by right-wing extremists and then abandoned, bleeding, at the roadside. This act of intimidation was the culmination of a series of politically motivated threats against her and Fo's lives.[17] Rame's rape, with its heavy ideological connotations and political implications, was defined as *stupro di stato* (state rape.) The 25-year statute of limitations in the Franca Rame case expired on February 3, 1998.

Wearing tight dark pants and a large sweater, Rame performs semi-prone on a table. As she mimes the victim's confinement and subjugation to her invisible aggressors' violence, she recites her monologue and dramatizes the various moments of the assault. Elin Diamond writes, "Rame demonstrates that the body cannot signify its brutalization: No writhing, flinching, or screaming can convey the horror of acute physical pain and the humiliation that feels, as she puts it, like someone had spit in her mind" (1988: 104). At the end of the performance, her wounded body on the stage, as the object of the dark narrative, succeeds in handing over the pain to the audience.

The Circeo Massacre: From Life Drama to Television

Another sensational episode of brutal sexual violence that did not become subject of a cinematic or theatrical representation, but did receive wide media coverage and shook the Italian public was the unforgettable and terrifying "Circeo Massacre." On September 29, 1975, two working-class girls from the outskirts of Rome, 16-year-old Donatella Colasanti and 19-year-old Maria Rosaria Lopez, accepted an invitation to a party from three well-off young men, Andrea Ghira, Giovanni Guido and Angelo Izzo, who they had met in a bar a few days earlier. The men instead took the girls to Ghira's abandoned villa in the town of San Felice Circeo where they repeatedly raped, beat and tortured the girls for two days. In the evenings, Donatella and Rosaria were locked in the bathroom because Guido had to return home to join his parents for dinner. Afterwards, he and his friends went back to the villa and continued to torture the girls. Lopez, exhausted by the torture, fainted and drowned in the bathtub, while Colasanti pretended to be dead and was spared. The girls were then wrapped in plastic bags and thrown into the trunk of a car. When the three murderers arrived in Rome, they parked the car next to Izzo's house on a quiet elegant street in the Salario neighborhood of Rome, planning to get rid of the girls' bodies the next day. Colasanti, lying next to her dead girlfriend, screamed to get attention and was heard by a man in a house nearby who called the police. Later she identified her torturers, who were upper-class *pariolini*[18] and politically active members of the extreme right. Demanding justice, women's groups and associations marched through the streets of Rome with large posters saying, "I am a woman. I am a person."[19] The trial was held in the Latina Assize Court in July 1976, and the late lawyer and jurist Tina Lagostena Bassi (1926–2008) represented Colasanti. Sentenced to 30 years in prison, Ghira absconded and was never caught. He was found dead in Spain years later.[20] Izzo[21] and Guido[22] were arrested, tried and sentenced to life imprisonment.

Colasanti never fully recovered from the trauma and died prematurely of breast cancer.[23]

Trial for Rape: The Courtroom on Screen

Trial for Rape[24] (1979), directed by Loredana Dordi, is an unprecedented documentary of an actual rape trial.[25] The trial, held in Latina in 1978, was the first open door trial in Italian history and the film includes the hearing, pleas and verdict. Permission was given to film the whole trial of the four men who had perpetrated sexual violence against Fiorella, a teenager from Rome.[26] The young woman, whose last name was not made public, not only agreed to face an open-door trial, she also accepted the filming. By entering the courtroom and being present at every stage, members of the Italian Women's Liberation Movement turned the case into an historic public and political event. The film was broadcast on the RAI network twice in 1979.[27]

This trial was one of the very few that reached the Italian courtroom because in most cases women would neither report the offence nor seek justice, afraid that they would not be recognized as victims and their assailants would not be prosecuted. In fact, Fiorella's trial was an overt attempt by a male-controlled legal system "to accuse the young woman of provoking male sexual rage"[28] (Zonta 2008: 94). Consequently, the victim "is violated a second time in the courtroom by indifference, prejudice and derision"[29] (Ghezzi 2008: 8). During Fiorella's trial, Lagostena Bassi listened to the closing remarks of the rapists' defense lawyer dejectedly, with her hand on her face (an image etched in history). She later declared, "People were shocked because nobody could imagine what really happened in a courtroom where justice was as violent towards the women as the rapists were."[30] She also wrote, "Everybody became aware that a woman who has been the victim of a tragedy that will change her life, is offended, slandered, vilified by a conniving world of men. Words, looks, winks from judges and lawyers: From being a victim, the woman becomes the accused"[31] (Lagostena Bassi and Monteverdi 2008: 92).

Anita Pasquali, from the *Associazione Federale Femminista Italiana* (Italian Feminist Federal Association), explains that paradoxically, "the injury done to an arm is considered a crime against a person, but rape, sexual violence, was considered a crime against a person's dignity, a concept, as we know, that, like morality, can be pushed and pulled in different directions."[32] Italian women protested that they were persons and, as written on a poster during one political march, asked "Can morality be raped?"[33] As journalist Liliana Madeo remembers, Fiorella's entire case showed that Italy "was a sex-phobic country with a strong discriminatory division between men and women."[34] Therefore, *Trial for Rape*[35] is an historical documentary that shook public opinion at a time when rape was still considered a crime against morality.

Lagostena Bassi is remembered in Italy as the "women's lawyer"[36] for her tenacious personal involvement in a vast number of cases of violence against women and for her professional commitment and contribution to legislative reforms for the protection of women. She recalls that in 1979, soon after the broadcast of *Trial for Rape*, she and the feminist collective gathered at the *Casa delle donne* (Women's House), in Rome to prepare a private bill that would include rape among offences against a person and inflict harsher punishments for crimes of sexual violence. Remembering those events, Lagostena Bassi wrote,

> The [Italian] Constitution allows its citizens to lay a bill signed by at least 50,000 voters, and for that occasion 300,000 official signatures were collected. These signatures were brought in carts and presented to the House of Deputies. They were kept and nothing happened. This was the first time that a bill had been prepared by citizens, or better female citizens, and not by the government or parliament[37] (Lagostena Bassi and Monteverdi 2008: 93).

One year later, in 1980 the book *Un processo per stupro*, based on the documentary of the same name, was published. In the preface, Franca Ongaro Basaglia wrote:

> This trial gives us a clear sense of the human squalor and baseness lying underneath our culture. [...] But there is an explanation for this squalor, [the fact that] women have dared to speak up, to say what has been created to control and silence them, what

their silence once concealed is now revealed. When exposed, power does not know what to say and gives a shameful show of itself, which confirms the strength of those who reject it[38] (cited in Lagostena Bassi and Monteverdi 2008: 92-93).

The Pack: From Reality, through Novel, to Film

A famous and highly dramatic depiction of gang-rape is the feature *The Pack* (1994),[39] directed by Marco Risi[40] who co-authored the screenplay with Andrea Carraro. The film is based on Carraro's novel *La baraccal Il branco*,[41] which was inspired by a real-life episode of violent gang-rape that took place ten years earlier in Marcellina, on the outskirts of Rome. The incident was one of the 12 rape cases officially reported and discussed by Lagostena Bassi (1991).[42] In this film, Risi makes the difficult choice of telling a brutal story from the point of view of the rapists—a group of teenagers and an adult, Raniero, Pallesecche, Ciccio, Brunello, Ottorino, Sola, with an older man, sor Quinto, as an accomplice. Raniero and Ciccio are the youngest and most innocent of the group, while Pallesecche is the meanest and most sadistic.

The film opens with a replay from the radio call-in show Radio Radicale, very popular among young people in the early 1970s, in which northern Italians bitterly insult southerners and vice versa. This introduction reveals the level of mutual and gratuitous anger and hatred, repressed violence and overt nastiness of a generation of young people, while setting the tone for the kinds of relationships among jobless teenagers living on the outskirts of Rome, and providing a disturbing opening to the massive and pervasive verbal, psychological and sexual violence that they will manifest in the story.[43]

One Sunday, in a small rural town outside Rome, Raniero, who aspires to become a police officer and is nicknamed "Carruba"[44] for this reason, meets his friends at the poolroom. He is engaged to Ernestina and lives with his family. His father dislikes his stupid and risky friends and regularly scolds him for hanging around with them. While the town celebrates its patron saint, Sola spreads the word that two young German hitchhikers, Sylvia and Marion, picked up by Ottorino, have been taken to an isolated shack in the woods and

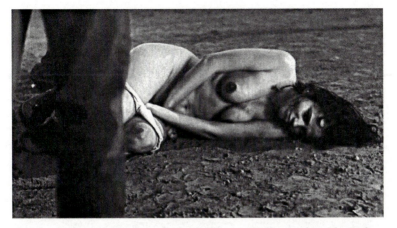

Sylvia cringes on the ground after being repeatedly raped in *The Pack* (1994)

are now available for fun. By the time Raniero and Ciccio get to the place, Sylvia has already been raped repeatedly, while Marion has been kept in Ottorino's car.

It is Raniero's turn to rape Sylvia, but he is unable to touch her, so he brings her to the car, telling the group that it is enough for her. His move, however, ignites rage towards Marion by the others. Sylvia attempts to run away in the woods, but Raniero runs after her, beats her and brings her back to the shack. Soon after, Pallesecche sodomizes Sylvia in front of Raniero, who lightly touches her hand during the rape. When two in the group start fighting, the girls attempt to escape but are caught. Unexpectedly, in the middle of this collective sexual euphoria, Raniero proposes to invite the rest of the town to join them and abuse the girls for money. A new party is held, but Marion dies as a result of the repeated violence. While the group wraps Marion's body in a blanket and dumps it in a lake, Sylvia runs away and Raniero chases after her on his moped. He reaches her, but Sylvia finds shelter and help from a railway level-crossing keeper. The police are immediately informed and they arrest Raniero.

Marco Risi deliberately chooses to tell the story "from the wrong side without ever taking sides with any of the men"[45] as they rape for sheer sadistic pleasure and are the ultimate icons of an unprecedented collective sexual fantasy. Neither Carraro's book nor Risi's film are psychologically introspective. Nonetheless, Risi seems to ask what possible explanation there could be for the delirious enactment of masculinity culminating in the scene of a village rave with collective rape, the perception of fun and sex in the woods as novelty and diversity, beyond the dismay and the senseless anger of his characters' actions. There is a dark atmosphere of rural *noir* hovering between horror and accusation of the perverse group dynamics, where the emotional violence is high, but the visual experience of the sexual violence is kept offstage. In *The Pack*, the director does not try to find plausible social causes for the criminal responsibilities of the subproletarian youth's unlawful behavior, and the director purposefully leaves out any conceivable reason and refuses to get involved in the psychology of his protagonists. Risi "does not attempt to understand or explain and takes a strong stand—there is nothing to understand as this is only gratuitous violence, expression of the nothingness of an empty generation adrift, [expression of] purely scabby and growling bestiality. The young men of the pack are ugly, dirty and nasty. The film does not even attempt to go beyond the horror of a brutal and degrading gesture, and the terrifying effect and simple condemnation"[46] (Causo 1994).

Deborah Young notes that Sylvia's "reactions are oddly muted, and she seems more concerned about the fate of her friend, Marion, who is a virgin. [...] The unfortunate tourists and helpless victims, [Sylvia and Marion] under-act, under-react, and do not connect emotionally with the rapists" (Young 1994: 71). The girls' silence and refusal to interact with the rapists are the symptoms of their voiceless terror and speechless trauma. Further, in the film, the men's attacks on the girls are often justified through a further degradation of them by asserting that the young women eventually enjoyed it, thus reinforcing cultural myths that only bad girls get raped and that women provoke rape by their behavior. So hitchhikers like Sylvia and Marion are seen as more prone and available, and therefore deserve or expect that it could happen to them, having put themselves in a position where they were asking for it.

The Wedding Dress: Getting over Sexual Trauma or What the Present Hides

Trauma theory, with its foregrounding concepts, including flashbacks and latency, has emphasized the continual damaging impact of trauma's past on the present. According to trauma theory, the present is held hostage to an over-present past. Cathy Caruth, who has developed the psychoanalytic concept of "belatedness," explains that "the impact of a traumatic event lies precisely in its belatedness, in its refusal to be simply located, in its insistent appearance outside the boundaries of any single space or time" (Caruth 1995: 9). The following discussion examines the relation of memory of a traumatic event with its belated impact on the present and the future, beyond spatial and temporal limits, as portrayed in the film *The Wedding Dress* (2003),[47] written and directed by Italian director Fiorella Infascelli.[48] In this film, the crime genre, psychological thriller, romance, and social commentary meet at a crossroads with trauma theory, thus providing a hybridization of narratives and aesthetics.

A three-minute-long scene involving the cruel gang-rape and sodomizing of a young woman on the eve of her wedding is explicitly rendered in the film *The Wedding Dress*. Inspired by the true story of a woman who brutally killed her lover after discovering that he was the rapist who had shattered her life, the film is an intense psychological thriller with a classical structure and dramatic ending, with the inevitable death of one of the rapists and imprisonment of the others. Infascelli explores the disturbing psychological effects of sexual violence on the victim, and addresses the depth and complexity of her existential drama. Moreover, the director follows her character's difficult emotional recovery from the shock and monitors the troubled process of her gradual social reintegration, while scrutinizing the psychological traits of the male rapists. Then, Infascelli reconnects the victim and one of her assailants through a tempestuous romantic relationship, and concludes the drama with the protagonist's disquieting discovery of the true identity of her new lover.

The film tells the story of Stella Algeri, a 25-year-old veterinary student spending the summer at her home in the beautiful, hilly countryside of central Italy. One day, while beneath an ancient oak tree, where just shortly before she had made love to her fiancé,

Andrea, Stella sits studying for an upcoming exam and is viciously as-
saulted by four masked hunters. The fiancé convinces Stella, possibly
out of fear, shame or honor, not to report the crime. Shaken by this
violent event, she is plunged into grief and despair, loneliness and
indifference, and withdraws into silence. Disoriented by the tragic
incident, unable to deal with Stella's trauma and incapable of providing her with adequate emotional support, Andrea suddenly leaves her
without offering any plausible reason or explanation. While slowly
recovering at home with her mother, Stella cancels her wedding arrangements, quits her studies, and decides to work in a local pastry
shop. When spring comes, Franco, who owns the shop where Stella
had commissioned her wedding dress, enters her life bringing the
promise of a new love story. Their difficult relationship is, however,
doomed to end tragically. One summer day, during a trip to the seaside, Stella accidentally discovers that Franco was one of her rapists,
but before she can confront him, he is struck by a bus while crossing
the road to join her, thus abruptly ending his life.

The Wedding Dress is a single, linear, narrative flashback spanning
over a 12-month cycle, where each season marks a different chapter
in the story. The film is introduced by the closing scene and ends full
circle with the same opening sequence followed by Stella's realization
of Franco's complicity in her rape a year earlier. The film starts on the
day of their summer trip to the seaside. Stella walks to Franco's car
to get something from her bag. A white wedding veil gently frames
the open trunk but, while she searches her bag, Stella is unexpectedly
distracted by a distinct smell. The more she goes through her bag, the
stronger the unpleasant odor becomes. Instinctively and somewhat
anxiously she looks for the source of the nauseating odor and finds
a jute bag hidden in the bottom of the trunk. In disbelief, she seeks
more evidence and finds a pair of hunting boots. She examines the
sack and brings it closer to her nose. This scene is interrupted by a
cut that brings Stella back to the previous summer on the day when
she went to try on her wedding dress in Franco's atelier. She enjoys
looking at her image reflected in the three mirrors as she rehearses her
marriage vows to Andrea. When Franco comes in for a final check on
her dress, they briefly talk and, before leaving, he greets her with a
polite "Goodbye,"[49] foreshadowing a cruel coincidence of events that,

on that very same day at dusk, will indeed bring them together again.

Infascelli's directorial choices establish striking tactile, olfactory and visual associations between Stella's delicate, white bridal tulle veil gently covering her face and the hunters' rough and stinking jute bag used as a hood during the ferocious rape scene. The parallelism linking these opposite symbols and emotionally loaded icons made of different fabrics, but characterized by the same threading, the veil fine and the sack harsh, constitutes the interweaving thread of the film's dramatic narrative. The tulle and the jute mark two fundamental and yet strikingly oppositional moments in Stella's life: her wedding day versus her rape experience. As the immaculate tulle and the stinking jute bag trigger the resurgence of past traumatic episodes and the re-emergence of bottled up and latent tormenting memories, they also prompt the belated realization of the trauma within the trauma.

The Wedding Dress depicts the psychological aftermath of a rape victim. The film revolves around a descriptive post-traumatic narrative while the story easily lends itself to the intersection of different discourses—trauma theory with a survivor-centered paradigm focusing on the symptomatology of sexual abuse (Stupiggia 2007; Lebowitz et al. 1993); and social denunciation of violence against women as a widespread criminal phenomenon. Thus the film encapsulates, in a single story, both a woman's private drama and the social accusation of the aberrant behavior of a wrecked generation of men. In this film Infascelli gives a perceptive view of her female protagonist's psychological shock derived from sexual violence, and offers a sensitive model of the character's difficult emotional recovery from brutal gang-rape and her exceptional resilience. Furthermore, the theme of the victim falling in love with her abuser is inspired by the trauma theory principle explaining the victim's fantasy of encountering the perpetrator and her dream of resolution as a possibility of transcending the trauma.

Central to Stella's experience is the fact that her trauma is frozen in time, perpetually re-experienced in a painful, dissociated traumatic present, through flashbacks, nightmares, emotional numbing, depression, guilt, explosive violence and tendency to hyper-vigilance, all symptoms of Post-Traumatic Stress Disorder (PTSD). These symptoms are manifested in her immediate sense of helplessness, meaninglessness, and disconnection from herself and others in her life. The film narrative initially focuses Stella's complex recovery on the establishment of a new form of safety as the protagonist attempts to regain control of her body and surroundings. Numbed by the pain that runs through her body and rips her soul, Stella experiences typical post-traumatic symptoms. She spends hours sleeping and lives day after day in her pajamas. She prefers darkness in her room to bright sunlight, and her aching body does not feel the unbearable heat of her room. She chooses total silence as she experiences typical "mute terror and the suspension of the word"[50] and prefers complete isolation feeling great "difficulty in relating with others"[51] (Stupiggia 2007: 80); she is often expressionless with a blank look in her eyes and cries frequently for no apparent reason.

In search of physical protection and emotional safety, she refuses to see her friends or go out with Andrea. She is easily irritable with her mother, shows intolerance for her fiancé's passive attention and lack of true understanding of her trauma. Not only is she afraid of possible further attacks, she is also frustrated by her inability to articulate her terrified thoughts and horrified feelings. One day, angered by the events that have destroyed her life, she hysterically eats the sugared almonds meant for her wedding day one by one, metaphorically cannibalizing the remains of her ruined nuptial plans.

She also confides in Andrea that she is afraid of herself, as she may not be able to control her own actions. She fears becoming violent and doing strange things. Her difficulty to fully explain her emotions and narrate the events of her experience are typical aspects of traumatic memory, which is usually less declarative or narrative, and more implicit or non-declarative, as it involves bodily memories of the violence (Van der Kolk et al. 1996: 47). Unfortunately, Andrea's ultimate cowardly response to Stella's attempt to communicate her state of panic and confusion is to leave her abruptly and without explanation. Later he will explain to her that he felt incapable of alleviating her pain and was frightened by her suffering.

Aware of the difficulty of Stella's healing as a survivor of sexual assault, Infascelli portrays, with insightful understanding, the protagonist's feelings of self-hate, self-blame and shame as unavoidable symptoms of post-traumatic stress. The director also addresses issues pertaining to Stella's accident and the latency inherent to her experience—what Cathy Caruth (1995) describes as the temporal delay that intervenes between the fright and the subsequent appearance of the traumatic symptoms: the belated, unmediated return of the traumatic event. Stella's subsequent improvement requires careful work uncovering the violent event in order to overcome painful memories. This process inevitably involves a period of intense grief and mourning, as she, the victim, contemplates the full extent of her losses—her fiancé, their wedding, and interest in her studies. Furthermore, Stella runs the risk of becoming a danger to herself by actively harming herself. This form of self-destructive behavior is explained by the psychology of recovery as symbolic or literal re-enactment of the abuse, and serves to regulate intolerable feelings in the absence of more adaptive, self-soothing coping strategies.

Stella's management of self-harm is represented in two effective dramatic scenes of projected and objectified destruction. The first is during a turbulent panic attack when she violently tears the pages out of her university books and destroys her bedroom. The second is a more symbolic illustration of a suicidal attempt expressed through calculated, mock self-inflicted injuries. The visually unsettling metaphor for slow, regular and painful cuts is rendered through Stella's irrational gathering of all her clothes, as an objectification of her disconnected body, followed by her quiet, solitary, ritualized ripping and cutting with scissors of her entire wardrobe into small pieces. When the mother enters, she finds Stella's room completely covered with what tangibly represents her physically dismembered, emotionally drained and psychologically dissociated self.

However, Stella is sustained through this process by the therapeutic influence of her mother's patient support, and she progressively

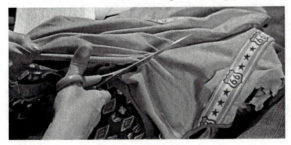

Stella cuts her clothes to shreds in *The Wedding Dress* (2003).

moves onward to reclaim control of her social network and natural environment, with the hope of restoring or building new relationships. Her suffering, as it unfolds over a series of crucial and clearly identifiable stages, is based on her gradual empowerment, the creation of different social connections, development of new interests, and engagement in new activities. In fact, the film narrative takes a new direction when Stella's gradual recovery leads her, during the winter, to actively pursue a healthy social and working life by getting a job in a pastry shop in town. Later, at the beginning of spring, as she regains control over her natural surroundings, she feels safe enough not to depend on her mother's car rides to the bus stop she uses to get to work, and is confident enough to walk freely through the familiar country lanes and hilly fields. As Infascelli explains, "Stella's country walks towards her healing, whether joyous, sad or angry, represent the emotional strength of the film."[52]

In the process of establishing mutual, non-exploitative relationships, Stella reassesses and renegotiates long-standing ties with Andrea and her new co-workers. At the end of the recovery, she assigns realistic meaning to the trauma and to herself as a survivor, the world around her and people in her life, as she is finally able to feel a renewed sense of optimism about her future. Infascelli's sensitive cinematography articulates a psychological model of recovery, which provides a solid narrative structure and a psychologically accurate journey of healing for the protagonist by first establishing Stella's safety, then exploring her drama, and lastly following her in regaining the ability to go on with her life. However, after creating a safe living situation, with attention to Stella's productivity at work and social reintegration sustained by a carefully considered plan for self-protection, the film narrative takes an unexpected and unsettling turn. As Stella achieves a level of emotional balance, she gets involved in a new and dangerous relationship.

At this point in the story, the director shifts her attention to the male rapists, thus providing a controversial and disturbing profile of the four assailants, and giving a sociocultural and psychological Identikit picture of the perverts. Defined as "a sample of degenerate and violent good-for-nothings"[53] (Zanetti: 84), Franco, Umberto, Augusto and Nicola are close, old friends, all single, healthy, good-looking men, approximately in their early to mid-30s, who (with the exception of one) are successful middleclass professionals. Free of steady romantic involvement, they spend their free time together and share a common pastime—hunting. Through these descriptive characterizations of the four men, Infascelli brings to light the alarming nature of the social and hedonistic elements of the crime. The bonds of solidarity and camaraderie between the rapists, as they jointly seek excitement and diversion in the distorted enactment of their goliardic sexual activities, provide a distressing picture of their perverted homosocial complicity. The men, experienced and well-equipped hunters, carefully choose their locations, employ well thought-out plans and target specific prey. These skills are then used to simulate wildlife hunts substituting young women as prey and gang-rape as an act of control and pleasure. Therefore, the team sport spirit takes a definite shift from the primordial instinct for the thrill of hunting aimed at wild prey to engaging in brutal sexual violence against human female victims. In the film, the archetype of the hunter unequivocally suggests nightmarish images of a ghostly rapist with feral instincts and predatory force.

Following Stella's recovery, Infascelli reintroduces Franco as a premeditated stalker and persistent seducer. Initially he observes Stella from distance—driving by her house at night, calling her home late at night without acknowledging his identity, and checking when she leaves home in the morning and work in the evening. Then, early one morning he approaches her while she is waiting for the bus into town, and offers her a ride. Reluctant and skeptical, Stella refuses, but Franco's reassuring and insistent invitation persuades her to accept his kind and harmless offer. This seemingly casual encounter marks the beginning of Franco's new role as Stella's seductive, romantic pursuer, and attractive and passionate future lover.

However, Franco and Stella's relationship, a kind of *amour fou*, is inevitably stormy from the very beginning with its mix of explosions of joy, expressions of tenderness, incomprehensible bursts of rage, and a series of hysterical reactions. Their encounters are mostly verbal duels and emotional battles, regularly troubled by Franco's excesses—the buying of an exorbitant number of pastries, sudden disappearances and equally unpredictable surprise reappearances, and his both voracious and impotent ways of approaching Stella sexually. Franco clearly experiences an uneasy relationship, suspended between his infamous crime of sadistic rape and his new feelings of love, as he flounders in a blurred magma of love and truth, violence and deceit. Therefore, he is unable to sustain an emotionally stable, loving relationship, while Stella is more willing to dream her new romantic fantasy and be seduced by this insane folly. Franco's dark and impenetrable personality makes him even more attractive to Stella, who is blinded by her need to trust and desire to love again, while incapable of perceiving Franco's revealing signals and disclosing messages.

Franco manifests a professional, perfectionist obsession when he inspects with arguably pathological care the wedding dresses in his atelier. The sensory seduction and sensual pleasure that he derives from the elegance and softness of the bridal gowns are subtle symptomatic evidence of his fetishistic attraction for women's clothes and suggestive signs of his inherent sexual tension with the feminine. Furthermore, Franco overtly reveals uncertainty about his gender self on two distinct occasions. Once, during a conversation with Stella in his shop, when he wears a large woman's hat, and provocatively assumes extremely feminized mannerisms, which inevitably disorient, irritate and alienate Stella; and the other when, in the company of his friend Umberto, he engages in an overacted feminized imitation of the graceless manners of one of his less refined young clients. Both incidents seem to suggest Franco's unsettling cross-gender ambiguities, unresolved identity issues and closeted conflicts about his own sexuality.

While Franco manifests uneasiness in dealing with a double lifestyle—the secret male socializing when raping women with his pals, and love-making in his new private and romantic relationship with Stella, he also feels the torture of shame and disempowerment in his turbulent feelings for Stella. His good side consciously longs for reconciliation with his victim and seeks her forgiveness in a desperate attempt to overcome guilt and remorse, while looking for a cure or distraction from his habitual, disturbing sexual practices. When Stella asks Franco, "Who was in your life before me?"[54] he candidly answers, "My mother."[55] On that occasion he also admits that he has never courted a woman before and confesses that he hangs out with terrible people. Although these hints are meant to send warning messages, Stella's heart is deaf, while their hunter-prey bipolarity brings them closer together than ever. The tangling bond of their love story lies in their sharing of a tragic past event, a horrifying secret that cannot be disclosed, but that paradoxically and dangerously keeps them together. In fact, when Franco asks Stella, "Why are you with me?"[56] she confidently replies, "Because I am like you."[57] Their conversations testify to their inseparability due to the intricate and inexplicable emotional attachment which irrationally unites them in a relationship that perpetuates the power struggle of an inextricable victim-abuser duality and dialectic psychological duplicity.

Their love story, however, is doomed to end tragically. Franco will not find redemption—his sudden, tragic death and Stella's tears of incredulity and anguish bring no final moral catharsis in the film. A *deus ex pullman*, as defined by Roberto Nepoti (cited in Prevosti 2003), will drive over their story, thus abruptly interrupting their relationship at a point where no justifications, nor vindication, are needed. Infascelli explains that she "was interested in telling the story of an impossible love, the encounter of two lonely people, whose lives were marked by tragic destinies and were tied by a painful truth that is necessary to know in order to move on with life"[58] (cited in Castellano 2003). The director also states that ending the story with Franco's death is "the solution most coherent with the premises. After all, the young man is trying to redeem himself, to repay Stella with his love, but he feels that he cannot do that, that he is heading towards a cruel destiny"[59] (cited in Castellano 2003). Zanetti, however, critically states that, although "only death can release the intensity of the situation, the director resolves it with an almost splattering expedient, and shows the man run over by a bus"[60] (Zanetti 2004: 85).

Conclusion

Directors De Sica and Dino Risi take inspiration from Moravia's literary text, set in devastated postwar Italy, to give the first dramatic representations of gang-rape in Italian cinema. Damiani's socially oriented cinematography, however, draws from a real case of collective sexual violence in Sicily in the mid-1960s. Rame's autobiographical monologue is the brutal testimony of gang-rape as the ultimate form of state rape against a militant woman in the politically turbulent mid-1970s. The widely reported events associated with the Circeo Massacre shook Italian society in the same period, and the first filmed rape trial in the late-1970s opened a new socio-political debate on cultural customs, traditional values, and legislative reforms in Italy.

Marco Risi and Infascelli also address the theme of gang-rape and tackle the problem from a sociological and a psychological perspective, respectively. While touching upon the complexities of the phenomenon, they remove the violence from the binary male versus female positions and take a prismatic point of view that more widely denounces the criminal behavior. Both their films take place in non-identifiable rural settings, but if socioeconomic marginalization cannot be pleaded as an extenuating factor for the criminal behavior of the young men in *The Pack*, the middle-class alienation, sport and sex activities in the woods of the adult men in *The Wedding Dress* can only be defined as aggravating circumstances. Risi's and Infascelli's groups of men represent a kind of *peggio gioventù* (worst youth)[61] seeking novel forms of entertainment through gratuitous sexual violence against female victims. While Risi does not try to rationalize, but simply provides a factual statement of his characters' behavior, Infascelli engages in the exploration of the sociocultural reasons behind rape and attempts to illustrate its irreparable consequences.

In conclusion, violence against women has been the focus of attention of artists, journalists, sociologists, psychologists, lawyers, legislators and political activists, and has been portrayed in cinematic representations, denounced through documentaries and televised in special programs. Such vast documentation of real life stories indicate the synergetic effort from a wide range of experts and artists to intervene swiftly and forcefully at educational, legal and legislative levels in order to inform people, prevent violence, protect women, assist victims of violence, and enforce more rigorous punishment. However, Italian legislators have realized that the 1996 law has become inadequate to address newly reported forms of violence against women, part of a rampant phenomenon that has produced an unprecedented number of victims in contemporary Italy.

NOTES

1 All translations of Italian citations are mine.
2 Formally known as CEDAW (Convention on the Elimination of All Forms of Discrimination Against Women) General Recommendation 19, titled "Violence against women," 1992.
3 Political parties were divided on several points, which caused a 20-year delay in passing the law. When Minister Alessandra Mussolini presented the Bill to the House of Deputies, it was strongly supported by a body of ministers from all parties. Law 66 passed on February 7, 1996.
4 The first bill, proposing to define sexual violence as a crime against a human being, was presented on 1976.
5 Dino Risi's adaptation of *Two Women* is a four-hour mini-series produced by Berlusconi's television network *Rete Italia*. Risi's film includes many episodes of Moravia's novel which were left out of De Sica's film.
6 In the film, the protagonist is a very poor 15-year-old girl, while her seducer is a young man protected by the local mafia.
7 She was freed on January 2, 1966.
8 The number of years was reduced to 10, of which two were spent in forced residence in Modena. Melodia was released in 1976 and was killed with a sawed-off shotgun on April 13, 1978.
9 (*Franca Viola getta un sasso nella storia lunghissima dei rapporti tra la donna in Sicilia e la legge, la donna e l'uomo, il sesso e il costume. L'episodio di Franca Viola è una luce che si è accesa in tanta oscurità.*) *Futuro femminile. Passioni e ragioni nelle voci del femminismo dal dopoguerra a oggi. Storia del movimento femminista in Italia: dal dopoguerra agli anni Sessanta.* Prima puntata. Directed by Luca Mancini and produced by Aleph Film for RAI Educational. Broadcast for RAI 3 for *La storia siamo noi*, a program by Piero A. Corsini, Massimiliano De Santis, Daniela Ghezzi, Marco Melega and Stefano Rizzelli. DVD, 2006, '55.
10 Franca Viola married Giuseppe Ruisi in 1968 and they moved to Monreale. They had three children and lived there for three years to avoid possible forms of revenge. They later returned to Alcamo.
11 The law was passed on August 5, 1981.
12 The monologue was presented at the RAI 1 show *Fantastico*, hosted by Adriano Celentano, on November 28, 1987. *The Rape* was also performed as part of the successful theater piece *Sesso? Grazie, tanto per gradire* (1995), on March 8, 1995, at the Teatro Smeraldo, in Milan.
13 The rapists Biagio Pitarresi, Angelo Angeli, a certain Patrizio, and a certain Muller, were all "*sanbabilini,*" residents of Milan's San Babila neighborhood. They were double dealers, provoking left-wing political groups, acting as police informants, trafficking in weapons and participating in organized crime.
14 Rame and Fo married in 1954 and since the 1950s have collaborated on

numerous theater pieces satirizing the Italian penal system, government bureaucracy, the military, the Catholic Church and, since the 1970s, sexism.

15   When Fo was awarded the Nobel Prize for Literature in 1997, Italian TV aired Rame's monologue *The Rape*.

16   (*Muoviti puttana, devi farmi godere.*)

17   "The police told us to rape Franca Rame," said the former neo-fascist Angelo Izzo (one of the three involved in the Circeo Massacre). This statement was confirmed by right-wing Biagio Pitarresi's statement to Judge Guido Salvini. His statement covers two of the 450 pages of the sentence of commitment for trial for fascist subversion in the 1970s. Pitarresi stated: "The action against Franca Rame was suggested by some police officers of the Division Pastrengo. Angeli and I had been in contact with the headquarters of the police." The judge comments in his sentence of commitment for trial: "The probable involvement of some officers of the Divison Pastrengo in suggesting [to rape Rame] should not surprise ... The headquarters of the Pastrengo Division had been heavily involved, in the 1970s, in activities of collusion with groups of subversives and in the heading off of several investigations in progress, such as covering up the traffic of weapons, hiding sources of information that could have led to find those responsible in the massacre of the neo-fascists Freda and Ventura" (Bellu, *La Repubblica* February 10, 1998).

18   *Pariolini* is an expression used to define young people residing in the upper-class Parioli neighborhood of Rome.

19   (*Sono una donna. Sono una persona.*)

20   Presumably died of an overdose in 1994, after joining the Legión Española.

21   Angelo Izzo murdered Maria Carmela Linciano and her 14-year-old daughter Valentina Maiorano on April 28, 2005.

22   Gianni Guido, after spending 30 years in prison, was released on August 26, 2009.

23   She died in Rome on December 30, 2005.

24   The trial took place in a courthouse in Latina on June 26, 1978.

25   The trial was filmed and produced by Maria Grazia Belmonti, Anna Carini, Rony Daopoulo, Paola De Martiis, Annabella Miscuglio and Loredana Rotondo, all members of the *Cooperativa maestranze del cinema*.

26   Fiorella was only 17 years old when the event took place in 1977. She had met a man she regularly saw coming out of school who, being married and mature, was a father-figure for her. She had told him that her family was poor and that she had to leave school and start working. He told her that he had a small business and could help her find a job as long as she met his partners in Anzio. When she replied that she did

not know how to get there, he offered to take her. Once there, Fiorella found herself in a small villa with four men who raped, beat and threatened her with a cricket bat throughout the entire day. The four men were Cesare Novelli, Rocco Vagnoni, Claudio Vagnoli and Roberto Palombo. The first three were arrested, the fourth gave himself up during the trial (Lagostena Bassi and Monteverdi 2008: 91).

27 Three million people watched the documentary when it was first broadcast by RAI 2, at 10 p.m. on April 22, 1979, but when aired again at 9 p.m. October 18, 1979, it was followed by 9 million viewers. Excerpts are available at www.youtube.com/watch?v=Nd4hKM62vwY.

28 (*Fare della ragazza la colpevole in quanto agente provocatorio della libido maschile.*)

29 (*Viene oltraggiata una seconda volta in aula dall'indifferenza, dal pregiudizio, dallo scherno.*)

30 (*Le persone rimasero esterefatte perché nessuno poteva immaginare che cosa realmente succedeva in un tribunale dove la giustizia era violenta verso le donne tanto quanto gli stessi stupratori*). *Storia del movimento femminista in Italia: gli anni Settanta.* Seconda puntata. Directed by Lorella Reale and produced by Aleph Film for RAI Educational. Broadcast for RAI 3 for *La storia siamo noi*, a program by Piero A. Corsini, Massimiliano De Santis, Daniela Ghezzi, Marco Melega and Stefano Rizzelli. DVD, 2006, '61.

31 (*Tutti si resero conto del fatto che una donna che ha subito una tragedia che la segnerà per tutta la vita, viene offesa, calunniata, denigrata da un connivente mondo di uomini. Parole, sguardi, ammiccamenti, anche di magistrati oltre che di avvocati: da vittima, la donna diventa imputata.*)

32 (*La ferita fatta ad un braccio è considerata un crimine contro una persona, ma lo stupro, la violenza sessuale, era considerata un crimine contro la dignità di una persona, un concetto, come sappiamo, che, come la moralità, può essere tirato in molte direzioni.*) *Storia del movimento femminista in Italia: gli anni Settanta.* Seconda puntata.

33 (*Si può stuprare la moralità?*)

34 (*Era un paese sessuofobo con una forte divisione discriminatoria tra uomini e donne.*) *Storia del movimento femminista in Italia: gli anni Settanta.* Seconda puntata.

35 The documentary, translated in several languages, was awarded several international prizes in 1979 (Lagostena Bassi and Monteverdi 2008: 92).

36 (*L'avvocato delle donne.*) Name given by Enzo Biagi when he introduced Lagostena Bassi in Lugano, for a TV program on *Sexual violence and the need for a new law.*

37 (*La nostra Costituzione, infatti, consente al "popolo", cioè ai cittadini, di predisporre una proposta di legge sottoscritta da almeno 50.000 elettori.*)

Vennero raccolte oltre 300.000 firme tutte autenticate dal notaio. Con delle carriole le portammo in cassazione e poi le depositammo alla Camera dei deputati. Le tennero per sé. Non successe nulla. È stata la prima e unica volta che una proposta di legge è stata predisposta da cittadini, anzi cittadine, e non dal governo o dal parlamento.)

38   (*L'esempio di questo processo ci dà la misura dello squallore e della miseria umana che stanno sotto alla nostra cultura. … ma questo squallore ha una spiegazione. È perché la donna ha osato parlare, ha osato dire ciò che è stato inventato per dominarla e farla tacere, viene svelato ciò che il suo silenzio copriva… Quando si smaschera, il potere non sa cosa dire e dà uno spettacolo di sé vergognoso che da solo conferma la forza di chi lo rifiuta.*) Primary source: AA.VV. 1980, ix.

39   Presented at the Venice Film Festival in 1994.

40   Marco, son of the late Dino Risi (1917–2008), started his career as assistant to his father, and later directed *I Am Going to Live by Myself* (*Vado a vivere da solo*, 1982), *Un ragazzo e una ragazza* (1984; no English title available), *Colpo di fulmine* (1985; no English title available), *Soldati 365 all'alba* (1987; no English title available). He has tackled difficult social and political themes in several of his films, such as *For Ever Mary* (*Mery per sempre*, 1989) and *Boys on the Outside* (*Ragazzi fuori*, 1990), both with young non-professional actors from the Palermo ghetto, and *Bambini al lavoro* (1996; no English title available) is a documentary on the exploitation of child labor. In the film *On the Dark Continent* (*Nel continente nero*, 1992) the director deals with lighter themes. He also directed *Humanity's Last New Year's Eve* (*L'ultimo capodanno*, 1998), the comedy-thriller and social satire *Three Wives* (*Tre mogli*, 2001), *Caro Vittorio* (2004; no English title available), and *Maradona: The Hand of God* (*Maradona: la mano de Dio*, 2007).

41   Sandro Veronesi suggested the novel *La baracca*, first published in a literary magazine, to Marco Risi as an idea for a film. When Risi's film was released, the book was republished in 1994 with the new title *Il branco* by Edizioni Theoria and was reprinted in 2005 by Gaffi Editore.

42   The book, published by Mondadori, was co-authored by Tina Lagostena Bassi and Emanuela Moroli. In 1996, Lagostena Bassi also wrote the screenplay adaptation of her book for a RAI television mini-series titled *L'avvocato delle donne*.

43   Risi devotes considerable attention to the rise of the Italian *radio libera* movement that characterized the 1970s. By 1978 there were about 1,000 independent radio stations in Italy, examples of a generational pervasive impulse to use the airwaves to spread an alternative, countercultural voice. Young people resorted to free radio channels to exercise freedom of speech denied to them in other public forums.

44   *Carruba* means carob, slang for police officer due to the black color of

their uniforms.

45 (*Dalla parte sbagliata senza prendere le parti di nessuno dei protagonisti.*) Interview with M. Risi, *Il Branco*, DVD.

46 (*Risi tiene le distanze, non entra in confidenza con i suoi giovani protago-nisti, non capisce, anzi ci dice che c'è poco da capire: la violenza è gratuita, espressione del nulla di una generazione allo sbando, pura bestialità rognosa e ringhiante. Brutti, sporchi e cattivi, dunque, i ragazzi del Branco.*)

47 Presented at the Locarno International Film Festival, in 2003.

48 Daughter of the famous producer Carlo and sister of the producer Ro-berto, Fiorella started as a photographer for *Sygma*, *L'Espresso* and *Il Mondo*. At the beginning of her cinema career she worked as assistant to Pasolini on *Salò o le 120 giornate di Sodoma* (1975), among others. Later she directed several TV productions including *Ritratto di donna distesa* (1980), *Lazio* (1995), *Italiani: alfabeto italiano* (1998), *Viaggio in musica* (1999) a portrayal of Yuri Bashmet, and *Conversazione italiana* (1999). Her first long feature is *Pa* (1981) a portrait dedicated to her father. She also directed the successful features *The Mask* (*La maschera*, 1987), *Fish Soup* (*Zuppa di pesce*, 1991), and *Ferreri I love you* (2000) dedicated to Italian director Marco Ferreri.

49 (*Arrivederci.*)

50 (*Terrore muto e la sospensione della parola.*)

51 (*Difficoltà relazionale.*)

52 (*Le camminate di Stella nella campagna verso la guarigione rappresentano un po' l'emozione del film—siano esse gioiose, tristi o rabbiose.*) Director's statement at the 56th Locarno International Film Festival, August 6–16, 2003.

53 (*Un campionario di vitelloni degenerati e violenti.*) *Il vestito da sposa*, DVD.

54 (*Chi c'era nella tua vita prima di me?*) *Il vestito da sposa*, DVD.

55 (*Mia madre.*) *Il vestito da sposa*, DVD.

56 (*Perché stai con me?*) *Il vestito da sposa*, DVD.

57 (*Perché sono come te.*) *Il vestito da sposa*, DVD.

58 (*A me interessava raccontare una storia d'amore impossibile, l'incontro tra due solitudini, tra due persone segnate da destini tragici, legate da una veri-tà dolorosa ma che è indispensabile conoscere per andare avanti.*)

59 (*La soluzione più coerente con le premesse. In fondo il giovane sta cercando di redimersi, di risarcire Stella con l'amore, ma sente che non ce la fa, che sta andando incontro a un destino spietato.*)

60 (*Solo la morte può sciogliere l'intensità della situazione. La regista la risolve con un espediente quasi splatter, che ci mostra l'uomo travolto da un pull-man.*)

61 From the title of Valerio Morucci's political book, *La peggio gioventù*, Rizzoli 2004.

BIBLIOGRAPHY

Chapter 1

Barzini, Luigi (1971). *From Caesar to the Mafia: Sketches of Italian Life* (New York, Bantam).

———— (1964). *The Italians: A Full-Length Portrait Featuring Their Manners and Morals* (New York, Atheneum).

Bianco e Nero (July 2007): 599.

Brunetta, Gian Piero (1998). *Storia del cinema italiano dal neorealismo al miracolo economico 1945–1959* (Roma, Editori Riuniti).

Burke, Frank (2005). "Homesick for the Unknown: Ulysses (1954) and Postwar Pressures to Re-domesticate the American Male" in Anthony Julian Tamburri (ed.) *Italian Cultural Studies 2002: Selected Essays* (Boca Raton, Florida, Bordighera Press): 51-73.

Il Cinema Ritrovato, 23rd edition, Bologna June 27-July 4. Festival Catalog. http://www.cinetecadibologna.it/cinemaritrovato2009/ev/Download.

Cohan, Steven (1997). *Masculinity and Movies in the Fifties* (Bloomington, Indiana UP).

Duggan, Christopher (1995). *A Concise History of Italy* (New York, Cambridge UP).

Dyer, Richard (1997). "The White Man's Muscles" in *White* (London, Routledge): 145-183.

Frayling, Christopher (2000). *Sergio Leone: Something to Do With Death* (London, Faber and Faber).

Ginsborg, Paul (1990). *A History of Contemporary Italy 1943–1980* (London, Penguin).

Günsberg, Maggie (2005). "Heroic Bodies: The Cult of Masculinity in the Peplum" in *Italian Cinema: Gender and Genre* (New York, Palgrave Macmillan): 97-132.

Jameson, Fredric (1991). *Postmodernism, or, The Cultural Logic of Late Capitalism* (London, Verso).

Lizzani, Carlo (1998). *Attraverso il novecento* (Roma, Biblioteca di Bianco e Nero/Torino, Lindau).

Lucanio, Patrick (1994). *With Fire and Sword: Italian Spectacles on American Screens: 1958–1968* (Metuchen, New Jersey, The Scare-crow Press): 1-52.

May, Elaine Tyler (1988). *Homeward Bound: American Families in the Cold War Era* (New York, Basic Books).

Overbey, David (ed. and trans.) (1979). *Springtime in Italy: A Reader on Neo-Realism* (London, Talisman Books).

Rondolino, Gianni (1980). *Vittorio Cottafavi: Cinema e televisione* (Bologna, Capelli).

Wyke, Maria (1997). *Projecting the Past: Ancient Rome, Cinema and History* (New York, Routledge).

Chapter 2

Fazzini, Paolo (2004). *Gli artigiani del terrore. Mezzo secolo di brivido dagli anni '50 ad oggi* (Roma, Un Mondo a Parte).

Günsberg, Maggie (2005). "Looking at Medusa: Investigating Femi-ninity in the Horror Film" in *Italian Cinema: Gender and Genre* (Basingstoke, UK, and New York, Palgrave, Macmillan): 133-172.

Re, Lucia (2008, January). "Futurism, Film and the Return of the Repressed: Learning From Thäis" MLN Vol. 123 no. 1 (Balti-more, The Johns Hopkins University Press).

Tentori, Antonio (1997). *Operazione Paura. I registi del gotico italiano* (Bologna, Punto Zero).

Chapter 3

Aquila, Richard (ed.) (1996). *Wanted Dead or Alive* (Urbana, Univer-sity of Illinois Press).

Beatrice, Luca (1996). *Al cuore, Ramon, al cuore!* (Florence, Italy, Tarab Edizioni/Dies Irae Records).

Bondanella, Peter (2001). *Italian Cinema: from Neorealism to the*

Present (New York, Continuum).

Brunetta, Gian Piero (1991). *Cent'anni di cinema italiano: dal 1945 ai giorni nostri* (Bari, Italy, Laterza).

—— (1982). *Storia del cinema italiano: dal 1945 agli anni ottanta* (Roma, Editori Riuniti).

Buscombe, Edward and Pearson Roberta E. (eds.) (1998). *Back in the Saddle Again* (London, British Film Institute).

Cameron, Ian and Pye Douglas (eds) (1996). *The Book of Westerns* (New York, Continuum).

Cawelty, John J. (1999). *The Six-Gun Mystique Sequel* (Bowling Green, Kentucky, Bowling Green University Press).

Coyne, Michael (1997). *The Crowded Prairie: American National Identity in the Hollywood Western* (London, I.B.Tauris).

Cumbow, Robert C. (1987). *Once Upon a Time: the Films of Sergio Leone* (Lanham, Maryland, Scarecrow).

Desilet, Gregory (2006). *Our Faith in Evil* (Jefferson, North Carolina, MacFarland & Company).

Forgacs, David (1996). *Italian Cultural Studies* (New York, Oxford UP).

Frayling, Christopher (2000). *Something to Do With Death* (London, Faber and Faber).

—— (1998). *Spaghetti Westerns* (London, I.B.Tauris).

French, Phillip (1977). *Westerns: Aspects of a Movie Genre* (New York, Oxford UP).

Garofalo, Marcello (1999). *Tutto il cinema di Sergio Leone* (Milano, Baldini e Castoldi).

Günsberg, Maggie (2005). *Italian Cinema* (New York, Palgrave).

Hughes, Howard (2004). *Once Upon a Time in the Italian West* (London, I.B.Tauris).

Kezich, Tullio (1975). *Il mito del Far West* (Roma, Bulzoni).

Loy, Phillip R. (2004). *Westerns in a Changing America 1955–2000* (Jefferson, North Carolina, MacFarland & Company).

—— (2001). *Westerns and American Culture 1930–1955* (Jefferson, McFarland & Company).

Micciché, Lino (2002). *Cinema italiano: gli anni '60 e oltre* (Venezia, Marsilio).

Parks, Rita (1982). *The Western Hero in Film and Television*

(Ann Arbor, Michigan, UMI Research Press).

Prince, Stephen (2003). *Classical Film Violence* (New Brunswick, New Jersey, Rutgers University Press).

—— (2000). *Screening Violence* (New Brunswick, Rutgers University Press).

Salizzato, Claver (ed.) (1989). *Prima della Rivoluzione: Schermi italiani 1960-69* (Venezia, Marsilio).

Slotkin, Richard (1992). *Gunfighter Nation: The Myth of the Frontier in Twentieth-Century America* (New York, Maxwell MacMillan).

—— (1973). *Regeneration Through Violence: The Mythology of the American Frontier 1600–1860* (New York, Atheneum).

—— (1985). *The Fatal Environment: The Myth of the Frontier in the Age of Industrialization 1800–1890* (New York, Harper and Collins).

Spinazzola, Vittorio (1974). *Cinema e pubblico—Lo spettacolo filmico in Italia 1945-65* (Milano, Bompiani).

Tompkins, Jane (1992). *West of Everything* (New York, Oxford UP)

Turner, Frederick Jackson (1969). *The Frontier in American History* (New York, Holt, Reinhart and Winston).

Walle, Half H. (2000). *The Cowboy Hero and Its Audience: Popular Culture as Market Derived Art* (Bowling Green, Kentucky, Bowling Green UP).

Wallmann, Jeffrey (1999). *The Western* (Lubbock, Texas Tech UP).

Williams, Linda, ed. (1994). *Viewing Positions: Ways of Seeing Films* (New Brunswick, Rutgers University Press).

Wright, Will (1975). *Six-Gun and Society* (Berkeley, University of California Press).

Chapter 4

Bondanella, P. (2007). *Italian Cinema. From Neorealism To the Present* (New York, Continuum): 31-141.

—— (1993). *The Films of Roberto Rossellini* (New York, Cambridge University Press).

—— (1991). *The Cinema of Federico Fellini* (Princeton University Press).

Brunetta, G.P. (1991). *Cent'anni di cinema italiano* (Bari, Italy, Laterza).

——— (2001). *Storia del cinema italiano. Dal neorealismo al miracolo economico 1945–1959* (Roma, Editori Riuniti).

——— (2000). "L'identità del cinema italiano" in AA.VV. [multiple authors] *Un secolo di cinema italiano* (Milano, Il Castoro): 17-30.

Camerini, C. (1986). "I critici e la commedia all'italiana: le occasioni perdute" in Napolitano, R. (ed.) *La commedia all'italiana. Angolazioni controcampi* (Roma, Gangemi): 179-92.

D'Agostini, P. (1991). *Romanzo popolare. Il cinema di Age e Scarpelli* (Napoli, Edizioni Scientifiche Italiane).

D'Amico, M. (2008). *La commedia all'italiana. Il cinema comico in Italia dal 1945 al 1975* (Milano, Il Saggiatore).

Della Fornace, L. (1983). *Il labirinto cinematografico* (Roma, Bulzoni).

De Vincenti, G. (2001). "Il cinema italiano negli anni del boom" in De Vincenti, G. (ed.) *Storia del cinema italiano. Volume X—1960/64* (Venezia, Marsilio): 3-27.

Di Marino, B. (2001). "Esterno/Interno giorno. Spazio urbano, design d'interni e immagine pubblicitaria" in De Vincenti, G. (ed.) *Storia del cinema italiano. Volume X—1960/64* (Venezia, Marsilio): 267-280.

Fanchi, M. (2001). "La trasformazione del consumo cinematografico" in De Vincenti, G. (ed.) *Storia del cinema italiano. Volume X—1960/-64* (Venezia, Marsilio): 344-357.

Fortini, F. (June 15, 1963). "Il realismo italiano nel cinema e nella narrativa" in *Cinema Nuovo*, no. 13.

Fusco, M.P. (1986). "Società, famiglia: e la donna?" in Napolitano, R. (ed.) *La commedia all'italiana. Angolazioni controcampi* (Roma, Gangemi: 131-140.

Giacovelli, E. (1995). *La commedia all'italiana. La storia, gli autori, gli attori, i film* (Roma, Gremese).

Grande, M. (2003). *La Commedia all'italiana* (Milano, Bulzoni).

Laura, E.G. (1980). *Comedy, Italian Style* (Roma, Anica).

Lizzani, C. (1975). "Il neorealismo. Quando è finito, quello che resta," in Miccichè L. (ed.) *Il neorealismo cinematografico italiano. Atti del convegno della X Mostra Internazionale del Nuovo Cinema.* (Venezia, Marsilio): 98-105.

Lapertosa, V. (2002). *Dalla fame all'abbondanza. Gli italiani e il cibo nel cinema italiano dal dopoguerra ad oggi* (Torino, Lindau).

Landy, M. (2008). *Stardom, Italian Style* (Bloomington, Indiana University Press).

Livi, G. (2005) "L'eroe negativo" in Goffredo Fofi (ed.) *Alberto Sordi. L'Italia in bianco e nero* (Milano, Mondadori).

Marcus, M. (2002). *After Fellini. National Cinema in the Postmodern Age* (Baltimore, the John Hopkins University Press).

—— (1986). *Italian Film in the Light of Neorealism* (Princeton, New Jersey, Princeton University Press).

Miccichè, L. (1975). "Per una verifica del neorealismo" in Miccichè, L. (ed.), *Il neorealismo cinematografico italiano. Atti del convegno della X Mostra Internazionale del Nuovo Cinema* (Venezia, Marsilio).

Monicelli, M. (1986). *Cinema italiano. Ma cos'è questa crisi?* (Roma, Laterza).

Napolitano R. (1986). *Commedia all'italiana. Angolazioni controcampi* (Roma, Gangemi).

Salizzato, C. Zagarrio, V. (1985). *Effetto Commedia. Teoria, generi, paesaggi della commedia cinematografica* (Roma, Di Giacomo Editore).

Pergolari A. (2004). *La fabbrica del riso: 32 sceneggiatori raccontano la storia del cinema italiano* (Roma, Un mondo a parte).

Pergolari A. (2002). *Verso la commedia. Momenti di cinema di Steno, Salce, Festa Campanile* (Firenze, Firenze Libri).

Pintus P. (ed.) (1985). *La commedia all'italiana. Parlano i protagonisti* (Roma, Gangemi).

Renzi, R. (1986). *Neorealismo e la sua eutanasia* in Napolitano (ed.) *Commedia all'italiana. Angolazioni controcampi* (Roma, Gangemi).

Spinazzola, V. (1974). *Cinema e Pubblico. Lo spettacolo filmico in Italia 1945–1965* (Milano, Bompiani).

Viganò, A. (2001). *La commedia all'italiana* in De Vincenti, G. (ed.) *Storia del cinema italiano. Volume X—1960/64* (Venezia, Marsilio): 235-52.

Chapter 5

Agamennone, M. and L. Di Mitri, (eds) (2003). *L'eredità di Diego Carpitella: etnomusicologia, antropologia e ricerca storica nel Salento e nell'area mediterranea* (Nardò, Besa).

Apolito, P. (2000). "Tarantismo, identità locale, postmodernità," in

G. Di Mitri (ed.) *Quarant'anni dopo De Martino* (Nardò, Besa) 135-43.

Attolini V., Marrese A., Abenante A. M. (2006). *Cineasti di Puglia. Autori mestieri storie* (Bari, Mario Adda Editore).

——— (2007). Abenante A. M. *Cineasti di Puglia. Film Paesaggi Associazioni* (Bari, Edizioni dal Sud).

Bandini, G. (2006). *Il bacio della tarantola* (Roma, Newton Compton Editori).

Bartholomew, R. (1994). "Tarantism, Dancing Mania and Demonopathy: the Anthro-political Aspects of 'Mass Psychogenic Illness'" *Psychological Medicine* Vol. 24: 281-306.

Biagi, L. (2004) *Spider Dreams: Ritual and Performance in Apulian Tarantismo and Tarantella* unpublished PhD disseration (New York University).

Cassano, F. (2006). *Il pensiero meridiano* (Bari, Sagittari Laterza)

Cupolo, M. (2006). Review of *The Land of Remorse. A Study of Southern Italian Tarantism.* Translated from Italian and annotated by Dorothy L. Zinn (London, Free Association, 2005, *Project Muse Scholarly Journals online*): 181-183.

De Martino, E. (1961). *La terra del rimorso* (reprint, Milano, Est, 1996).

Del Giudice, L. (ed.) (2003). "Healing the Spider's Bite: Ballad Therapy and Tarantismo" in T. Mckean *The Flowering Thorn* (Logan, Utah State University Press): 23-33.

Del Giudice, L., N. van Deusen (eds) (2005). *Performing Ecstasies: Music, Dance and Ritual in the Mediterranean* (Ottawa, Institute of Mediaeval Music).

D.E.U.M.M.—*Dizionario Enciclopedico della Musica e dei Musicisti* (1983). (Torino, UTET).

De Simone, L. G. (1996). *La vita nella terra d'Otranto* (Lecce, Italy, Besa).

Di Lecce, G. (1994). *La danza della Piccola Taranta: Cronache da Galatina 1903–1993* (Roma, Edizioni Sensibili alle Foglie).

——— (2001). *Tretarante: taranta/pizzica/scherma. Le tarantelle-pizziche del Salento* (Nardò, Besa).

Durante, D. (1999). "Pizzica e techno-pizzica," in V. Ampolo and G. Zappatore (eds.) *Musica, droga e transe* (Rome, Sensibili alle foglie): 167-90.

Gouk, P. (ed.) (2000). *Musical Healing in Cultural Contexts* (Aldershot, Ashgate).

Gramsci, A. (1996). *Lettere dal carcere, 1926–1937* (1947) (Reprint: Palermo, Sellerio).

Hecker, J. F. K. (2001). *Danzimania. Malattia popolare del Medioevo.* G. Di Lecce (ed.) (New Edition: Nardò, Besa).

Horden, P. (ed.) (2000). *Music as Medicine: the History of Music Therapy since Antiquity* (Aldershot, Ashgate).

Inchingolo, R. (2003). *Luigi Stifani e la pizzica tarantata.* (Nardò, Besa)

Lanternari, V. (1995). "Tarantismo: dal medico neopositivista all'antropologo, alla etnopsichiatria di oggi," *Storia, antropologia e scienze del linguaggio,* Vol. 3: 67-92.

La Penna, D. (2005). "The Cinema of Giuseppe M. Gaudino and Edoardo Winspeare: Between Tradition and Experiment," in W. Hope (ed.) *Italian Cinema New Directions* (Oxford, Peter Lang): 175-200.

Laviosa, F. (2005). "ESTetica: la Puglia nel cinema," in A.Vitti (ed.) *La Scuola Italiana di Middlebury (1996–2005) Passione Didattica Pratica* (Pesaro, Italy, Metauro Edizioni): 233-263.

Lüdtke, K. (2000). "Tarantism in Contemporary Italy: the Tarantula's Dance Reviewed and Revived" in P. Horden (ed.) *Music as Medicine* (Aldershot, Ashgate): 293-312.

——— (2005). "Dancing towards Well-Being: Reflections on the *Pizzica* in Contemporary Salento, Italy" in L. Del Giudice and N. van Deusen (eds.), *Performing Ecstasies* (Ottawa, Institute of Mediaeval Music): 37-53.

——— (2009. *Dances with Spiders. Crisis, Celebrity and Celebration in Southern Italy* (Oxford & New York, Berghahn Books).

Nacci, A. (ed.) (2001). *Tarantismo e neo-tarantismo. Musica, danza, transe. Bisogni di oggi, bisogni di sempre* (Nardò, Besa).

——— (2004). *Neotarantismo* (Viterbo, Nuovi Equilibri).

Rossi, A. (1970). *Lettere da una tarantata* (Bari, De Donato).

Tarantino, L. (2001). *La notte dei tamburi e dei coltelli. La danza-scherma nel Salento* (Nardò: Besa).

Zinn, L. D. (2005). *The Land of Remorse. A Study of Southern Italian Tarantism.* Translation of De Martino's *La terra del rimorso* (London, Free Association).

Chapter 6

Aquila, Richard (ed.) (1996). *Wanted Dead or Alive* (Urbana, University of Illinois Press).

Beatrice, Luca (1996). *Al cuore, Ramon, al cuore!* (Florence, Italy, Tarab Edizioni/Dies Irae Records).

Blake, Michael F. (2007). *Hollywood and the O.K. Corral* (London, McFarland).

Bondanella, Peter (2001). *Italian Cinema: from Neorealism to the Present* (New York, Continuum).

Brunetta, Gian Piero (1991). *Cent'anni di cinema italiano: dal 1945 ai giorni nostri* (Bari, Italy, Laterza).

———— (1982). *Storia del cinema italiano: dal 1945 agli anni ottanta* (Roma, Editori Riuniti).

Buscombe, Edward and Pearson Roberta E. (eds.) (1998). *Back in the Saddle Again* (London, British Film Institute).

Cameron, Ian and Pye Douglas (eds) (1996). *The Book of Westerns* (New York, Continuum).

Carmichael, Deborah A. (2006). *The Landscape of Hollywood Westerns* (Salt Lake City, Utah UP).

Cawelty, John J. (1999). *The Six-Gun Mystique Sequel* (Bowling Green, Kentucky, Bowling Green University Press).

Coyne, Michael (1997). *The Crowded Prairie: American National Identity in the Hollywood Western* (London, I.B.Tauris).

Cumbow, Robert C. (1987). *Once Upon a Time: the Films of Sergio Leone* (Lanham, Maryland, Scarecrow).

Desilet, Gregory (2006). *Our Faith in Evil* (Jefferson, North Carolina, MacFarland & Company).

Forgacs, David (1996). *Italian Cultural Studies* (New York, Oxford UP)

Frayling, Christopher (2000). *Something to Do With Death* (London, Faber and Faber).

———— (1998). *Spaghetti Westerns* (London, I.B.Tauris).

French, Phillip (1977). *Westerns: Aspects of a Movie Genre* (New York, Oxford UP).

Fridlund, Bert (2006). *The Spaghetti Western: A Thematic Analysis* (London, McFarland).

Garofalo, Marcello (1999). *Tutto il cinema di Sergio Leone* (Milano, Baldini e Castoldi).

Giusti, Marco (2007). *Dizionario del Western all'Italiana* (Milano, Mondadori).

Günsberg, Maggie (2005). *Italian Cinema* (New York, Palgrave).

Hughes, Howard (2004). *Once Upon a Time in the Italian West* (London, I.B.Tauris).

Joyner, Courtney C. (2009). *The Westerners* (London, McFarland).

Kezich, Tullio (1975). *Il mito del Far West* (Roma, Bulzoni).

Kitses, Jim (2004). *Horizons West: Directing the Western from John Ford to Clint Eastwood* (London, British Film Institute).

Leutrat, J.L., Guigues S. Liandrat (eds.) (1993). *Le carte del Western: percorsi di un genere cinematografico* (Genova, Le mani). Translation by Carlo Alberto Bonadies and Enrica Zaira Merlo of *Les cartes de l'Ouest — Un genre cinématographique: le western* (1990) (Paris, Arman Colin Éditeur).

Loy, Phillip R. (2004). *Westerns in a Changing America 1955–2000* (Jefferson, North Carolina, MacFarland & Company).

——— (2001). *Westerns and American Culture 1930–1955* (Jefferson, McFarland & Company).

McMahon, Jennifer L., Steve B. Csaki (eds.) (2010). *The Philosophy of the Western* (Lexington, Kentucky UP).

Micciché, Lino (2002). *Cinema italiano: gli anni '60 e oltre* (Venezia, Marsilio).

Parks, Rita (1982). *The Western Hero in Film and Television* (Ann Arbor, Michigan, UMI Research Press).

Pippin, Robert B. (2010). *Hollywood Westerns and American Myth: The Importance of Howard Hawks and John Ford for Political Philosophy* (New Haven, Connecticut, Yale UP).

Prince, Stephen (2003). *Classical Film Violence* (New Brunswick, New Jersey, Rutgers University Press).

——— (2000). *Screening Violence* (New Brunswick, Rutgers University Press).

Rollins, Peter C., John O'Connor (eds.) (2005). *Hollywood's West: The American Frontier in Film, Television, and History* (Lexington, Kentucky UP).

Salizzato, Claver (ed.) (1989). *Prima della Rivoluzione: Schermi italiani 1960-69* (Venezia, Marsilio).

Slotkin, Richard (1992). *Gunfighter Nation: The Myth of the Frontier in Twentieth-Century America* (New York, Maxwell MacMillan).

—— (1973). *Regeneration Through Violence: The Mythology of the American Frontier 1600–1860* (New York, Atheneum).

—— (1985). *The Fatal Environment: The Myth of the Frontier in the Age of Industrialization 1800–1890* (New York, Harper and Collins).

Spinazzola, Vittorio (1974). *Cinema e pubblico—Lo spettacolo filmico in Italia 1945-65* (Milano, Bompiani).

Tompkins, Jane (1992). *West of Everything* (New York, Oxford UP).

Turner, Frederick Jackson (1969). *The Frontier in American History* (New York, Holt, Reinhart and Winston).

Walle, Half H. (2000). *The Cowboy Hero and Its Audience: Popular Culture as Market Derived Art* (Bowling Green, Kentucky, Bowling Green UP).

Wallmann, Jeffrey (1999). *The Western* (Lubbock, Texas Tech UP).

Williams, Linda, ed. (1994). *Viewing Positions: Ways of Seeing Films* (New Brunswick, Rutgers University Press).

Wright, Will (1975). *Six-Gun and Society* (Berkeley, University of California Press).

Chapter 7

AA.VV. [multiple authors] (1980). *Un processo per stupro*. Turin, Einaudi Editore.

Bellu, Giovanni Maria (1998). "'I carabinieri ci dissero: stuprate Franca Rame.' E il giudice accusa cinque neofascisti" *La Repubblica*, February 10.

Carraro, Andrea (2005). *Il branco* (Roma, Gaffi Editore).

Caruth, Cathy, ed. (1995). *Trauma Exploration in Memory* (Baltimore, The Johns Hopkins University Press).

Castellano, Alberto (2003). "Quello stupro dietro 'Il vestito da sposa.'" *Il Mattino on line*, August 10, 2003. *www.ilmattino.caltanet. it* (accessed on September 29, 2003).

Causo, Massimo (1994). "Il branco" *Cineforum* 337, September. *www.municipio.re.it/cinema/catfilm.nsf/PES_perTitolo/0B6F8* (accessed on December 3, 2008).

Diamond, Elin (1988). "Female Parts: An Open Couple, the Rape, Medea, by Franca Rame; Dario Fo" *Theatre Journal*, Vol. 40, March: 102-105.

Ghezzi, Daniela (2008). "Premessa." In *Futuro Femminile. Passioni e ragioni nelle voci del femminismo dal dopoguerra a oggi,* ed. Lorella Reale (Roma, Luca Sassella Editore): 7-8.

Il branco. Directed by Marco Risi. Italy, 1994.

Il vestito da sposa. Directed by Fiorella Infascelli. Italy, 2003.

Infascelli, Fiorella (2003). "Dichiarazione della regista" Locarno International Film Festival August 6-16, 2003. *www.2003.pardo. ch/2003/sito/program.director* (accessed on September 29, 2003).

La ciociara. Directed by Vittorio De Sica. Italy, 1960.

La ciociara. Directed by Dino Risi. Italy, 1989.

Lagostena Bassi, Tina and Moroli, Emanuela (1991). *L'avvocato delle donne: dodici storie di ordinaria violenza* (Milan, Mondadori).

Lagostena Bassi, Tina (1993). "Violence Against Women and the Response of Italian Institutions" in *Visions and Revisions Women in Italian Culture,* eds. Mirna Cicioni and Nicole Prunster (Providence, Rhode Island, Berg Publisher): 199-213.

Lagostena Bassi, Tina and Cappiello, Agata Alma (1998). *Violenza sessuale. Venti anni per una legge* (Istituto Poligrafico dello Stato: Dipartimento dell'Editoria).

Lagostena Bassi, Tina and Monteverdi, Giordana (2008). *Una vita speciale* (Casale Monferrato, Piemme).

La sposa più bella. Directed by Damiano Damiani. Italy, 1970.

Lebowitz, Leslie, Harvey, R. Mary and Herman, Judith Lewis (1993). "A Stage-by-Dimension Model of Recovery From Sexual Trauma" *Journal of Interpersonal Violence,* Vol. 8, (3) September: 378-391

Lo stupro. In *Sesso? Grazie, tanto per gradire.* Written and performed by Franca Rame. Italy, 1995.

Nerenberg, Ellen (2004). "*La Ciociara/*Two Women" in *The Cinema of Italy,* ed. Giorgio Bertellini, (London, Wallflower Press): 83-90.

Ongaro Basaglia, Franca (1980). "Prefazione" in *Un processo per stupro,* AA.VV., I-XVII (Turin, Einaudi Editore).

Prevosti, Carlo (August 2003). "Il vestido da sposa. L'altra metà del cielo, solo quella" *Cinemavvenire* website, 12. *www.cinemavvenire.it/magazine/articoli* (accessed on September 29, 2003).

Processo per stupro. Directed by Loredana Dordi. Italy, 1979.

Robinson, Mary (2004). "The United Nations Has Helped Reduce Worldwide Violence Against Women" in *Violence Against Women,* ed. Karen F. Balkin (Farmington Hills, Minnesota,

Greenhaven Press): 159-165.

Storia del movimento femminista in Italia: dal dopoguerra agli anni Sessanta. DVD, part I, directed by Mancini, Luca. Produces by Aleph Film for Rai Educational. Italy, 2006.

Storia del movimento femminista in Italia: dal dopoguerra agli anni Settanta. DVD, part II, ibidem.

Stupiggia, Maurizio (2007). *Il corpo violato. Un approccio psicocorporeo al trauma dell'abuso.* (Molfetta [Bari], Edizioni La Meridiana).

Van der Kolk, Bessel A., McFarlane, Alexander C. and Weisaeth, Lars, eds. (1996). *Traumatic Stress: The Effects of Overwhelming Experience on Mind, Body, and Society* (New York, Guilford Press).

White Stewart, Mary (2002). *Ordinary Violence. Everyday Assaults Against Women* (Westport, Connecticut, Bergin & Garvey).

Young, Deborah (1994). "The Pack" *Variety Movie Reviews*, October 24, 1971.

Zanetti, Alberto (2004). "Il Vestito da Sposa" *Cineforum*, vol. 435: 84-85.

Zonta, Dario (2008). "Chi è cosa … Vogliamo anche le rose e il cinema underground italiano" in *Le rose*, ed. Alina Marazzi (Milan, Feltrinelli Editore): 83-97.

NOTE: Internet URL addresses cited herein were correct at the time this work was written.

INDEX